# AMERICA GOES TO PRESS

# AMERICA GOES TO PRESS

# The News of Yesterday

### The History of the United States as Reported in the Newspapers of the Day from the Boston Tea Party to the World War

By
LAURENCE GREENE

*Essay Index Reprint Series*

**BOOKS FOR LIBRARIES PRESS**
FREEPORT, NEW YORK

First Published 1936
Reprinted 1970

INTERNATIONAL STANDARD BOOK NUMBER:
0-8369-1929-7


LIBRARY OF CONGRESS CATALOG CARD NUMBER:
74-128252


PRINTED IN THE UNITED STATES OF AMERICA

# CONTENTS

# CONTENTS—*Continued*

# CONTENTS—*Concluded*

THIS BOOK IS GRATEFULLY DEDICATED
TO THE MEN AND WOMEN
WHO WROTE IT

# AUTHOR'S NOTE

This book has certain purposeful shortcomings, whose presence makes this brief explanation necessary.

All material quoted herein is from newspapers. The stories furnished their readers by those newspapers were prepared in great haste, and consequently often contained inaccuracies. The author feels that in presenting this collection it would be presumptuous to burden its text with corrective footnotes, on the theory that the errors themselves are a badge of authenticity. Therefore, in its factual detail, this book is not to be regarded as reliable. The quoted material has been edited only by the correction of obviously typographical errors and by condensation.

Two questions governed the selection of the individual happenings described: "Was it news?" and "Was it interesting?" In answering yes to both, it became necessary to treat history very shabbily: many significant events are ignored because of their failure to furnish exciting first copy. In addition, the matter of space required a ruthlessness of selection. Many readers no doubt will be disappointed that stories they know are not represented—to such readers, the author can say only that their regret is but a fraction of his own. To another possible criticism—that the contents of this book are bloody— the response is that ours has been a bloody history, and blood often makes the best *Extras*.

Finally, the author would suggest that this work be read as a scrapbook—as the sort of book an inveterate reader of newspapers who lived in three centuries might have compiled.

It is designed, that the Countrey shall be furnished once a moneth (or if any Glut of Occurrences happen, oftener) with an account of such considerable things as have arrived unto our notice.

In order hereunto, the Publisher will take what pains he can to obtain a Faithful Relation of all such things; and will particularly make himself beholden to such Persons in Boston whom he knows to have been for their own use the diligent Observors of such matters.

The which is herein proposed, is, First, That Memorable Occurrents of Divine Providence may not be neglected or forgotten, as they too often are. Secondly, That people every where may better understand the Circumstances of Publique Affairs, both abroad and at home; which may not only direct their Thoughts at all times, but at some times also to assist their Businesses and Negotiations.

Thirdly, that something may be done toward the Curing, or at least the Charming, of that Spirit of Lying, which prevails amongst us, wherefore nothing shall be entered but what we have reason to believe is true, repairing to the best fountains for our Information. And when there appears any material mistake in any thing that is collected, it shall be corrected in our next.

From the First American Newspaper:
*Public Occurrences,*
Boston, September 25, 1690

# BULLDOG

On Monday last, at Twelve o'clock, the Declaration of Independence was proclaimed at the State House in this city, in the presence of many thousand spectators, who testified their approbation by repeated acclamations.

——Pennsylvania *Gazette*

# AMERICA GOES TO PRESS

---

## I

## FRIENDS! BRETHREN! COUNTRYMEN!

(Massachusetts *Gazette*)

---

In that day they stood over cases and fumbled crude types into sentences. What they composed had for the 's' the symbol that looks like an 'f' and is to us so difficult to read. The types themselves were old and worn, bought second hand for the large part in England and serving for official documents and handbills until their faces were mashed almost into illegibility. When the printers had finished setting up whatever items they thought should be presented to the public, they mounted their forms upon unhandy wooden presses, and tugged on a lever for each impression. If the newspaper was a double sheet of four pages, four tugs were necessary for each copy. The result was a tiny, smeared thing, half the size of a modern tabloid, poorly written and worse displayed, no more than quaint to us sophisticates, accustomed as we are to stereotyped, photoengraved, multiple-unit-pressed journals.

They have been dust these hundred years and more. The Revolution is so long ended that even its warriors are almost legendary, and its war correspondents seem never to have existed. But if dust can feel, the editors of the Revolutionary press should lie quietly—almost smugly—in their graves. Printing upon presses which a modern letter-duplicator would put to shame, telling their stories in awkward and un-incisive types, hampered by the primitive communications that brought them domestic news weeks late and foreign news months after it had happened, they recorded with clear proph-ecy the significance and the drama of their times. If their dust could become living flesh again, they would know pride that when history was in the making they recognized and iden-tified it.

At the beginning (in 1704, say, when John Campbell first "Published by Authority" his Boston *News Letter*) news-papers trod a hard road. The printers were poor and forever pleading for payment of subscriptions. They had to be printers and editors and circulation men and advertising managers all in one. They took what gossip reached their offices and, if they believed it, prepared it in the best form they knew. They watched eagerly for a sail in the harbor, because a sail meant foreign newspapers and such casual correspondence as ac-quaintances abroad would give them; and the Colonies were as yet no more than a part of England. Thus, the news of Par-liament provided the occasional sensation for the Colonial printer, and after 1765, when the Stamp Act was passed, Par-liament became even more important. Through its actions there came the war, which the editors reported with great as-surance. And when the war was over, there was a new and expanding nation whose lusty activities provided all manner of exciting news.

The editors took the Stamp Act, their first really big story, in their stride. It affected their papers, and they protested against it with editorial intelligence: issues with the column rules turned in mourning, like that of the Pennsylvania *Journal* and the *Weekly Advertiser;* mock stamps printed upon the paper, showing skull and bones, or the tools of a gravedigger; epitaphs, such as the Pennsylvania *Journal's*: "EXPIRING:

In hopes of a resurrection to LIFE again" or the Maryland
*Gazette's:* "The Times are Dreadful, Dismal, Doleful, Dolo-
rous and Dollarless"; anonymous newspapers, carrying in place
of their mastheads the brave and false legend: "No Stamped
Paper to Be Had."

The Colonies grew bolder in voicing their protests against
the Crown. The Stamp Act was repealed, but America suffered new indignities. The most significant of these was
reported in the *Massachusetts Gazette and Boston Weekly
News-Letter* (the same *News-Letter* started by John Campbell,
but no longer "published by authority") for December 2, 1773.
It was a call to arms:

> Monday morning the following notification was posted up
> through the town:
>
> FRIENDS! BRETHREN! COUNTRYMEN!
> That worst of plagues, the detested T E A, shipped for
> this Port by the East-India Company, is now arrived in this
> Harbour; the Hour of Destruction or manly Opposition to
> the Machinations of Tyranny stares you in the Face; every
> Friend to his Country, to himself, or to Posterity, is now
> called upon to meet in Faneuil-Hall, at Nine oClock T H I S
> D A Y (At which Time the Bells will ring), to make a
> united, and successful Resistance to the last, worst and most
> destructive Measure of Administration.

Boston held a series of meetings, to decide what should be
done about the "detested T E A." The three vessels bearing
it lay at their wharves, guarded by the citizens so that none of
the boxes could be unloaded. After two weeks nothing had
been attained; the precise form of the protest had not yet
been determined by the protestants. The Boston *Gazette* went
to press with the account of the final meeting, held on December fourteenth:

On Tuesday last the body of the people of this and all the adjacent towns, and others from the distance of twenty miles, assembled in the Old South Meeting-House, to inquire the reason of the delay in sending the ship Dartmouth, with the East-India Tea, back to London; and having found that the owner had not taken the necessary steps for that purpose they enjoined him at his peril to demand of the collector of the customs a clearance of the ship, and appointed a committee of ten to see it performed: after which they adjourned to the Thursday following, ten o'clock. They then met, and being informed by Mr. Rotch, that a clearance had been refused him, they enjoined him immediately to enter a protest and apply to the Governor for a passport by the castle, and adjourned again till three o'clock for the same day. At which time they again met, and after waiting till near sunset, Mr. Rotch came in and informed them that he had accordingly entered his protest and waited on the Governor for a pass, but his excellency told him he could not consistent with his duty grant it until his vessel was qualified. The people finding all their efforts to preserve the property of the East-India Company and return it safely to London frustrated by the tea consignees, the collector of the customs, and the Governor of the Province, DISSOLVED their meeting.—But, BEHOLD, what followed:

And we BEHOLD from the columns of the *News-Letter:*

Just before the Dissolution of the Meeting, a Number of brave and resolute Men, dressed in the Indian Manner, approached near the Door of the Assembly, and gave the War-Whoop, which rang through the House and was answered by some in the Galleries, but Silence being commanded, and a peaceable Deportment was again enjoined till the Dissolution; the Indians, as they were then called, repaired to the Wharf, where the Ships lay that had the Tea on board, and were followed by Hundreds of People, to see the Event of the Transactions of those who made so grotesque an Ap-

pearance.—They, the Indians, immediately repaired on board
Capt. Hall's Ship, where they hoisted out the Chests of
Tea and when upon Deck, stove the Chests, and emptied the
Tea overboard; having cleared this Ship, they proceeded to
Capt. Bruce's and then to Capt. Coffin's Brig—they applied
themselves so dextrously to the Destruction of this Com-
modity that in the Space of three Hours they broke up 342
Chests, which was the whole number in those Vessels, and
Discharged their Contents into the Dock; when the Tide rose
it floated the Chests and the Tea insomuch that the Surface
of the Water was filled therewith a considerable Way from
the South part of the Town to Dorchester-dock and lodged
on the Shores.—There was the greatest care taken to prevent the Tea from being purloined by the Populace:   One
or two being detected in endeavoring to pocket a small Quantity were stripped of their Acquisitions and very roughly
handled.—It is worthy of Remark that although a considerable quantity of Goods were still remaining on board the
Vessels, no Injury was sustained; Such Attention to private
Property was observed that a small Padlock belonging to
the Captain of one of the Ships being broke, another was
procured and sent to him.—The Town was very quiet during the whole Evening and the Night following: Those
Persons who were from the Country returned with a merry
Heart; and the next Day Joy appeared in almost every
Countenance, some on Occasion of the Destruction of the
Tea, others on Account of the Quietness with which it was
effected.—One of the Monday's papers says that the Masters and Owners are well pleased that their Ships were thus
cleared.

## II

# AMERICANS! LIBERTY
# OR DEATH! JOIN OR DIE!

(Massachusetts *Spy*)

---

Of all the editors in the rebelling Colonies, perhaps the one most nearly approximating today's definition of a newspaperman was Isaiah Thomas, of Boston. Isaiah had done well in Boston with his Massachusetts *Spy*, because it was well-written and consistently edited. There came a day when his field was too limited for his talents; in his shrewd New England mind there was a glimmering of the lust certain of his successors were to know for "chain papers." He looked about for new territory: Worcester was near by and without a paper; it was a fine and growing town. Isaiah totted up columns of figures in his angular script and presently felt himself ready to bring out an edition for Worcester alone.

His decision coincided with some of the more drastic regulations of the British General Gage, who ruled Boston. Embargoes were in effect: Isaiah found that if he were to print his Worcester edition, he would have a poor chance of sending it to the subscribers, and, what was less to his liking, it would be a censored journal. So he loaded his box of a press and his fonts of type into a wagon, and on May 3, 1775, the Massachusetts *Spy* appeared with Worcester in its date line instead of Boston.

This first edition of the Massachusetts *Spy and ORACLE of Liberty* to be printed in Worcester was a bargain in news and sensation. It contained one of the first streamers in American journalistic history, spread across the top of the

masthead in large type: "AMERICANS! LIBERTY OR
DEATH! JOIN OR DIE!" There was an explanation of
the reasons for transferring the entire plant from Boston.
There was also a moving and accurate description of the battle
of Lexington. No more need be said for the talents of Isaiah
Thomas than this: obscurely laboring with the sorry equipment of his day, he told of this conflict with a complete sense
of its importance and implications.

AMERICANS! forever bear in mind the BATTLE OF
LEXINGTON!—where British troops, unmolested and unpro-
voked, wantonly and in a most inhuman manner, fired upon
and killed a number of our countrymen, then robbed, ran-
sacked and burnt their houses! nor could the tears of defenceless women, some of whom were in the pains of childbirth,
the cries of helpless babes nor the prayers of old age, confined to beds of sickness, appease their thirst for blood!—or
divert them from their DESIGN of MURDER and ROBBERY!

The particulars of this alarming event will, we are cred-
ibly informed, be soon published by authority, as a Committee of the Provincial Congress have been appointed to
make special enquire and to take the depositions, on oath,
of such as are knowing in the matter. In the meantime, to
satisfy the expectations of our readers, we have collected
from those whose veracity is unquestioned the following
account, viz.

A few days before the battle, the Grenadier and Light-
Infantry companies were all drafted from the several regi-
ments in Boston; and put under the command of an officer,
and it was observed that most of the transports and other
boats were put together, and fitted for immediate service.
This manœuvre gave rise to a suspicion that more formidable expedition was intended by the soldiery, but what or
where the inhabitants could not determine—however, town
watches in Boston, Charlestown, Cambridge, &c., were ordered to look well to the landing place. About 10 o'clock
on the night of the 18th of April, the troops in Boston were

disclosed to be on the move in a very secret manner, and it was found they were embarking of boats (which they privately brought to the place in the evening) at the bottom of the Common; expresses set off immediately to alarm the country, that they might be on their guard. When the expresses got about a mile beyond Lexington, they were stopped by about fourteen officers on horseback, who came out of Boston in the afternoon of that day, and were seen lurking in bye-places in the country till after dark. One of the expresses immediately fled, and was pursued two miles by an officer, who when he had got up with him presented a pistol, and told him he was a dead man if he did not stop, but he rode on till he came up to a house, when stopping of a sudden his horse threw him off, having the presence of mind to hollow to the people in the house, *Turn out! Turn out! I have got one of them!* the officer immediately retreated and fled as fast as he had pursued; the other express, after passing through a strict examination, by some means got clear.* The body of the troops, in the meantime, under the command of Lieut. Colonel Smith, had crossed the river and landed at Phipp's Farm; They immediately, to the number of 1000, proceeded to Lexington, about 6 miles below Concord, with great silence: A company of militia, of about 80 men, mustered near the meeting-house; the troops came in sight of them just before sunrise; the militia upon seeing the troops began to disperse; the troops then set out upon the run, hallooing and huzzaing, and coming within a few rods of them, the commanding officer accosted the militia, in words to this effect, *Disperse, you damn'd rebels!—Damn you disperse!* Upon which the troops again huzzaed and immediately one or two officers discharged their pistols, which were instantaneously followed by the firing of four or five of the soldiers; and then there seemed to be a general discharge from the whole body;

*Paul Revere's letter to Dr. Jeremy Belknap, founder of the Massachusetts Historical Society, indicates that it was he who, "after passing through a strict examination" escaped and that his companion, Doctor Prescott, was the express who reached Concord.

it is to be noticed they fired on our people as they were dispersing, agreeable to their command, and that we did not even return the fire; Eight of our men were killed and nine wounded;—The troops then laughed, and damned the Yankees, and said they could not bear the smell of gunpowder. A little after this the troops renewed their march to Concord, where, when they arrived, they divided into parties, and went directly to several places where the province stores were deposited. Each party was supposed to have a tory pilot. One party went into the gaol yard and spiked up and otherwise damaged two cannon, belonging to the province, and broke and set fire to the carriages—Then they entered a store and rolled out about an 100 barrels of flour, which they unheaded and emptied about 40 into the river; at the same time others were entering houses and shops, and unheading barrels, chests, &c., the property of private persons; some took possession of the town house, to which they set fire, but was extinguished by our people without much hurt. Another party of the troops went and took possession of the Northbridge. About 150 provincials who mustered upon the alarm, coming toward the bridge, the troops fired upon them without ceremony and killed two on the spot!—(Thus had the troops of Britain's king fired FIRST at two separate times upon his loyal American subjects, and put a period to ten lives before one gun was fired upon them)—Our people THEN fired and obliged the troops to retreat, who were soon joined by their other parties but finding they were still pursued the whole body retreated to Lexington, both provincials and troops firing as they went. During this time an express from the troops was sent to General Gage, who thereupon sent out a reinforcement of about 1400 men, under the command of Earl Piercy, with two field pieces. Upon the arrival of this reinforcement at Lexington, just as the retreating party had got there, they made a stand, picked up their dead and took all the carriages they could find and put their wounded thereon; others of them to their eternal disgrace be it spoken, were robbing and setting houses on fire, and discharging their cannon at the meeting-house. . . . The enemy having halted about an hour at Lexington, found it necessary to make a second retreat, carrying with them many of their dead and wounded. They continued their retreat from Lexington to Charleston with great precipitation; our people continued their pursuit, firing till they got to Charlestown neck (which they reached a little after sun-set), over which the enemy passed, proceeded up Bunker's Hill, and the next day went into Boston, under the protection of the Somerset man-of-war of 64 guns.

A young man, unarmed, who was taken prisoner by the enemy, and made to assist in carrying off their wounded says that he saw a barber who lives in Boston, thought to be one Warden, with the troops and that he heard them say he was one of their pilots; he likewise saw the said barber fire twice upon our people and heard Earl Piercy give the order to fire the houses: He also informs, that several officers were among the wounded who were carried into Boston, where our informant was dismissed. They took two of our men prisoners in battle who are now confined in barracks.

Immediately upon the return of the troops to Boston, all communication to and from the town was stopped by Gen. Gage. The provincials, who flew to the assistance of their distressed countrymen, are posted in Cambridge, Charlestown, Roxbury, Watertown, &c., and have placed a guard on Roxbury neck, within gunshot of the enemy; guards are also placed everywhere in view of the town to observe the motions of the King's troops: the Council of War, and the different Committees of Safety and Supplies set at Cambridge, and the Provincial Congress at Watertown. The troops in Boston are fortifying the place on all sides, and a frigate of war is stationed at Cambridge River, and a sixty-four gun ship between Boston and Charlestown.

Deacon Joseph Loring's house and barn, Mrs. Mulliken's house and shop, and Mr. Joshua Bond's house and shop, in Lexington, were all consumed. They also set fire to several other houses, but our people extinguished the flames. They pillaged almost every house they passed by, breaking and destroying doors, windows, glass, &c., and carrying off cloath-

ing and other valuable effects. It appeared to be their design
to burn and destroy all before them, and nothing but our
vigorous pursuit prevented their infernal purposes from
being put in execution. But the savage barbarity exercised
upon the bodies of our unfortunate brethren who fell is almost incredible; Not content with shooting down the unarmed, aged and infirm, they disregarded the cries of the
wounded, killing them without mercy, and mangling their
bodies in the most shocking manner.

We have the pleasure to say, that notwithstanding the
highest provocations given by the enemy, not one instance
of cruelty that we have heard of, was committed by our militia; but, listening to the merciful dictates of the Christian
religion, they "breathed higher sentiments of humanity". . . .

The public most sincerely sympathize with the friends and
relations of our deceased brethren, who sacrificed their lives
in fighting for the liberties of their country. By their noble
intrepid conduct, in helping to defeat the force of an un-
grateful tyrant, they have endeared their memories to the
present generation, who will transmit their names to posterity with the highest honor. . . .

III

# IMPORTANT INTELLIGENCE!

(Boston *Gazette*)

The Declaration of Independence, to the men who wrote it
and to the citizens who were affected by it, was a splendid document. The Pennsylvania *Gazette,* on July tenth, devoted nearly
all its first page to the text, dismissing the story of its proclamation with the item:

On Monday last, at twelve o'clock, the Declaration of Independence was proclaimed at the state house in this city, in

the presence of many thousand spectators, who testified their approbation by repeated acclamations.

In his efforts to justify this document, General Washington gave the editors much to print in that year—and little of it was cheering to the citizenry. The newspapers for the autumn and early winter of 1776 are filled with notices of deserting soldiers, offers of rewards for whole batches of them sometimes appearing in a single block of type. The army was poorly disciplined and underequipped. In one paper there was published an official plea for more vigilance against the volunteers who collected their bounty for service, deserted and reënlisted for another bounty. On the sea, Great Britain harassed the rebels; one editor, describing the capture of a ship bearing lead, said that it was no great loss as "we have lately received great supplies, so that we can provide every red or blue coated plunderer with a pound of it, if an ounce should not prove sufficient to make him honest."

In this period, news was a haphazard thing. The papers printed information in the form in which it was received: actual stories, advertisements, proclamations and letters. Thus, throughout the Revolution, many of the more important events were described in official dispatches. The rewrite man, today's blessing and curse to the copy desk, was yet to be journalistically born. The Boston *Gazette* for January 6, 1777, presented its readers with a most significant letter, which did much to revive the waning morale of the citizens:

The following is a copy of a letter from Major General Heath, forwarded by express by Jonathan Trumble, Esq., Governor of the State of Connecticut, to the President of the Council of the State, received last Saturday afternoon, dated,

Peeks Kill, Dec. 30, 1776

By Col. Chester, this moment arrived from his Excellency, General WASHINGTON, who was at Newtown, I have the pleasure to acquaint you, that early on the morning of Thursday last, his Excellency in Person at the Head of about 3000 of our troops, crossed the Delaware, attacked the enemy at Trenton, consisting of about 1,600 men; and after a brisk action of thirty-five minutes, entirely routed them, taking 1 Colonel, 2 Lieutenant-Colonels, 3 Majors, 4 Captains, 3 Lieutenants, 12 Ensigns, 1 Judge Advocate, 2 Surgeon's Mates, 92 Sergeants, 20 Drummers, 9 Musicians, 25 Officers' Servants, and 740 Rank and File prisoners, (Total 919) exclusive of killed and wounded. Together with 6 Brass Pieces, 2 of which were Twelve Pounders.—1,200 Small Arms, 4 Standards, 12 Drums, a number of Trumpets, &c., 6 Waggons, a number of Swords, Capes, &c., are Trophies of Victory. We had not more than 4 killed and 8 wounded.

All the Prisoners, except one, were Hessians.

Our Troops behaved with the greatest Bravery.

This Signal Victory, at this time, will be productive of the best Consequences. Ardour glows in every Face, and I hope she shall soon return all our losses.

And on January thirteenth, in the same paper:

Further IMPORTANT Intelligence!

Last Saturday night an express arrived in town, containing an account of General Washington's attaining a victory over the Hessians on the 26th of December at Trenton; as lately mentioned, with the following further particulars, viz. That the number of the enemy taken prisoner (including those at Trenton) amounts to about 1,200.—That our loss does not exceed 20 killed and wounded.—That our troops behaved with the utmost bravery.—That the General gave the Hessians all their luggage, with their packs unsearch'd, who were so amazed at this act of generosity, and so contrary to their own conduct, that they called him a very good rebel, but they are since sent to the western counties of Pennsylvania.—That on or about the 16th of December there was scarce a town in the Jersies the enemy did not occupy or overawe; whereas on the first instant there was scarce one in West Jersey they were in possession of.—That the Pennsylvanians were arming with spirit.—That the Generals Cadwallader, Putnam and Mifflin, with 1,800 men each, had crossed at Philadelphia, some of whom had arrived in Trenton, and been joined with 700 of the Jersey militia.—That on the 20th ult. a junction of the American army was expected which would then be 10,000 (a vast alteration in 5 days) who were to march for Princeton.— That the captains of the frigates at Philadelphia, with their brave tars and a number of pieces of cannon had join'd them, who were willing to beat the enemy by land as well as by sea, provided the General would let them be commanded by their own officers, whose request was granted, and they swear they will never flinch while the General finds them in Rum, Beef and Biscuit.—That a train of artillery is to accompany the army.—That the eastern troops had agreed to tarry six weeks longer, before which time our army would be formed.—That on the first of January the enemy was at Princeton, and preparing to retreat to Brunswick, one division of our army being close to their heels.—And the rest following.—That matters had not gone right.—That the Congress had given our worthy General ample power to rectify all abuses.—That New England must exert herself, or she will repent in Dust and Ashes.—That it is not the turning out for six weeks, but it must be an Army engaged for a considerable Term of Time.—That it will ever be the Policy of the Enemy to push us at the Expiration of the Men's Time.—That the New Englanders have done themselves immortal honor in generally continuing for a further Space of Time.—That these brave Lads will and are able to combat an equal number of Troops of any Nation.—That our present wins are great.—And that we are near some important Event, it must be, and oh, our GOD! most earnestly do we entreat Thee to favor America against the urgent claims of Tyrants.

In its enthusiasm after this victory, the army borrowed a leaf from the book of the British and brought from the pen of Washington this warning, published February twelfth, in the Pennsylvania *Gazette* (which contained "the Freshest Advices, Both Foreign and Domestic") :

> Head Quarters, Morris Town, Jan. 22, 1777
> The General prohibits, in both the militia and continental troops, in the most positive terms, the infamous practices of plundering the inhabitants, under the specious pretence of their being Tories. Let the persons of such who are known to be enemies of their country be seized and confined, and their property disposed of as the State directs.—It is our business to give protection and support to the poor, distressed inhabitants, not to multiply and increase their calamities. After the publication of this order, any officer, either militia or Continental, found attempting to conceal the public stores, plundering the inhabitants under the pretence of their being Tories, or selling at vendue plunder taken from the enemy, or in any other manner than that these orders may direct, may expect to be punished in the severest manner, and be obliged to account for everything so taken and sold.
>
> J. Reed, Adjutant-General.

## IV

# BE IT REMEMBERED!

(Freemen's *Journal*)

———————————

The newspapers had improved only in the amount and quality of their news, by 1781. They continued to be blotchily printed. There was no attempt at display and an almost complete lack of headlines. To the reader of today's super-head-lined paper, they would be impossible as a regular diet. Items were set into type and then piled into the forms as they came to hand, so that sometimes the most important story of a month was to be found buried beneath a column of marine advices.

Then, in October, 1781, the editor of the *Freemen's Journal, or the North American Intelligencer,* of Philadelphia, received an item of such great importance that he cast about for a means to display it suitably. The result of his efforts was an approximation of the modern headline. In a heavy border and printed in type three or four times the size of that in the body of the paper, the subscribers read on October twenty-fourth this brief bulletin:

### BE IT REMEMBERED!

That on the 17th day of October, 1781, Lieut. Gen. Charles Earl Cornwallis, with above 5000 British troops, surrendered themselves prisoners of war to His Excellency, Gen. GEORGE WASHINGTON, Commander-in-Chief of the allied forces of France and America.

*LAUS DEO!*

Apparently, there was time to print no more than the box and this half-stick on an inside page:

#### ANECDOTE

A Watchman of this city, after having conducted the express rider to the door of his Excellency, the President of Congress, on Monday evening last, the honest old German continued the duties of his function, calling out, "Basht dree o'—glock, und Gorn—wal—lis isht da—ken!"

A week later, the *Freemen's Journal* had a complete account of the surrender. Following a long introduction in official documents, containing the terms offered by Washington and the correspondence between him and Cornwallis, there appeared the full story, in the words of the General himself:

Head Quarters, Near York, 19 October, 1781

I have the honor to inform Congress that a reduction of the British Army under the command of Lord Cornwallis is most happily effected. The unremitted ardour which actuated every officer and soldier in the combined army on this occasion has principally led to this important event, at an earlier period than my most sanguine hopes had induced me to expect.

The singular spirit of emulation which animated the whole army from the first commencement of our operations has filled my mind with the highest pleasure and satisfaction and has given me the happiest presage of success.

On the 17th a letter was received from Lord Cornwallis, proposing a meeting of commissioners to consult on terms for the surrender of the posts of York and Gloucester.

This letter (the first which had passed between us) opened a correspondence—a copy of which I do myself the honor to inclose—that correspondence was followed by the definite capitulation, which was agreed to and signed on the 19th, a copy of which is also herewith transmitted, and which, I hope, will meet with the approbation of Congress.

I should be wanting in the feelings of gratitude, did I not mention on this occasion, with the warmest sense of acknowledgments, the very cheerful and able assistance which I have received in the course of our operations, from his excellency, the Count Rochambeau, and all officers of every rank, in their respective capacities. Nothing could equal this zeal of our allies, but the emulating spirit of the American officers, whose ardour would not suffer their exertions to be exceeded.

The very uncommon degree of duty and fatigue which the nature of the service required from the officers of the engineers and artillery of both armies, obliges me particularly to mention the obligations I am under to the commanding and other officers of these corps.

I wish it was in my power to express to Congress how much I feel myself indebted to the Count de Grasse and the officers of the fleet under his command, for the distinguished aid and support which had been afforded me by them; between whom and the army the most happy concurrence of sentiments and views have subsisted and from whom every possible co-operation has been experienced which the most harmonious intercourse could afford.

The return of the prisoners, military stores, ordnances, shipping and other matters I shall do myself the honor of transmitting to Congress as soon as they can be collected by the heads of the departments to which they belong. . . .

Your excellency and Congress will be pleased to accept my congratulations on this happy event, and believe me to be, with the highest esteem and respect, Sir,

Your excellency's<br>Most obedient, humble servant,<br>G. Washington

His Excellency, the President of Congress.

P. S. Though I am not possessed of the particular returns, I have reason to suppose that the number of prisoners will be between 5 and 6,000 men, exclusive of seamen and others.


The editors spread this news, as fast as it reached them. They wrote in superlatives of their general. So highly did the Pennsylvania *Gazette* speak of him that a reader—writing not to that paper, but to the *Freemen's Journal*—voiced a grave fear:


### TO THE PRINTER

Having read Mr. Bradford's paper of November 28, these words struck me, "WASHINGTON, THE SAVIOUR OF HIS COUNTRY", I trembled and said, "Shall we attribute to the

arm of flesh," what the Almighty has done for America?
I respect our great General "but let us not make a GOD of
him!" It must give him pain and cause him to blush, when
he finds that "what is due to our Creator is attributed to
him."

MARY MEANWELL

V

# DIED

(Philadelphia *Aurora*)

One thinks of Washington retiring to Mount Vernon a tran-
quil man. Perhaps he was; perhaps his victories in the field and
his two terms as president pleased him. But he could not and
did not ignore the attacks against him in the press. The newspapers of this country have been curiously consistent in their
treatment of public men, particularly those elected to the presidency: the inauguration calls for pæans and bright prophecies;
the end of the second year in office brings criticisms; the end
of the term or terms is hailed as the salvation of Democracy.
Washington, retiring to Mount Vernon in 1797, was pushed
toward oblivion (so the editors hoped) by this comment in the
Philadelphia *General Advertiser:*

. . . When a retrospect is taken of the Washingtonian administration for eight years, it is a subject of the greatest
astonishment that a single individual should have cankered
the principles of republicanism in an enlightened people, just
emerged from the gulf of despotism, and should have carried his designs against the public liberty so far as to have
put into jeapordy its very existence——Such, however, are
the facts, and with these staring us in the face, this day
ought to be a Jubilee in the United States.

In two short years, the same paper reported the death of Washington with a simple tribute:

### DIED

At Mount Vernon, on Saturday evening, December the 14th, at 11 o'clock, of an illness of 24 hours

#### GEORGE WASHINGTON

Commander in chief of the American armies during the Revolution, caused by the tyranny of Great Britain; in this distinguished character his name will live to the latest posterity among the greatest men who have ornamented history, by the support of Liberty and their country against tyranny.—As we can offer no higher Eulogium to the memory of a character elevated by fortune, talents and the voice of his country to so high a station, among the benefactors of mankind—we confine ourselves to that alone, recommending the principles for which he fought with so much honor to himself and his fellow citizens, and to the freedom of his country, to the careful and steadfast conservatism of those who survive him.

## VI

# TO THE EDITOR

*(American Citizen)*

---

Fulton's Folly, which in 1807 steamed up the Hudson to Albany and back to New York, was regarded very casually by the journalists of the time. With the exception of a brief paragraph in the *Commercial Advertiser* of New York, nothing much was said of his achievement in the New York press, until the inventor himself sought publicity. Then, on an inside page, and apparently without too much enthusiasm for the possibilities the voyage suggested, the editor of the New York *American Citizen* printed this letter:

New York, August 20, 1807.

To the Editor of the *American Citizen:*

Sir,

I arrived this afternoon at 4 o'clock, in the steam boat, from Albany. As the success of my experiment gives me great hope that such boats may be rendered of much importance to my country, to prevent erroneous opinions, and give some satisfaction to the friends of useful improvements, you will have the goodness to publish the following statement of facts:

I left New York on Monday at 10 o'clock and arrived at Clermont, the seat of Chancellor Livingston, at 10 o'clock on Tuesday, time 24 hours, distance 110 miles; on Wednesday I departed from the Chancellor's at 9 in the morning, and arrived at Albany at 5 in the afternoon, distance 40 miles, time 8 hours, the sum of this is 150 miles in 32 hours, equal near 5 miles an hour.

On Thursday at 9 o'clock in the morning, I left Albany, and arrived at the Chancellor's at 6 in the evening; I started from thence at 7, and arrived at New York on Friday at 4 in the afternoon; time 30 hours, space run through, 150 miles, equal 5 miles an hour. Throughout the whole way my going and returning the wind was ahead; no advantage could be drawn from my sails—the whole has, therefore, been performed by the power of the steam engine.

I am, Sir,

Your most obedient,

ROBERT FULTON

---

We congratulate Mr. Fulton and the country on his success in the Steam Boat, which cannot fail of being very advantageous. We understand that not the smallest inconvenience is felt in the boat either from heat or smoke.

# STATE EDITION

*Congress*—twenty days from this date Congress is to come together, but at what place is not known!—No arrangements can be made for bringing on the President's message by express; for no one knows where it will be delivered. But let it be delivered where it may, we hope it will contain the resignation of the President! . . .

—New York *Herald*

# I

# DESTRUCTION OF THE AMERICAN CAPITOL

(Georgetown *Republican*)

---

Of the six major wars in which the United States has had a part, that fought with Great Britain beginning in 1812 was the most inept. Outraged and offended by the impressment of American sailors, the blockading of the coast, the campaign to restrict our commerce and the Indian attacks along the northern border, the small boy that was America tried to be a man. Unfortunately, the country was divided on the wisdom of this official step and as a result the actual fighting of the war was halfhearted—so much so that disasters dotted the records of the campaigns. History books remember Perry on Lake Erie, which is a more impressive victory in its color than in its facts, for Perry captured but six ships and of these one was a schooner and another a sloop.

The unhappy land campaigns along the lakes made many an editor bite his nails and fume through his quill. For two years the ill-fought war dragged along, with militiamen trying stupidly to fight like regulars, until the affair that was to prove their inability was prophesied in a New York *Spectator* dispatch:

Norfolk, August 16, 1814.
11 o'clock.

The following report has this moment reached Head-Quarters by Express from Cape Henry, August 16, 5 o'clock A. M.

"A list of vessels off Rudia (10 miles to the Southward of Cape Henry). 5 Seventy-Fours; 6 Frigates; 1 Sloop-of-War; 10 Transport; 1 Tender; a Ship in the offing rating unknown."

1 o'clock P. M.—Another express from the Pleasure House—The Fleet have all come in from the Capes and gone up the Bay.

In Washington, close to the scene of this maneuver, and soon to suffer as a result of it, the *National Intelligencer* printed a series of worried items, beginning with

## THE ENEMY

The menacing aspect which the enemy has assumed in the adjacent waters, has again called our citizens into the field. As soon as the intelligence which we announced yesterday from Point Lookout reached this city, General Winder issued the necessary orders for embodying the several volunteer corps of this district, and for parading and holding the remaining companies in readiness.

We do not pretend to be acquainted with the measures which have been for some time maturing for the defence of this district, and which, were we able, it would be improper to make public; yet we have full confidence in the zeal and ability of the officers to whom, for six weeks past, the protection of this district has been entrusted; and doubt not that provision has been made to meet the present crises.

The latest authentic news from the enemy's fleet states that a very strong force had entered the Patuxent on Thursday, and indicated an intention to ascend that river.

We shall lose no time in publishing such intelligence of the enemy's movements as may safely be relied on. In the present state of things, however, the various rumors that will be daily circulated should be received with caution.

[*August 20, 1814.*]

### NOTICE

The Captains of companies of the Militia of the City of Washington, are hereby notified that such arms belonging to the Militia of the 1st and 2d Wards, as are out of order, will be repaired with all possible expedition, at the expense of the Corporation, at the shop of Hollenbach on Pennsylvania Avenue, nearly opposite T. Ringold's, Esq.—and those of the 3d and 4th wards at the shop of Capt. William McKee, near the Navy Yard.

By order of the Mayor,<br>
PETER LENOX,<br>
Superintendent.

[*August 20, 1814.*]

---

Nearly all the rumors that reach us from the scene of action below, are evidently so exaggerated and so contradictory, that it is impossible to form from them anything like a correct or satisfactory opinion either of the strength or operations of the enemy. Each man brings the tidings dictated by his own fears and impressions; consequently we are inundated with numerous reports that bear no likeness to the truth.

The only intelligence which we can venture to give to our readers, as authentic, will be found in the letter that follows. It is the latest news we have received, and may be confided in. . . .

"*Long Old Fields,*<br>
"*Monday, 2 o'clock P. M.*

"Our army is about two miles from the Woodyard, the enemy's flankers (as we suppose) have advanced near the farm of Mr. Benjamin Oden, and his main body to Upper Marlborough; his force is not exactly known, but presumed to be from 5 to 6000. Commodore Barney and his men are now with us. From a very heavy firing or explosion that we heard about 11 or 12 o'clock, it was the opinion that the flotilla had been burnt, or that the Militia, Majors Warren and ———'s batallions had met them.  We are all in fine spirits.  I shall lose no time in giving you information."

In the present circumstances of this District, our readers will find a sufficient apology for the leanness of today's paper.  A single object at this time occupies all hands and hearts.
[*August 23, 1814.*]

We feel assured that the number and bravery of our men will afford complete protection to the city.  The Baltimore troops, about 2,500, completely equipped, have arrived in our city; and last night 700 men reached the city from Virginia.  These, and reinforcements every moment expected, added to our other forces, will secure the safety of the metropolis.  In a few hours we believe the enemy's object will be developed and the issue perhaps determined.
[*August 24, 1814.*]

The *Intelligencer* spoke truly.  In a few hours the issue was determined, not only for the Capital itself, but for the *Intelligencer*.  The British invaders seized the plant, destroyed much of the printing material, and carried off the press.  As a result, it remained for other papers to give an

## AUTHENTIC ACCOUNT OF THE CAPTURE OF WASHINGTON

(The following is a correct, and very interesting account of the loss of Washington, from unquestionable authority. The concluding suggestions are such as ought to receive the

most serious attention from all officers who are entrusted
with the defence of the country.)

TO THE EDITORS OF THE BALTIMORE PATRIOT:

Friday Evening, August 26, 1814.

GENTLEMEN—Having witnessed the unhappy occurrence at Washington, I will, agreeably to your request, put
them on paper; that, if necessary, they may be used to correct some of the many erroneous reports, which are circu-
lating.

I arrived at Washington on Sunday the 21st inst. At that
time the officers of government and the citizens were very
apprehensive of an attack from the British, who had landed
a force on the Patuxent. The numbers had not been ascertained, but reports were various, stating them from 4000 to
16,000. Gen. Winder was stationed near the Wood Yard,
with about 2000 men, hourly expecting large reinforcements
from every quarter, particularly from Baltimore, 3000 having been ordered to march immediately from that place. On
Sunday, the public offices were all engaged in packing and
sending off their books, and the citizens their furniture. On
Monday, this business was continued with great industry, and
many families left the city. The specie was removed from
all the Banks in the District. Reports were very current that
Winder had received large reinforcements; so that it was
believed by many well-informed persons that he would have
10,000 men embodied in the course of the week. In the expectation that there was a very considerable force collected,
the President, accompanied by the Secretary of War and of
the Navy, left the city for the camp. They arrived there late
that night; and the next morning, finding but 3000 men and
learning that the Baltimore troops were encamped at Bladensburg, they returned to the city on Tuesday to make further arrangements. All the books and papers were sent off,
and the citizens generally left the place.

In the course of that day a scouting party from General
Winder's army had a skirmish with the British advance
guards, and returned to camp with such tidings as induced

General Winder to retire to the city, with his army, which he accomplished by 9 o'clock in the evening, burnt the old bridge which crossed the Potomac, and encamped on the hill, directly above the other bridge about one mile and a half from the Navy Yard, and prepared to defend that passage. In the event of the British being too strong, the bridge was to be blown up, for which he had everything prepared. At this post he remained the whole night, expecting the enemy's forces. On Wednesday morning, I walked through the army, and remained at the bridge until 10 o'clock, when advice was received that the enemy had taken the Bladensburg road. The troops were immediately put in position, and by 12 o'clock the whole were on their march, in the hope of forming a junction with the Baltimore troops, before the enemy reached Bladensburg. This was only partially accomplished, when the battle commenced, and was contested, by the Baltimore troops and the men from the flotilla, with great spirit and gallantry, until it appeared useless for so small a force, very badly supported, to stand against *six thousand regulars, all picked men and well supplied*—a retreat was ordered, when the President, who had been on horseback with the army the whole day, retired from the mortifying scene, and left the city on horseback, accompanied by Gen. Mason and Mr. Carroll. At Georgetown the President met his lady, she having left the city only a half hour before him, having remained with great firmness and composure at the President's house, until a messenger brought her the tidings that the British were within a few miles of the city, and that our army were retreating without any chance of being rallied, so as to check their march.

The President and Secretary of State went to Virginia with their families—*the other officers of government went to Fredericktown, where the government is to be formed, and where the President intends to meet his Secretaries next week.*

I remained at the President's house until our army had passed, and ninety-nine hundredths of the citizens gone, leaving nothing but empty walls. I fell into the trail of the army and marched about four miles on the Frederick road. Being much fatigued, I turned off into a wood, and found good quarters in a farm house, on the hill back of Pearce's. Soon after reaching there, at nine o'clock on Wednesday evening, a signal gun was discharged, and the President's house, the capitol and many other public buildings were at the same moment in a blaze, which continued nearly all night.

On Thursday morning, I proceeded on with the army to Montgomery Court House where Gen. Winder's headquarters were established. I had some conversation with him. He appeared to regret very much that he had not been enabled to have made a greater resistance, although he was perfectly satisfied that a successful resistance could not have been made with the force in the neighborhood of Washington, since, if it had all been brought together before the action, it would not have been so large as that opposed to him, and our force was principally militia, and that of the enemy all regulars and picked men.

The uncertainty on which road the enemy intended to attack the city compelled him to keep his forces divided, and their being divided, occasioned frequent marches and countermarches, which at this hot season was quite too much for our militia, *particularly as the Quarter-Master's department was either shamefully neglected, or the officers unable to procure supplies;* for it is a fact, that our men suffered severely, not only for accommodations, but for bread and meat; and after retreating to the Court-House at Montgomery, *they could not get quarters nor provisions, not even a tent to cover them from the rain.*

It is to be hoped, that the officers of the army in every part of the United States, will take warning from this sad lesson, and provide an abundance of provisions and of tents, for it is impossible for men to fight if they are not well fed; and if they are not sheltered from the rains and the fog when they sleep. Our army may with truth be said to have been beaten by fatigue, before they saw the enemy. It is indeed a very bad plan to march troops far in the hot sun the day on which they are to fight; and it is still worse not to have them well supplied with provisions, especially bread, which can so easily be baked hard, and each man furnished with a competency for several days. And, as all armies are liable to be defeated, provision should be made for such a state of things, and the requisite deposits made at the proper places for the army to retire to; as, when they retire, it is to be presumed, that they are much fatigued and many of them wounded, and after having lost a great portion of their baggage and provisions—at such a time they require immediate food and repose more than at any other. Consequently, more pains should be taken to provide quarters and make seasonable deposits of provisions.

The Georgetown *Republican* for August thirtieth added to this certain colorful details by its own reporter:

The retreat was rapid and disorderly. At capitol hill, the district volunteers and some companies of militia were rallied, but orders were given to continue the retreat, and the inhabitants of Washington and Georgetown had the mortification to see the whole body pass through their streets in disgraceful flight.

The retreat was continued till the troops reached Montgomery courthouse, 18 miles from the battleground, almost exhausted with fatigue and without camp equipage, the baggage wagons having been sent across the Potomac bridge and ordered up the Virginia shore.

Before the retreating troops reached Georgetown, the Secretary of the Navy passed through the place, and recommended to the citizens to make the best terms they could with the enemy. The President made his escape by crossing Mason's ferry into Virginia. The second day after the battle he passed through Rockville, Montgomery county, to Brookville, in the same county, where he arrived at nine in the night, escorted by twenty dragoons. He was taken in at the house of one of the Society of Friends, having "rode thirty miles since breakfast, as he stated, over a dreadful road, without any dinner". The next day, being joined by Col. Monroe, he found his way to the District, late in the evening, and his quarters have since been at the houses of his different friends.

No pursuit was kept up by the enemy, who entered Washington at his leisure, and in the evening, with ONE HUNDRED MEN, destroyed the capitol, the president's house, and the treasury office. A few of our men left at the Navy Yard destroyed, by order, the sloop of war Argus, the frigate on the stocks, and the public buildings there, and the arsenal at Greenleaf's point.

The General Post Office was spared on the representation of Dr. Thornton, that a part of the building was a museum of the arts, containing models of the patent machines, and the cause of general science would suffer by its conflagration.

On Thursday the War-Office and two rope walks in Washington were burnt. In the evening a party was despatched to Greenleaf's point, and while employed in burning a number of gun-carriages, a quantity of powder which had been thrown into a well, exploded and destroyed a considerable number of men and mangled many others. . . .

At a late hour on Thursday night, the British troops evacuated the city, leaving behind them the men wounded by the explosion.

This was a story truly calculated to make journalistic opponents of the war cry out. The Baltimore *Federal Gazette,* against the conflict from its beginning, said:

Thus, after being upwards of two years at war, so very provident have been our rulers of the general defence committed to their care, that a small force of six thousand men have landed on our shore, and in one short week taken possession of the seat of government of the United States; destroying the Capitol in which our legislature had just been invited to assemble; all the offices in which the functionaries transacted the business of the nation; and the very house in which the chief magistrate had the day before declared such an attack from them impracticable.

But although the Capitol is in the possession of the enemy, the existence of the Republic is not endangered. The destruction of Moscow roused the Russians to an exertion which led to the downfall of the invader. A nation of freemen will not be less powerfully excited or prove less energetic in defence of their homes, and of all that is dear to man.

Roused from their lethargy, the American people will make such a change in the conductors of their affairs as will ensure that able and energetic defence . . . which all candid men must agree is necessary to retrieve our situation.

And the Georgetown *Republican,* also a Federalistic paper, in the same edition in which it described the looting of Alexandria by the British, had a pertinent question to ask editorially:

Are there no troops and no munitions of war after the millions that have been borrowed and squandered? There are, but they are on the Lakes in Canada. Admiral Cockburn was told in the city the night of the conflagration, "If Washington were alive, you could not have done this." "No," said the Admiral, "we should not have been at war, nor would *he* have left his capital defenceless for the purpose of making conquests abroad."

The reluctance to be at war was not alone an American conviction. England, too, felt that it was a senseless strife, and England agreed with the Federalist editors in placing the blame squarely upon President Madison. In the London *Times* for October sixth, the burning of Washington was defended thus:

We observe in one of the *Paris* papers, which have reached
us to the 3d instant, a lamentation over the fall of Washington and an attempt to represent the conduct of the British forces on that occasion as bordering on barbarism.  The
writer is not one of those Frenchmen who see nothing in
the conduct of England but Machiavelian policy and Punic
faith; on the contrary, he gives us due credit for the perseverance with which we fought the battle of Europe, in
Europe.  It is for this reason that we are the more anxious
to reply to his mistaken imputations; and to prove that we
are now fighting the battle of Europe, and fighting it hon-
orably, in America.  Mr. MADISON, as the writer justly ob-
serves, has espoused the cause of the tyrant, who was the
truest enemy of France.  With an inconsistency merely
apparent, he at the same time proclaims himself the advocate of the most democratic and disorganizing principles;
and he defends this double cause by a series of the most disgraceful equivocations, lies, meannesses, and frauds, that
ever disgraced a Government calling itself civilized.  It was
not sufficient, therefore, that BUONAPARTE should fall; it
was and still is necessary that Mr. MADISON's principles
should be exposed to contempt and himself to infamy.  It
is besides necessary—we repeat the word, strictly necessary—that an indemnity be procured to England for the
losses of a war brought on her by the crooked policy, the
wilful and wicked falsehoods of this man.  We could not,
therefore, in common sense have closed the war, as no
doubt every person of humanity would have wished to do
with the fall of BUONAPARTE.  We had still a long account
to settle with an enemy, whose guilt was infinitely aggra-
vated by the very circumstances that he was sprung of
English blood.  In pursuing this war, then, it happened,
that a division of our army became masters of Washington.
It was not occupied with a view to hold it as a military post;
still less as the seat of a civil administration; but there were
two objects to be attained by its occupation—the destruction
of a most formidable naval arsenal belonging to the enemy,
and a retribution which should have the effect of stopping

the barbarities authorized and encouraged by the American
Government.   With these views, our forces destroyed the
Dockyard with its stores and store-houses; and they also
burnt the yet unfinished public edifices of a capital which is at
present little more than traced out in the wilds of America.
But mark this lesson, which we read to the hypocritical
philanthropist and sophistical philosopher, by whose rule
America is cursed!  Whilst his Generals on the borders of
Canada mercilessly burnt whole towns to the ground, ex-
posing their wretched inhabitants to the miseries of an in-
clement season and a dreary wilderness, private property
was scrupulously respected by our troops at Washington, not
a family was disturbed in its dwelling, not a hair of any
individual's head was touched.   The palace, indeed, so
unworthily occupied by a political imposter, was destroyed;
and he was rendered ridiculous in the eyes of his fellow-
citizens by being driven from the fancied security of the
seat of government, at the moment when he was indulging
the most gigantic dreams of distant conquest.   We have
not made war on the weak and defenceless.  We have pun-
ished pride and insolence by appropriate disgrace; we have
wrested from a perfidious foe a most formidable weapon of
destruction.

## II

# IN THE TENT OF WASHINGTON
### (Baltimore *Morning Chronicle*)

---

Forty years after he had left its shores, an aging Frenchman
arrived in the United States, to be received by the people he
had helped emancipate.  The Marquis de LaFayette, after a
voyage of thirty-five days from Le Havre, arrived in New
York on August 15, 1824, aboard the ship *Cadmus*.  On the

seventeenth, the welcome he was accorded was described in
the New York *Patriot:*

The reception of LA FAYETTE in this city yesterday
was a fair exhibition of the feelings entertained toward
him by the AMERICAN PEOPLE.   Never was there a
display more brilliant, nor a reception more warm—the former did as much honour to the taste and spirit of the
citizens as the latter was creditable to their hearts.

At an early hour the multitudes thronged from all quarters to the Battery—every tree, housetop, fence and other
eminence in the vicinity of which was loaded with persons
of all ages and sexes, every one eager to witness the landing
of the LAST GENERAL OFFICER OF THE AMER-
ICAN REVOLUTION.

The steam ship Robert Fulton, the Chancellor Livingston,
Oliver Ellsworth, Connecticut, and several other elegant
steamboats, decorated with the banners of all nations, proceeded to Staten Island about 11 o'clock to receive the General, who had resided at the Vice-President's house since
his landing in this country.   Between one and two o'clock
LA FAYETTE marched on board the Chancellor Livingston, escorted by a detachment of MARINES under the
command of Major Smith, with the excellent band attached
to the West Point establishment. . . . The CADMUS, the
vessel in which the General arrived, was tastefully decorated
with colours, and was towed up by two steam boats, ornamented in like manner.   It was a grand sight to see all those
vessels propelled by steam and thus adorned, moving in a
body through our waters, among hundreds of pleasure boats,
and others of all descriptions.

The departure of the General from Staten Island was
announced by discharges of artillery from various quarters,
and particularly from the potent fortress that bears his
name.   The usual salutes were fired by the citizen soldiery
and the United States brig Spark, on his arrival at Castle
Garden.   The waving of handkerchiefs, hats and banners

on the wall of this place, and around the stairs where he landed, was continued for a long time. . . .

The veteran hero, after partaking of some refreshment, marched on foot along the lines of troops that were drawn up on the Battery. . . . His aged face was irradiated with pleasure at the appearance of the men under arms, who but for his own exertions (in a measure) heretofore might possibly have been the vassals of a foreign despot. . . .

The countenance and gait of LA FAYETTE would lead a person unacquainted with him to form an erroneous idea of his age. With the exception of a slight HALT in one of his legs, occasioned it is said, by a wound he received at Brandywine, and a subsequent accident in the same leg, he walked as erect and stately as any man of thirty; his tall figure (full six feet in height, we should think) distinguishes him from the generality of those who surround him. His face gives evidence that it has witnessed many a storm, but nevertheless the vigour of his eye seems to be unimpaird. Having lost his hair when in the dungeon at Olmutz, he is compelled to wear a wig.

Although he had shaken hands probably with thousands in the beginning of yesterday, the cordial squeeze he gave those who saluted him in the evening gave evidence that his physical powers have as yet decayed but little.

The City Hotel was illuminated last evening in a beautiful manner.

Lafayette's journey was a triumphal march. He visited Boston, returned to New York and proceeded thence to Philadelphia, Baltimore, Washington, Mount Vernon, Yorktown and Monticello, where the aging Jefferson was his host.

The poet is as enthusiastic a reporter as the greenest cub, and so, in the columns of the Baltimore *Morning Chronicle*, there appeared, from an anonymous pen, one of the many tributes to the great Frenchman:

## IN THE TENT OF WASHINGTON*

I will rest in the war-house, that shelter'd the form
Of my hero, my friend, and his country's preserver-—
That guarded his care-stricken head from the storm—
That caught the warm sighs of the patriot's fervor.

I will count, by the threads that I find in its woof,
The throbs, in his head and his heart that were beating,
While his thoughts were, when midnight enshrouded its roof,
Reliving defeat, or a victory greeting.

I will sleep in the house of the soldier, and view
In my dreams, his achievements, unequall'd in story;
My visions the hopes of my youth shall renew,
Till I wake to the real fruition of glory.

### III

# CANAL CELEBRATION

### (New York *Evening Post*)

---

In 1817, there was no depression of long standing. The federal government, therefore, had no alphabetical agency to provide funds for the mighty dream of DeWitt Clinton of New York. Governor Clinton felt that, if the government at Washington would assist with funds, a waterway could be constructed to link the lakes with the sea, thus opening new markets for the products of East and West. Failing to get the eight million dollars he needed, Clinton persuaded the state of New York to build the Erie Canal. Eight years later, on November 4, 1825, this project had been completed and the

---

*Baltimoreans prepared for the returning warrior the campaign tent of Washington, which was set up at Fort McHenry.

day of fete to celebrate it was described next day in the New
York *Evening Post:*

> *Canal Celebration*—Yesterday the celebration of uniting
> the waters of the Grand Erie Canal with the Atlantic Ocean
> took place, and a proud day it was for the city and state of
> New York. The morning was ushered in by firing of can-
> non and the bells rang a joyous peal. All business was
> suspended, and the day being remarkably fine and pleasant,
> the whole population of our city, male and female, lined the
> walks and filled the windows of the buildings on the streets
> through which the procession passed. The Battery was
> literally crammed with spectators to witness the aquatic part
> of the celebration. The shipping in port displayed their
> colors, and the United States ships of war at the Navy Yard,
> Brooklyn, were most tastefully and beautifully dressed in
> the flags of all nations. The British sloops of war, *King
> Fisher,* Lieut. Henderson, and the *Swallow,* Lieut. Baldock,
> on the approach of the aquatic procession off the Battery, and
> on their return from Sandy Hook, fired a national salute of
> 24 guns. They had an American Ensign displayed at the
> foretop as a mark of respect. The East and North rivers
> and the Bay were covered with watercraft of every descrip-
> tion. There were several canal boats in the procession,
> towed by steam boats. On the deck of one of them were to
> be seen a number of live wild beasts and wild fowl, such as
> the bear, wolf, fox, bald headed eagle, &c. &c. The beautiful
> boat, *Noah's Ark,* met with an accident in coming through
> the Locks, which prevented her joining the procession. She
> has since arrived and is now at Castle Garden, with animals
> and birds of various descriptions, and two young Indian
> Hunters of the Seneca tribe, dressed in their costume. The
> boat will remain there a few days.
>
> The societies formed their procession about half past 10
> o'clock and marched on to the Battery, then wheeled and
> moved up Greenwich street to Canal street, up Canal street
> to Broadway, up Broadway to Broome street, through
> Broome street to the Battery. along the Battery to Broad-

way, and up Broadway to the Park. At the Battery, the honorable Corporation, with their guests, on their return from the ocean, joined in the procession.

At the head were four buglemen on horse back, a band of music, and the Grand Marshal with his aids, who preceded the

Agricultural and Horticultural Societies, many of whose members wore nose-gays of flowers.

The Journeymen Tailors, with emblematic banners, on one of which was "*I was naked and ye clothed me.*"

Measures of grain-Millers and Inspectors of flour; of pot and pearl ashes, and of provisions.

Brewers and Distillers.

Coopers and Journeymen Coopers Society.

The Bakers, with white hats.

The Butchers, mounted and wearing aprons, with the banners of their Society, and two cars, each drawn by 4 horses. The first was covered with a roof, decorated, and contained a calf and a sheep; the other a fine white ox and four large sheep, and over it, on a second stage, a resemblance of another with several butchers' boys.

The Typographical Society had a car drawn by four horses on which were mounted two presses. These were kept in operation, striking off copies of the following Ode, written by Mr. Woodworth, of which they distributed between five and six thousand. Between the presses stood Dr. Franklin's arm chair, occupied by Mr. James Oram, the oldest printer in the city, surrounded by two Heralds and two Mercuries, who assisted him in folding the sheets and throwing them from the car to the public. The presses were handsomely gilt, and are beautiful specimens of American workmanship and taste. One of them is the invention of Mr. Rust, and the other of Mr. Smith. A large banner with the representation of a Clymer Printing Press, and other implements of the great art, with the motto "THE ART PRESERVATIVE OF ALL ARTS" followed immediately after the car. Another banner bore a picture of the Aqueduct over the Mohawk at Little Falls, with the inscription *"Exegi monumentum ære perenius"*—and a likeness of His Excellency, Governor Clinton.

### ODE

'Tis done! 'tis done! The mighty chain
Which joins the bright ERIE to the MAIN
For ages, shall perpetuate
The glory of our native State.
'Tis done! Proud ART o'er NATURE has prevailed!
GENIUS and PERSEVERANCE have succeeded,
Though selfish PREJUDICE assailed,
And honest PRUDENCE pleaded.
'Tis done! The monarch of the briny tide,
Whose giant arm encircles earth,
To virgin ERIE is allied,
A bright-eyed nymph of mountain birth.
Today, the *Sire of Ocean* takes
A sylvan maiden to his arms,
The goddess of the crystal lakes,
In all her native charms!
She comes! Attended by a sparkling train;
The Naiads of the WEST her nuptials grace;
She meets the sceptered father of the main,
And in his heaving bosom hides her virgin face.

### IV

# ARTS AND IMPROVEMENTS

(New York *Mercury*)

---

The success of the Erie Canal led to an excess of canal building. But before the novelty of this form of progress had worn off, the railroad arrived on the American scene. It would be pleasant to record that the average editor of the Thirties realized the importance of the things that clanked and puffed their way along the crude rails, but unfortunately available papers indicate that the iron horse was regarded with contempt and some skepticism.   The first locomotive to run on the rails of the Baltimore and Ohio is supposed to have been paced and outdistanced by a horseman; at least one story of this experimental passage concerned itself not at all with the horse.   It appeared in the Washington *Daily Intelligencer,* as a dispatch from Baltimore, on September 2, 1830:

BALTIMORE, Aug. 30—The first Rail-Road Car, propelled by steam, proceeded the whole distance from Baltimore to Ellicott's Mills on Saturday last, and tested a most important principle, that curvatures of 400 feet radius offer no material impediment to the use of steam power on Railroads, when the wheels are constructed with a cone, on the principles ascertained by Mr. Knight, Chief Engineer of the Baltimore and Ohio Rail-Road Company, to be applicable to such curvatures.   The Engineers in England have been so decidedly of the opinion that locomotive steam engines could not be used on curved rails, that it was much doubted whether the many curvatures on the Baltimore and Ohio Rail-Road would not exclude the use of steam power.   We congratulate our fellow-citizens on the conclusive proof which removes forever all doubt on this subject, and establishes the fact that steam power may be used on our road with as much facility and effect as that of horses, at a very reduced expense.

A few days after this successful journey, curious Philadelphians could have seen a locomotive.   Poulson's *American Daily Advertiser* for September first advised that

The Rail Road and Locomotive Steam Engine, which is now exhibiting at the Masonic Hall, is a curiosity in which amusement, novelty and instruction are so intimately blended that no one would return from a visit there without high gratification.

We cordially wish the inventor success.

# EARLY HOME

(New Orleans *Commercial Bulletin*)
San Jacinto, 26 April, 1836
"Tell our friends all the news, and that
we have beaten the enemy. . . .
Tell them to come on and let the
people plant corn." . . .
SAMUEL HOUSTON

# DIRECT FROM THE FIELD OF GLORY

(Mobile *Mercantile Advertiser*)

The life span of the Republic of Texas covered less than ten years. As a nation, it furnished little in the way of news; as a section of Mexico in rebellion, it gave us some of the great war stories of all history.

Stephen Fuller Austin led three hundred colonists into that section of the state of Coahuila known as Texas in 1822. The land on which this band of immigrants settled had been ceded to Austin's father some years before. From the first, the newcomers found themselves out of tune with the Mexicans, until at last—in 1836—they declared their independence, and formed a government of the Republic of Texas.

Mexico made haste to crush this rebellion. It found itself fighting against tiny but fierce armies composed of handfuls of men—but those handfuls were under the leadership of some of the most resourceful of frontiersmen: such men as David Crockett, Sam Houston, Jim Bowie, "Deef" Smith, and Colonels Travis and Fannin. The warfare occurred in a fairly restricted area of southwest Texas: the Alamo massacre took place on the outskirts of what is now San Antonio, the butchery at Goliad was only a few days' march away, and Houston's final coup was on the Brazos River to the **east**.

Before the Republic was established, there was dissension among the patriots. Governments were formed sometimes in pairs, with each attempting to minimize the efforts of the other. Fannin, theoretically under the command of Houston, ignored orders and pursued his own military course. From his stronghold, the New Orleans *Journal of Commerce* published in March, 1836, this account of the difficulties facing the new nation:

FORT DEFIANCE, GOLIAD, TEXAS,
March 9, 1836

A brief retrospect of our hitherto bloodless campaign will perhaps be interesting to you. I write in great haste, and may possibly omit events necessary to elucidate our conduct. Indeed, it is impossible, within the compass of a single letter, to give you any idea of the manner in which our little army has been influenced by the politics of the country; though most of them are strangers to it, and consequently unable to realize the motives which actuate the different parties; for Texas is not, as you would probably suppose, united in the great struggle before her. Party spirit has taken a form here even more malignant than in the United States; and to such an extent has domestic cavilling been carried, that the council have deposed, impeached and arrested the Governor, while he, by an official fiat, has dissolved the council; and thus we see the striking anomaly of two Governors, created by different authorities, ruling in the same country.

But to return: On the 24th of January, 1836, the Georgia battalion of volunteers, in which I held a responsible office, sailed from the Brazos, under the command of Col. J. W. Fannin, Jr. The object of this expedition was to take the city of Metamoras, to revolutionize the State of Tamaulipas, to form a nucleus or point of rendezvous for volunteers from the United States; to harass the enemy at home; to relieve ourselves from the burden of the war by carrying it out of the country, and to give employment to the volunteers who had lately arrived.

On the fourth day we arrived at Campano, at the head of the Aransassos bay, where we debarked, and landed our stores, munitions and artillery. After a day's march, we pitched our tents at the Mission of Refugio, in Mr. Powers' grant, and remained a few days in order to make cartridge and prepare our artillery, which was defective, for service. In the mean time, a scout who had been sent ahead, returned with information that Santa Ana had already commenced the concentrating of his army on our frontiers. They were rendezvousing at Metamoras, Monclova, Saltillo, Monterrey and Loreda, to the number of from 6,000 to 10,000 men, and designed attacking Bexar and Goliad simultaneously, with two divisions of his army, and marching the third between these points to San Felipe, where he intended fortifying. We immediately apprized the Government of these facts, and fell back to Goliad with our small force of 450 men, and commenced repairing the fort. Bexar was garrisoned by·150 to 200 men; and with this handful of 600 or 700 volunteers, we are left by the generous Texians to roll back the tide of invasion from their soil.

On the 23d ult. the Mexicans' advance reached Bexar, and attacked it on the subsequent morning, with 1,800 men. The gallant little garrison retired to the Alamo, a fortress in the suburbs, resolved to hold out to the last. The Mexicans made several assaults, and were repulsed with loss in every instance. On the receipt of the intelligence in Goliad, we promptly marched with 320 men, and four pieces of artillery, to their aid. In marching a few miles, our men became wearied, and we were compelled to halt or leave our baggage and artillery. While consulting on what course to pursue, we received news of the successive defeats of the parties of Cols. Johnson and Grant, and of the approach of the lower division of Santa Ana's army on our position at Goliad. A council of war was held in the bushes, and it was determined to return to the post we had vacated in the morning, as its abandonment would leave the road open to the settlements and completely uncover our depot of provisions, the only one now in Texas, and consequently the main stay of the army.

The Mexicans, to the number of 700, are now in San Patricio, about 60 miles in front of our position, and another party of 200 have been discovered within 18 miles of us, between us and Gonzales. Everything indicates that an attack will be speedily made upon us. Their scouts, well mounted, frequently push up to our walls, and from the want of horses we are unable to punish them.

We have again heard from Bexar. Santa Ana has arrived there himself with 3,000 men, making his whole force 4,800 men. He has erected a battery within 400 yards of the Alamo, and every shot goes through it, as the walls are weak. It is feared that Bexar will be taken and that the devoted courage of its brave defenders will be of no avail.

We have had no bread for several days. I am nearly naked, without shoes and without money; we suffer much; and as soon as Bexar falls, we will be surrounded by 6,000 infuriated Mexicans. But we are resolved to die under the walls rather than surrender.

Even as this volunteer, naked and shoeless and hungry, sat writing this dispatch, doom had come to Texas. More, the writer was to know doom himself: he was to be one of the three hundred and more who fell in a field on Palm Sunday. Perhaps he was to run from the Mexicans, perhaps he was to stand and look coldly at them as they blasted the soul from his body with their guns, perhaps he was to escape and hide in the bushes. But he wrote without knowing of all this tragedy, while the ashes of the funeral pyre at San Antonio de Bexar cooled and grew gray. . . .

The New Orleans *True American* was next to give a picture of the apparent hopelessness of the Texans' cause. In an edition late in March, 1836, this account of the fall of the Alamo was offered:

We learn by a passenger of the schooner *Camanche,* eight days from Texas, that the war has assumed a serious character. On the 25th February the Texian garrison in Bexar, of 150 men, commanded by Lt. Colonel B. Travis, was attacked by the advance division of Gen. Santa Ana, consisting of 2,000 men, who were repulsed with the loss of many killed, between 500 to 800 men, without the loss of one man of the Texians. About the same time, Colonel Johnson, with a party of 70 men, while reconnoitring the westward of San Patricio, was surrounded in the night by a large body of Mexican troops. In the morning the demand of a surrender was made by the Mexican commander unconditionally, which was refused, but an offer of surrender was made as prisoners of war; but no sooner had the Texians marched out of their quarters and stacked their arms, than a general fire was opened upon them by the whole Mexican force. The Texians attempted to escape, but only three of them succeeded, one of whom was Col. Johnson.

Between the 25th February and 2d March, the Mexicans were employed in forming retrenchments around the Alamo, and bombarding the place; on the 2d March Col. Travis wrote that 200 shells had been thrown into the Alamo without injuring a man. On the 1st March, the Garrison of Alamo received a reinforcement of 32 Texians from Gonzales, having forced their way through the enemy's lines, making the number in the Alamo consist of 180 men.

On the 6th March about midnight, the Alamo was assaulted by the whole Mexican army, commanded by Santa Ana in person. The battle was desperate until daylight, when only seven men belonging to the Texian garrison were found alive, who cried for quarter, but were told that there was none for them. They then continued fighting until the whole were butchered. One woman (Mrs. Dickinson) and a negro of Col. Travis', were the only persons whose lives were spared. We regret to say that Colonel David Crockett, his companion, Mr. Jesse Benton, and Col. Bonham, of South Carolina, were among the number slain. Col. Bowie was murdered in his bed, sick and helpless. Gen. Cos, on entering the fort, ordered the servant of Col. Travis to point out the body of his master. He did so, when Cos drew his sword and mangled the face and limbs with the malignant feelings of a camanche savage. The bodies of the slain were thrown into a heap in the center of the Alamo and burnt. The loss of the Mexicans in storming the place was not less than one thousand killed and mortally wounded, and as many wounded; making, with their loss in the first assault, between two and three thousand men. The flag used by the Mexicans was a blood-red one, instead of the constitutional flag. Immediately after the capture, General Santa Ana sent Mrs. Dickinson and servant to Gen. Houston's camp, accompanied by a Mexican with a flag, who was the bearer of a note from Gen. Santa Ana, offering the Texians peace and a general amnesty if they would lay down their arms and submit to his government. Gen. Houston's reply was, "True, sir, you have succeeded in killing some of our brave men, but the Texians are not yet conquered." . . .

General Houston had burnt Gonzales and fallen back on the Colorado with about 1,000 men; Col. Fannin was in the fort at Goliad, a very strong position, well supplied with munitions and provisions, with from 400 to 500 men.

The general determination of the people of Texas is to abandon all their occupations and pursuits of peace, and to continue in arms until every Mexican east of the Rio del Norte shall be exterminated.

Colonel Travis' negro body servant lived to describe the massacre, in this story published by the Memphis *Enquirer* for April sixth:

The negro states that the attack was suddenly made at 3 o'clock in the morning, after 14 days' siege. It was unexpected, as no alarm except a single voice crying out, "Col. Travis, the Mexicans are coming!" was heard from the guard on the wall; the picket guard, from whom nothing was heard, having probably been killed. Col. Travis sprang from his blanket with his sword and gun, mounted the rampart, and seeing the enemy under the mouths of the cannon with scaling ladders, discharged his double-barrelled

gun down upon them; he was immediately shot, his gun falling down upon the enemy and himself within the fort.   The
Mexican General leading the charge mounted the walls by
means of a ladder, and seeing the bleeding Travis, attempted
to behead him; the dying Colonel raised his sword and
killed him! . . . The lady of Lieut. Dickinson was within
the fort, and begged to share the honorable fate of her husband; Santa Ana, honor to his name—thrice honor to his
name!—here proved himself a soldier and protected her; he
replied: "I am not warring against women."   He sent her
away with the servant who carried this news, and who left
her safely near Washington.

He has raised the blood-red flag of extermination and no
quarters, and swears he will not stop until he has planted his
banner upon the Capitol of our Washington, if he under-
stands our Government in the least abets the Texians; if his
bones bleach upon any other field than that of Texas, our
prophesy fails.

The loss of the Alamo was a blow very nearly fatal to the
land so soon to be a Republic.  Houston, trying to keep his
pitiful army together, marched through a deserted country.
Colonists fled from the menace of Santa Ana; Americans who
had left their country turned and scuttled for home, casting
frightened glances back over their shoulders.  Before Houston
was to reassure them, and before they would return to the
homes they had built for themselves under another flag, they
were to be further spurred in their flight.  They were to hear
of Fannin and his fate, a few days before the readers of the
New Orleans *Bee* were told of it.

After the first fragmentary accounts of the massacre at
Goliad had been told, the *Bee* recounted "The subjoined tale
of Fannin's massacre . . . a tale of horror":

Col. Fannin evacuated Goliad on the 19th March, by
order of General Houston, commander in chief; his force

was between 209 and 340; about eight miles east of the fort they were surrounded by the enemy with 2,000 cavalry and infantry. The advance guard were cut off, 28 in number. The attack was made by the enemy between 4 and 5 o'clock P. M. Fannin fought them until late in the evening, and repulsed them with a small loss on his part, while that of the enemy was 190 killed, and many wounded. After the enemy had fallen back, Colonel Fannin entrenched himself during the night. On the following morning the enemy showed a white flag. Fannin went out to meet the commanding General, who represented to Col. Fannin that he knew the force opposed to him; that he [Fannin] was entrenched in an open prairie without water; that he was surrounded, and that his men must perish; that he wished to show him quarters, &c. A capitulation was made with the usual forms of honorable warfare, Colonel Fannin was to lay down his arms and march back to Goliad, where they were to remain six or eight days as prisoners of war, to be shipped to New Orleans from Copano. They surrendered on these conditions, on the ninth day after their arrival at Goliad; they were assured that a vessel was ready to receive them at Copano, to embark for New Orleans, and Colonel Fannin marched out in file; the Mexicans each side of him. They were marched down about five miles, and the order was given to fire upon them. At the first fire, nearly every man fell; a Mr. Hudden of Texas, and three others succeeded in reaching some bushes about 100 yards distant. They were pursued by the enemy into the high grass, where they lost sight of them. Hudden remained in the grass all night; in the morning he succeeded in making his escape.

Houston fell back. He marched his troops inhumanly. He lied to them and denied there had been a massacre. He retreated with the skill of a great general, drawing his enemy from its base of supplies and tiring it, training his men with thirty-mile marches and iron discipline, waiting . . . waiting. . . .

There came the proper hour and jubilantly the Mobile *Mercantile Advertiser* described the battle of San Jacinto:

## DIRECT FROM THE FIELD OF GLORY!

On the 21st April, the Texians, under Houston, and 600 strong, had manoeuvred so as to get above and within some two miles and in sight of the Mexicans, under Santa Ana, who were 1,270 strong, and near down to the fork of the two rivers, the Brassos and Sabine. Houston, having the enemy thus snugly hemmed in, had his little army drawn up for the purpose of addressing it in person. "Soldiers," said he, "there is the enemy—do you want to fight?" "Yes!" was the universal shout. "Well, then," said he, "let us eat our dinner, and then I will lead you into battle!" They obeyed the order to eat, and immediately thereafter, at about 4 o'clock P. M. were marched to the attack. They bore down upon the Mexicans at the top of their speed, reserving their fire until near enough to have every shot tell. A hot engagement was kept up about twenty minutes, when the Mexicans began to break and retreat in great disorder and confusion. The Texians carried all before them. Although they had but half the number of the Mexicans, and but two pieces of cannon [the famous "Twin Sisters"] of four pounds each, while the enemy had a six and a nine pounder, yet in fifteen minutes after the engagement commenced, many of the Mexicans called loudly for quarter. After the rout of the Mexicans, Houston's men continued to follow up and pour in upon them for about two hours. Upwards of *six hundred and fifty* Mexicans were killed, and about six hundred taken prisoners. There were *six* or *seven* Texians killed and about twenty wounded. Generals Cos and Almonte were among the first prisoners taken. The former was pale and greatly agitated, but the latter displayed, as he had done during the fight, great coolness and courage.

Santa Ana fled among the earliest who retreated. He was seen by two boys, one about 15 and the other about 17 years of age, to go into a thicket of wood. They kept watch of the place during the night, and the next morning a man came out dressed like a common Mexican soldier. Not suspecting him to be Santa Ana, they took him prisoner. He offered no resistance, but wished to be taken to General Houston. He was conducted to that officer, when he made himself known as Santa Ana, asked the respect due officers of rank, and made the offers for his liberty which had been published. Santa Ana, Mr. Andrews says, is apparently about 45 years of age, of rather small stature, dark complexion, black hair, black bright eyes, and altogether a good looking man.

When questioned as to the murder of Cols. Fannin and Ward, and the men under their command, he stated that, in the battle of the evening previous to their surrender, about 1000 of the Mexicans were killed, while not more than 20 Texians had fallen—that the Texians had exhausted their ammunition and were without water; that they surrendered upon the terms of capitulation since published, but that he had been induced to violate those terms for two reasons— first, because, the day after the surrender of Col. Ward and those under his command, the number of prisoners became so great in consequence that he had not provisions sufficient for them and his own army; and, secondly, he had not men enough to keep them securely. Consequently, Col. Ward and almost all his soldiers were shot with Col. Fannin.

There was born the short-lived Republic of Texas. In less than a decade it ceased to be. Its admission into the Union may be found recorded in the Washington *Daily National Intelligencer* for December 23, 1845, in a singularly naive editorial. The author could not see six months ahead, to the imperialistic war with Mexico, nor could he remember that President Polk had yearned publicly for the annexation of California. In view of the following events, the "unseemly precipitancy" that surprised this editor is not so strange.

The Joint Resolution for the admission of Texas into the Union, which last week passed the House of Representatives, yesterday passed the Senate, after a debate, brief but of great interest, of which a full report will be placed before our readers.

The die having been cast at the last session, the consummation of "annexation" in one form or another, at the present session of Congress, was to have been expected. But the act of admission is exceptional in several particulars, and especially in its contravention of the spirit, if not of the letter of the Constitution, in giving to Texas, without any intermediate term of probation such as other Territories have all undergone before being admitted into the Union, a right to send *two* Representatives to Congress, her population not being sufficient to entitle her to even one, except under the special provision in the Constitution that "each state shall have at least one Representative". What there is in the case of Texas, or in the claims of her population to the peculiar favor of Congress, that should give to her, a State just born, privileges which are not yet even enjoyed by the older States of Arkansas and Florida—which were not enjoyed by other new States before them, and will assuredly not be extended to the State of Iowa when she comes into the Union—it required the assembled wisdom of the nation to discover.

In the Senate, the privilege of debate upon the subject, or of proposing amendments, we are happy to say, was not refused, as it had been in the House of Representatives. In both Houses, however, this act of admission of a Foreign Territory into the Union—an act for solemn deliberation, if any act can be—appears to us to have been pressed to a decision with, to say the least of it, an unseemly precipitancy.

II

# DEATH OF AARON BURR

(New York *Evening Post*)

---

It is said that when news of the battle of San Jacinto reached him, Aaron Burr cried, "I was thirty years too soon!" Old and living in the grandiose dreams that had governed his life, he thought of Texas as he had thought of it in 1804, when the tragedy of his quarrel with Alexander Hamilton forced him to seek a kingdom of his own, and to plot great conquests on Blennerhasset Island and elsewhere.

Politics was no more heated in 1804 than it is today, but the methods of obtaining satisfaction varied. Hoodlums did not destroy ballots and shoot their protectors on election day; instead, the principals—in this case Burr and Hamilton—exchanged wary and graceful notes, offered and accepted challenges, met in the dawn.

The readers of the New York *Morning Chronicle* read, on the morning of July 13, 1804, a brief story beneath one of the favorite headlines of the early nineteenth century: "MELANCHOLY INTELLIGENCE":

> We publish with regret the melancholy intelligence that General Hamilton expired yesterday afternoon about half after two o'clock. Few circumstances have awakened such general sympathy as the sudden decease of this gentleman, so distinguished for his talents, so warmly esteemed by his friends, and so highly respected in extensive circles of society. . . .
>
> We are authorized to state, as the declaration of the two gentlemen who attended Col. Burr and Gen. Hamilton to the field, that the conduct of both parties was correct, gentlemanly and honorable.

And, four days later, the *Chronicle* contained the full details. Meanwhile, the New York *Press* had printed the correspondence between Burr and Hamilton preceding the duel, from which can be gathered the simple reasons for the quarrel: Hamilton's cutting criticism of Burr as too dangerous a man to be entrusted with government and Burr's inability to force a retraction of the words. The story of the duel itself recreates the early morning tableau of two gentlemen settling a disagreement:

Col. Burr arrived first on the ground, as had been previously agreed; when General Hamilton arrived the parties exchanged salutations, and the seconds proceeded to make their arrangements. They measured the distance, ten full paces, and cast lots for the choice of position as also to determine by whom the word should be given, both of which fell to the second of General Hamilton. They then proceeded to load the pistols in each other's presence, after which the parties took their stations. The gentleman who was to give the word then explained to the parties the rules, which were to govern them in firing, which were as follows: "The parties being placed at their stations—the second who gives the word shall ask them whether they are ready; being answered in the affirmative, he shall say 'present' after this the parties shall present and fire when they please—if one fires before the other, the opposite second shall say one, two, three, fire—and shall then fire or lose his fire." He then asked if they were prepared, being answered in the affirmative, he gave the word *present,* as had been agreed upon, and both parties took aim and fired in succession, the intervening time is not expressed, as the seconds do not precisely agree on that point. The fire of Col. Burr took effect, and General Hamilton almost instantly fell. Col. Burr then advanced toward General Hamilton with a manner and a gesture that appeared to General Hamilton's friend to be expressive of regret, but without speaking, turned about and withdrew, being urged from the field by his friend as has been subsequently stated, with a view to prevent his being recognized by the surgeon and bargeman, who were then approaching. No further communication took place between the principals, and the barge that carried Col. Burr immediately returned to the city. We conceive it proper to add that the conduct of the parties in this interview was perfectly proper as suited the occasion.

New York took no more than moments to supplant its shock at the loss of Hamilton with anger against his destroyer. Crowds gathered in the streets to discuss the crime; indictments for murder began to be drafted in the minds of officials; and Burr found himself in the stage for Philadelphia, jouncing over the execrable roads for three days, riding into the pages of another fantastic chapter of his life. From the fatal Weehawken the Vice-President of the United States went to the Mississippi, and floated down it upon a commodious boat, telling those with whom he stopped, and who might help, of his plan for the conquest of Mexico. The tragedy that stalked through the life of this man is reflected in the phrase: "I was thirty years too soon!" Theodosia, who died in the storm off the Capes, the daughter who meant more to this lover of many women than any or all of them . . . the trial for high treason before the court at Richmond . . . futile search for the key to the chamber that would give him power, in New York, New Orleans and Europe . . . and finally, in retirement, poor and nearly forgotten:

(New York *Evening Post*, September 15, 1836)

## DEATH OF AARON BURR

This distinguished individual, who has for a length of time resided at Richmond house, in Bristol, expired yesterday at about 3 o'clock P. M.

The New York *Evening Post* had been founded, three years before he fell with Burr's bullet in his body, by Alexander Hamilton, as a staff to support his political travelings. It was to be expected that the editors of the *Post*, even thirty-two years after their founder had died, would not feel too kindly toward his killer. Four days after its announcement of the death of Burr, the *Post* appraised him, without regard for the false reverence we give the dead:

*FUNERAL OF AARON BURR*—The remains of Aaron Burr were on Friday committed to the earth at Princeton, New Jersey, beside the graves of President Edwards and President Burr, his father and grandfather. It was natural enough that the relatives of this man should wish to perform his obsequies with decency and propriety, but we protest against the puffery of which he is made the object in the publick prints, and the effect of which is to confound all moral distinctions. When we read of "admiration for his greatness", "respect for his memory", and "condolence for his loss", we are tempted to ask ourselves if the community have ceased to discriminate between the good and bad actions of men. The truth is, nobody is to be condoled with for his loss, no respect is entertained for the memory of one so profligate in private and publick life, and though Colonel Burr was a man of acute and active mind, he did not rise to the measure of intellectual greatness—as he certainly was at a deplorable distance from moral greatness. We would willingly have passed by this subject in silence, but these remarks are forced from us by what we must regard as a shameful prostitution of the voice of the Press.

Some of the publick prints are indulging in anticipation of the posthumous record of Colonel Burr's political and personal adventures, prepared under his direction for the press, and are essaying to awaken a prurient curiosity concerning them, by the intimation that they contain disclosures of things which ought never to be revealed. We have no expectation of advantage to the cause of truth or of morals from the appearance of such a work. It were better that the memory of his intrigues should die with him.

## III

# THE MAGNETIC TELEGRAPH
### (Baltimore *Clipper*)

———————

The editors paid sketchy tribute to the device of Samuel F. B. Morse, after he had fought the long fight, and had wrested from a reluctant Congress thirty thousand dollars for his first line. Within a decade of that May day in 1844 when the wire between Baltimore and Washington was first tested, the editors were to accept telegraphic dispatches as a matter of course. But in its beginnings they had little space for articles on Professor Morse's invention; from the appearance of their newspapers, they were still mentally in the "Special Express to the *Gazette*" era. They seemed not to realize, at the beginning, that the first messages passing over the line were news—the proceedings of the 1844 Democratic National Convention in Baltimore. The Baltimore *Clipper* for May 23, 1844, gave one of the earliest accounts of the invention:

MAGNETIC TELEGRAPH—This telegraph has been completed from Washington city to the railroad depot in Pratt street, where it will stop for the present. It has excited considerable attention, people being curious to see it in operation. The wire (perfectly secured against the weather by a covering of rope yarn and tar) is conducted on the top of posts about twenty feet high and about 100 yards apart. We understand that the nominations on Monday next will be forwarded to Washington by means of this telegraph.

We have no doubt that the government will deem it expedient to continue this telegraph to Philadelphia, New York and Boston, when its utility shall have been fully tested. When understood, the mode of operation is plain and simple.

A week later the line was in full operation, reporting happenings of the Convention to eager listeners at the Washington end. On the twenty-eighth, the Washington correspondent for the New York *Herald* put into very few words what 1844 thought of the telegraph:

In the matter of news, Washington is now altogether an importer and not an exporter. The exchanges are largely against us. Little else is done but watch Professor Morse's Bulletin from Baltimore, to learn the progress of doings at the Convention. Nothing will be done of any interest or importance until after the adjournment of the Convention.

Professor Morse's telegraph is not only an era in the transmission of intelligence, but it has originated in the mind an entirely new class of ideas, a new species of consciousness. Never before was anyone conscious that he knew with certainty what events were at that moment passing in a distant city—40, 100 or 500 miles off. For example, it is now precisely 11 o'clock. The telegraph announces as follows:

"11 o'clock—Senator Walker is *now* replying to Mr. Butler upon the adoption of the two-thirds rule."

It requires no small intellectual effort to realize that this is a fact that *now is,* and not one that *has been.* Baltimore is 40 miles from Washington. It is a most wonderful achievement in the arts.

# FINAL HOME

GOLD HUNTING IN 1843—"The gold is found in the earth in a pure state in particles from the size of a pea up to an ounce weight. . . . I have worked ten days, during which I got eight ounces. . . ."

—Boston *Transcript*

# I

## HO! HO! FOR CALIFORNIA
(New York *Herald*)

---

James W. Marshall was delayed by the silt that gathered in the tailrace he was constructing for John Sutter's mill. It made frequent cleanings necessary, dull and stupid work—until a morning early in 1848. On that morning—January twenty-fourth—the eyes of Marshall caught a glitter reflecting the sunlight, and he delved more deeply into the dirt. He picked up particles of yellow gold, and doubted that it could be anything so precious: he pounded bits of it and it did not crumble, but instead mashed flat into a pliant, strong wafer. As soon as he was sure, he mounted his horse and rode the forty miles to the fort.

He and Sutter tried to keep their secret: as well try to quench the light of the sun. The gold fever swept California, a happy plague. San Franciscans read in their newspapers that the reports of the strike were exaggerated, and when they finished reading they dropped the papers, their wives and children and businesses, and rushed for the fields. Six months after the discovery on the American Fork, San Francisco had one quarter of its population left, and the first of the flood of emigrants from the East had not yet arrived.

The East learned of the fortunes to be had for the stooping in a letter to the New York *Tribune,* published August 19, 1848:

San Francisco, Alta California, April 1, 1848—The gold mine . . . is only three feet below the surface, in a strata of soft sand rock. From explorations south twelve miles and north five miles, the continuance of this strain is reported, and the mineral said to be equally abundant, and from twelve to eighteen feet in thickness: so that, without allowing any golden hopes to puzzle my prophetic visions of the future, I would predict for California, a Peruvian harvest of the precious metals, as soon as a sufficiency of miners, &c., can be obtained.

A few reckless ones started at once.  Others waited, disbelieving the Peruvian harvest and being not quite willing to help make the sufficiency of miners.  It remained for President Polk, in his message to the Thirtieth Congress in December, to convince thousands that in California lay the fulfillment of fabulous dreams.  The New York *Herald* for December sixth printed the message in full; in it, speaking of the gold, the President said:

It is known that mines of the precious metals existed to a considerable extent in California at the time of its acquisition. Recent disclosures render it probable that these mines are more extensive and valuable than was anticipated.  The accounts of the abundance of gold in that territory are of such an extraordinary character as would scarcely command belief were they not corroborated by the authentic reports of officers in the public service, who have visited the mineral districts, and derived the facts which they detail from personal observation.  Reluctant to credit the reports in general circulation as to the quantity of gold, the officer commanding our forces in California visited the mineral district in July last, for the purpose of obtaining accurate information on the subject.  His report to the War Department of the result of his examination, and the facts obtained on the spot, is herewith laid before Congress.  When he visited the country, there were about four thousand persons engaged in collecting gold. There is every reason to believe that the number of persons so employed has since been augmented. The explorations already made warrant the belief that the supply is very large and that gold is found at various places in an extensive district of country. . . .

The effects produced by the discovery of these rich mineral deposits, and the success which has attended the labors of those who have resorted to them, have produced a surprising change in the state of affairs in California. Labor commands a most exhorbitant price, and all other pursuits but that of searching for the precious metals are abandoned. Nearly the whole of the male population of the country have gone to the gold district. Ships arriving on the coast are deserted by their crews and their voyages suspended for want of sailors. Our commanding officer there entertains apprehensions that soldiers cannot be kept in the public service without a large increase of pay. Desertions in his command have become frequent, and he recommends that those who shall withstand the strong temptation, and remain faithful, should be rewarded.

This abundance of gold, and the all-engrossing pursuit of it have already caused in California an unprecedented rise in the price of the necessaries of life.

By January of 1849, the Eastern newspapers were crowded with advertisements addressed to the gold seekers. The New York *Herald* and other newspapers ran whole columns of them, under the heading "HO! FOR CALIFORNIA!", offering steamship passage via the Nicaraguan crossing between the oceans, portable houses, clothing, tin roofing, pistols and pistol holsters, machinery for mining gold, compressed foods, rifles and everything else a pioneer might need. Here is one advertisement, whose author may have profited by his cynicism:

HO! HO! HO! FOR CALIFORNIA! HO! LAST
NOT LEAST!—Persons going out to the gold regions are
seriously advised to take, among other necessaries, a good
lot of Monuments and Tombstones. A great saving can be
effected by having their inscriptions cut in New York be-
forehand. These articles can be had in all variety to suit the
gold country, at short notice, at the marble yard of R. E.
LAUNITZ, 536 Broadway.

Fortune is fortune wherever men live. England, too, caught
the fever, and the matter of an ocean was no deterrent to the
Britons. So serious became the lust for gold and the eagerness
to make a start that the Liverpool *Mail,* on January thirteenth,
tried to warn away its readers from what it felt was certain
fraud:

> Gold! It is the God of this world. Only whisper the word
> and its worshippers fall down on their knees. Breathe it in
> the valley and it is heard at the mountain top. Tell where it
> can be found, and the millions rush to the spot faster than
> they would go to heaven.
> California! That is the newest "South Sea Bubble" of
> the day. There, they say, it is to be had in bucketsfull for the
> gathering—there it is strewed "thick as the leaves in Vallam-
> brosa." Mr. Jonathan Polk, of the United States, is one of
> the most remarkably cute tradesmen of these times. He
> wants money, but he scorns the idea of picking it up, which
> act of picking, perhaps, he would consider a fraud upon the
> public spirit and patriotism of this republican era. He, there-
> fore, in a fervent spirit of true munificence, invites the
> citizens of the world to gather it for themselves. "Go to Cali-
> fornia," he says, "there is gold." The eyes of the idolators
> glisten—the gulls flap their wings—and it is well that they
> are gulls for a large portion of the imaginary gold district
> of California is six months of the year under water. But go
> they will without any mistake, with their pickaxes and melt-
> ing pots, and if they find only copper instead of gold, or

nothing at all of any value, the object of Mr. Polk will be accomplished. He will relieve New York of a few thousand reckless adventurers, whom his Mexican War has made penniless and desperate, attract other adventurers from this and other countries, and he will procure settlers and inhabitants sufficient for his purpose.

The London *Times* only a few days before it was forced to endorse the authenticity of the strike, tried a more subtle form of discouragement. An anonymous poet prepared a jingle which appeared in the Sunday edition of that newspaper on January sixth: He called it "A NEW GOLD SONG" and suggested it be sung to the air *Yankee Doodle.*

> *"What is here?*
> *Gold—yellow, glittering precious gold?"*
> *—Timon of Athens.*

Now's the time to change your clime,
  Give up work and talking;
All who choose be rich as Jews,
  Even without asking,
California's precious earth
  Turns the new world frantic;
Sell your traps and take a berth
  Across the wild Atlantic.

> Every one who digs and delves,
>   All whose arms are brawny
> Take a pick and help yourselves—
>   Off to Californy.

Yankee Doodle all agog,
  With the golden mania,
Debts no longer prove a clog—
  Happy Pennsylvania!
Those who about stocks and loans
  Kicked up such an old dust,
Live to see the very stones
  Come down with the gold dust.

Every one who digs and delves,
Joins the Indians tawny;
Take a pick and help yourselves—
Off to Californy!

Shakespeare, of undying fame,
Whom they're going to play so,
Gave to gold a naughty name,
Or made Timon say so.
And the mob their true lands leave,
Corn, and canes, and 'taters,
To appear, lest it deceive,
As Californicators.

Every one who digs and delves,
Wear your hands quite horny,
Take a pick and help yourselves—
Off to Californy!

Gold is got in pan and pot,
Soup tureen or ladle,
Basket, birdcage and what not,
Even to a cradle!
El Dorada's found at last,
*Turba sed virorum*
Lose their dazzled heads as fast,
As Raleigh did before 'em.

Choose your able bodied men,
Navvies bold and brawny;
Give them picks and spades, and then
Off to Californy!

How this flush of gold will end
We have statements ample;
Perhaps a few sacks they will send,
Only for a sample.
But we hope the golden move
Really is all true, sirs,
Else will Yankee Doodle prove
A Yankee Doodle doo, sirs.

Every one who digs or delves
　Stout, and tough, and brawny,
Buy a pick and help yourselves—
　Off to Californy!

Such ridicule was not alone English. Under the imprint of Baker and Scribner appeared a book by Cantell A. Bigly: *AURIFONDA, or Adventures in the Gold Regions.* The New York *Tribune* reviewed this book, the reviewer apparently not displeased with Mr. Bigly's humor:

The Californimania has brought to light many adventures and experiences in that hitherto half known region, and the volume before us has, we doubt not, as good claims to notice as some of them. It describes the adventures of *Can-tell-a-big-ly,* a trapper, who was *not* connected with the Exploring Expedition, and found his way into the southern part of the Great Basin of California. Here he discovered a region of gold, where the most valuable metal was iron— where the princes were magnificently habited in cotton and the laborers in cloth of gold. We copy the author's description of the capital of this region, named *Aurum,* with a few corrections of our own:

"We had now reached an open square, surrounded by a heavy gold railing, and containing many ornamental trees. It was thronged with people. Toward the farther extremity of it was a great golden fountain. In the middle stood the royal palace, all one blaze of light and gold. *Mideer* pointed out various buildings and told me their names; the palace is called *Sitioll;* on the east of the square is another great palace called *Tamanioll*—this is a great national school of oratory and manners. On the west is the *Hastarowse,* a princely structure occupied by *Ztetzn,* First Lord of the Commisariat Department and Curator of Delegates from the various provinces. All these buildings were now brilliantly illuminated, and the whole square was one blaze of splendor, almost too dazzling to be looked at without pain.

"South of *Tamanioll* was a large edifice called *Trybnbil-dens* where the couriers from all parts of the kingdom were constantly arriving with news of whatever took place. It was, in fact, very similar to the office of a daily paper in our country. The intelligence thus collected was printed on thin golden sheets and distributed by a class of beings peculiar to the region. They were called *Nuzboiiz* and possessed very remarkable voices. In all quarters we heard them crying *Sonerelden-Trybewn* which was the name of the paper they carried. The population of *Aurum* looked anxiously every morning for the appearance of these *Nuzboiiz* and gave them in return for the auriferous sheets pewter, tin and other precious metals."

The British forgot to ridicule after a bit, but their editors were far from admitting that in California lay the answer to their readers' hopes. A Liverpool dispatch to the New York *Herald* reported on January thirtieth:

The gold excitement here and in London, exceeds anything ever before known or heard of. The extravagent tales told at first about the glittering chunks were regarded as visionary, and called a "Yankee humbug." Subsequently, however, but not until endorsed by the London *Times* did the people of this country believe it. But the reports having been duly authenticated by official correspondence, which places the matter beyond doubt, John Bull has been actually mad, crazy and bewildered. Nothing is heard or talked about but the new El Dorado. Companies are organizing in London, in great numbers, for the promised land; and we hear it stated that not less than fourteen vessels have already been chartered, and nearly or quite filled with passengers and freight. . . .

An editor in one of the Liverpool papers, yesterday, more scared than hurt, winds up a long article by saying, "The bones of thousands of these deluded creatures are doomed to mix with the gold dust of the plains. Already there are more deaths than burials among the gold finders, and murder and rapine diversify the process of acquirement. The gold fever in California may this year number as many victims as Cholera."

James Gordon Bennett, the elder, writing in his *Herald,* took issue with the "more scared than hurt" editor abroad, when he wrote on February fourth:

We allude to the vast discoveries of mineral wealth recently made in California. Now, what will be the effect of these discoveries on this country and on Europe? We have seen that the gold mania has completely thrown in the shade the agitation and excitement caused by the slavery question in Congress, and out of it; that it is at the present time producing an emigration of our best classes of population, who, even if they do not find all the gold they expect, will effect an entire revolution on the western shores of the American continent. They are, in either event, laying the foundation of greatness, that will, in due course of time, rival that of the Atlantic side. They will found a western empire, that will change the whole course of trade and make San Francisco on the Pacific, and New York on the Atlantic, the great receiving and distributing reservoirs of the wealth, commerce, manufactures and productions of the whole commercial world. What further changes it will effect, time alone can tell.

San Francisco, nearly depopulated at first by the departure of gold seekers, became in a year the great city of the West. Gamblers, suckers, pimps, murderers, whores, fathers of happy families, remittance men, professional killers tumbled off every boat and emerged from Conestoga wagons. There was no law, except in name. Murders were cheap and common—it was not unusual for a man to be killed for a couple of thousand dollars, and for the murderer to buy his freedom with half the loot. The city essentially was a respectable one, but with money paving the streets there had to be crime, and for two years the citizens were too busy enriching themselves to bother greatly about corpses in alleys. But in 1851, urged on by the editors, summary law came into being. In the beginning—in June of that year—it was the quick and undisciplined hanging of a thief. The California *Courier* for June tenth reported this, and added:

> Our predictions have been most signally verified, and most terribly have the bands of murderers, thieves and criminals visited their vengeance upon the devoted city. We have lost millions of dollars and the lives of some thirty men. . . . What now shall be done? Are we to continue to threaten, and nothing more? . . . Where the guilt of the criminal is clear and unquestionable, the first law of nature demands that they be shot, hung or burned alive. Delay is dangerous. Some terrible visitation must be meted out to these villians. . . .

On the following day there appeared, under the paper's masthead, this notice—a summons to be answered by what has become famed as the Committee of Vigilance of San Francisco:

### Public Meeting

All citizens of San Francisco, favorable to adopting some measures to protect themselves from the depredations of the villains who infest the city, are requested to meet on the Plaza, at the Adobe Building, This Afternoon, at 4 o'clock.

The Vigilantes wasted no time. Only three days later there appeared, also in the *Courier,* the report of the coroner's verdict in the death of one Jenkins, who had the dubious distinc-

tion of being the first criminal executed formally by the
Vigilantes :

> The verdict of the jury is as follows :
> "We, the Jurors of a Jury of Inquest empaneled by the
> Coroner of the county of San Francisco, to inquire into the
> cause of the death of one John Jenkins, alias Simpton, do
> find upon their oaths that the said Jenkins, alias Simpton,
> came to his death on the morning of the 11th of June, be-
> tween the hours of two and three o'clock, by violent means,
> by strangulation, caused by being suspended by the neck,
> with a rope attached to the south end of the Adobe Building
> on the Plaza, at the hands of and in pursuance of a precon-
> certed action on the part of an association of citizens, styling
> themselves the Committee of Vigilance. . . ."

As quickly as the cry of "Gold!" had been raised, that of
"Law!" now echoed.

The Vigilantes functioned for a year. Then, with some
thieves and killers hanged and others banished, quiet settled
upon the city and the committee was disbanded. Elsewhere in
the state other committees remained active; there appeared in
the papers of 1851 dispatches from such places as Sonora,
where :

> Yesterday, near the second crossing of the Calavaras, a
> man named Mickey was hung for theft. From what I can
> learn of his career in this community, hanging was decidedly
> a compassionate way of depriving him of his worthless
> life. . . .

And in the case of Jim Hill, another thief in the same
town :

> A large crowd was gathered round; but all was still as
> death. The signal was given and in an instant the wretched

man was hanging by the neck. There was scarce a struggle. The crowd was deeply impressed, but all were satisfied of the righteousness and necessity of the punishment.

The Vigilantes were dormant until May 14, 1856. The murder of a man named James King-of-William by James Casey on that day aroused them. The leaders of the community suddenly realized that their work was not done: that four thousand murders in California and twelve hundred in San Francisco, in the five years between 1849 and 1854, demanded further summary action. Casey, in the jail, saw through the bars a mob of ten thousand demanding his death and three thousand armed guards holding them off.

The Vigilantes numbered thirty-five hundred when they appeared before the jail on May twenty-second. The guards melted; Casey and another murderer named Charles Cora were neatly hanged. It was a quiet ceremony. And law came to California. . . .

## II

## JENNY LIND'S FIRST CONCERT

(New York *Tribune*)

---

Phineas Taylor Barnum, the Connecticut Yankee who put teeth in the word ballyhoo, vexed and plagued nearly every newspaper man of his time. In 1835, the year of the great New York fire, he purchased Joice Heth, his first major attraction. Joice Heth was a negro slave, wizened and crippled, who had nothing to recommend her except the legend that she was one hundred and sixty-odd years old and had been nurse to George Washington. Barnum sold Joice Heth (at a luscious profit) to the public. The tricks he used on the gullible Fourth

Estate seem too transparent today ever to have been possible, but they worked. He started quarrels in the newspapers about the slave, with scientific gentlemen debating her authenticity. He prayed (and his prayers were answered) that editors would berate him as a humbug—spelling his name correctly, of course. And finally, when Joice Heth died, and an autopsy revealed that she was possibly ninety years of age, but no older, the showman made publicity out of that.

But the list of Barnum's achievements is too long to be treated here in full length. Among the attractions he offered were Tom Thumb, and Jumbo, the elephant; the Feejee Maid (a phony mermaid, singularly ugly, except in Barnum's advertising) and Zip, the What Is It?; the American Museum and the Greatest Show on Earth. The tour of Jenny Lind in this country under his management is perhaps the best example of Barnum's skill as a producer. Never having heard the Nightingale, Barnum negotiated with her and signed a contract for the then stupendous figure of one thousand dollars a concert for one hundred and fifty appearances. What Jenny Lind had to give the people of the New World was, her European admirers believed, high art; under the Barnum banner her appearances in New York and elsewhere were sawdusty and tinseled.

For weeks before her arrival, Barnum flooded the press with accounts of her movements abroad. When her ship finally crept through the harbor to its wharf, dense thousands of hysterical New Yorkers packed the streets. Every day there appeared a column concerning the Nightingale, with the result that when she sang for the first time all the newspapers set off rhetorical roman candles in her honor.

The New York *Tribune* for September 12, 1850, printed this account of her appearance in Castle Garden, at the Battery:

Jenny Lind's first concert is over, and all doubts are at an end. She is the greatest singer we have ever heard, and her success is all that was anticipated from her genius and her fame. As this is something of an era in our history of Art, we give a detailed account of all that took place on the occasion.

All the preparatory arrangements for the Concert were made with great care, and from the admirable system observed, none of the usual disagreeable features of such an event were experienced. Outside of the gate there was a double row of Policemen extending up the main avenue to the Battery grounds. Carriages only were permitted to drive up to the gate from the Whitehall side, and pass off into Battery-place. At one time the line of carriages extended to Whitehall and up State street into Broadway. The order specified in yesterday's *Tribune* was observed, by which means everything was accomplished in a quiet and orderly manner. The Chief of Police, with about 60 men, came on the ground at 5 o'clock and maintained the most complete order to the end.

Mr. Barnum, according to promise, had put up a substantial frame-work, and thrown an immense awning over the bridge, which is some 200 feet in length. This was brilliantly lighted, and had almost the appearance of a triumphal avenue on entering the gate.

There was an immense crowd on the Battery clustering around the gates during the whole evening, but no acts of disorder occurred. When Jenny Lind's carriage came, but very few persons knew it, and no great excitement followed. The principal annoyance was occasioned by a noisy crowd of boys in boats, who gathered around the outer wall of the Castle, and being by their position secure from the Police, tried to disturb those within by a hideous clamor of shouts and yells, accompanied by a discordant din of drums and fifes. There must have been more than 200 boats and a thousand persons on the water. They caused some annoyance to that portion of the audience in the back seats of the balcony, but the nuisance was felt by none in the parquette.

By 10 o'clock they had either become tired or ashamed of the contemptible outrage they were attempting, and dispersed. We may here remark that if the River Police asked for by Chief Matsell had been in existence, this attempt could not have been made.

On entering the Castle a company of ushers distinguished by their badges were in readiness to direct the visitors to that part of the hall where their seats were located. Colored lamps and hangings suspended to the pillars indicated at a glance the different divisions, and the task of seating the whole audience of near seven thousand persons was thus accomplished without the least inconvenience. The hall was brilliantly lighted, though from its vast extent the stage looked somewhat dim. The wooden partition which was built up in place of the drop curtain, is covered with a painting representing the combined standards of America and Sweden, below which are arabesque ornaments in white and gold. Considering the short time allowed for these improvements, the change was remarkable. The only instance of bad taste which we noticed was a large motto, worked in flowers, suspended over the pillars of the balcony directly in front of the stage. "Welcome, Sweet Warbler" (so ran the words) was not only tame and commonplace, but decidedly out of place.

The sight of the grand hall, with its gay decorations, its glittering lamps, and its vast throng of expectant auditors, was in itself almost worth a $5 ticket. We were surprised to notice that not more than one-eighth of the audience were ladies. They must stay at home, it seems, when the tickets are high, but the gentlemen go, nevertheless. For its size the audience was one of the most quiet, refined and appreciative we ever saw assembled in this city. Not more than one-third were seated before 7 o'clock, and when the eventful hour arrived, they were still coming in. A few of the seats were not taken when the orchestra had assembled and Mr. Benedict, who was greeted with loud cheers on his appearance, gave the first flourish of his baton.

Now came a moment of breathless expectation. A moment more, and JENNY LIND clad in a white dress which well became the frank sincerity of her face, came forward through the orchestra. It is impossible to describe the spontaneous burst of welcome which greeted her. The vast assembly rose as one man and for some minutes nothing could be seen but the waving of hands and handkerchiefs, nothing heard but a storm of tumultuous cheers. The enthusiasm of the moment, for a time beyond all bounds, was at last subdued, after prolonging itself by its own fruitless efforts to subdue itself, and the divine songstress, with that perfect bearing, that air of all dignity and sweetness, blending a child-like simplicity and half-trembling womanly modesty with the beautiful confidence of Genius and serene wisdom of Art, addressed herself to song, as the orchestra symphony prepared the way for the voice in *Casta Diva*. A better test piece could not have been selected for her debut. Every soprano lady has sung it to us; but nearly every one has seemed only trying to make something of it, while Jenny Lind *was* the very music of it for the time being. We would say no less than that; for the wisest and honestest part of criticism on such a first hearing of a thing so perfect, was to give itself purely up to it, without question, and attempt no analysis of what too truly fills one to have yet begun to be an object of thought.

If it were possible we would describe the quality of that voice, so pure, so sweet, so fine, so whole and all-pervading, in its lowest breathings and minutest *fioriture* as well as in its strongest volume. We never heard tones which in their sweetness went so far. They brought the most distant and ill-seated auditor close to her. They *were* tones, every one of them, and the whole air had to take the law of their vibrations. The voice and the delivery had in them all the good qualities of all the good singers. Song in her has that integral beauty which at once proclaims it as a type for all, and is most naturally worshipped as much by the multitude.

But not all Americans were swept along to such a state as the *Tribune* man by the Barnum tidal wave. Among the doubters was the author of *Letters from Paumanok,* one Walt Whitman, who wrote to the New York *Evening Post* on August 14, 1851:

> The Swedish Swan, with all her blandishments, never touched my heart in the least. I wondered at so much vocal dexterity; and indeed they were all very pretty, those leaps and double somersets. But even in the grandest religious airs, genuine masterpieces as they are, of the German composers, executed by this strangely over-praised woman in perfect scientific style, let the critics say what they like, it was a failure; for there was a vacuum in the head of the performance.

## III

# THE JAPAN EXPEDITION
### (New York *Tribune*)

The brother of the Commodore Perry who defeated the British fleet on Lake Erie sailed for Japan in 1852, to open that remote nation to the Yankee traders. In that day Japan was farther away than could be computed in miles, and Christian peddlers were sternly excluded.

America thought little of the project when it was first suggested. The New York *Tribune* said in an editorial on March seventeenth:

> It seems we are to send a fleet to Japan, and to enter the Capital City at all hazards. The interests of American trade require that commercial communications be opened with that recluse region, and a numerous array of armed vessels will proceed to state that fact to the Japanese Govern-

ment and to open the gates of its ports. It is a fair suspicion that the greatness of America is better understood at Washington than at Jeddo,* and that the Japanese will be unable immediately to discern the advantage of trading with a nation which makes the overture from the cannon's mouth. . . .

In this state of things, going thus to pagan realms, it behooves us not to lose the opportunity of laboring for the spiritual benefit of these benighted Japanese. Let not these misguided men, fighting for their own, perish without benefit of clergy. . . . To this end, and to impart a moral luster to the expedition, we suggest that some of the many chaplains in the United States, now unemployed, be despatched to Japan with the fleet, and while the ships lie before Jeddo, bombarding the city, and stray boatsfull of obstinate Japanese are captured and brought on board our ships, the reverend gentlemen might exert all their genius in the conversion of such natives. . . .

We should, indeed, be truly sorry to see the American government engaged in any undertaking of this magnitude to which it would be unwilling to give the ameliorating aspect of a solicitude for the moral welfare of the people concerned. . . .

The *Herald* of the twenty-first echoed the *Tribune's* irony with:

. . . In paying his compliments to the inhabitants of Jesso, Sikof, Niphon and the great number of other islands comprising the kingdom of Japan, Com. Perry will be specially instructed to induce these benighted pagans to enter into friendly commercial intercourse with their more enlightened Christian brethren of the United States. . . . In case they are found to be dull of comprehension, or do not

---

*Only one of the several versions of this name. So little did the editors know of Japan that the spelling of its cities' names baffled them. The Jeddo of 1852 has become the Tokyo of today.

understand the Commodore's language . . . then, of course, the Commodore will urgently remonstrate, and in a very friendly manner—in order to make himself better understood—introduce to them his interpreters, whose language cannot be mistaken, as they speak with forty-two pound lungs.  However, should the Japanese King be so rude as to take offense at the prying propensities of this expedition, and attempt to forcibly expel it from his dominion—after an ample apology had been made for the intrusion—why, then, he should have to take the consequences which his own ungenerous inhospitality would bring upon him and his people.  The Yankees are merely desirous of ascertaining what these pagans are about, learning whether they have anything to trade, and what their opinions are concerning the Maine Liquor law; and if they should have the audacity to attack Com. Perry's ships, there may be a fight.  Upon the whole, it is more than possible that there will be considerable fuss, anyhow.

Two years and one month later, Mr. Bennett was still upset. He thought on April 19, 1854, that "it is a pity that Commodore Perry should have been occupied over a year with his squadron in taking a letter to the Emperor of Japan, and in calling for an answer.  But we presume that our administration will be satisfied if an answer of any kind is received."

Then, the *Herald* found space for reports from the expedition.  The gifts of the United States to the Emperor were described in the first story, printed June thirteenth:

. . . Four days after the interview, the presents were interchanged, time having been required to erect places for their reception.  Those for the Emperor consisted of, among other things, a railway with a steam engine, an electric telegraph, a surf boat, a life boat, a printing press, a fine lorgnette, a set of Audubon's *American Ornithology,* splendidly bound, plates of American Indians, maps of different states of America, agricultural implements, with all the modern improvements, a piece of cloth, a bale of cotton, a stove, rifles, pistols, and swords, champagne, cordials and American whiskey.

A similar list of gifts for the Empress, "if there be one," was described.

The following day there appeared a somewhat dubious report, reprinted from the London *Times'* Far Eastern correspondence:

### THE AMERICANS IN JAPAN
*(Correspondence of the London Times)*

. . . On the 7th of February we sailed for Japan [from China where the squadron had been wintering] and on Sunday the 13th we anchored within about twenty-five miles of Jeddo, where no foreign vessel had ever anchored before. After a good deal of diplomacy on the part of the Japanese and firmness on the part of the Americans, we told them that we did not like the place appointed for the negotiations, and would go nearer to Jeddo. They assented as gracefully as children go to bed before time, and we proceeded to Yokohama, off which village within ten miles of the imperial city we anchored. . . . We had passed our word to negotiate there and we made a new era in Eastern diplomacy by keeping it. . . .

As for any advantage to be immediately derived from commerce with these people, I am doubtful on that point; we saw no evidence of any wants or of any superfluities; but who can anticipate the wants which commerce can create? . . . But, if our first adventurers come here under the impression that the Japanese are ignorant because they are inexperienced in commerce, they will find themselves mistaken, for not even the Chinamen understand the art of making things appear to the greatest advantage with more skill than the Japanese. The presents of fruits and sweetmeats were so arranged in the boxes as to appear of thrice the real quantity, and everything is so contrived as to be overestimated by all but the closest observer.

Three thousand miles away and two days later, there was placed on the press a periodical edition of the San Francisco *Alta Californian.* Until the opening of the telegraph, many of the Pacific Coast newspapers printed what were called the "steamer editions," to be dispatched on the next boat leaving for Atlantic ports and so in some measure to keep the East informed of the West's progress. The *Alta Californian* offered "NEWS FROM JAPAN":

By arrival of the schooner *Restless*, we have a slip from the *"Polynesian"*, Sandwich Islands, of 21st May, from which we take the following very important news:
"The American Sloop-of-War, *Saratoga,* Capt. Walker, arrived at Honolulu on the 29th Ult. in 25 days from Japan, which is the shortest passage ever made.
"The *Saratoga* brings Capt. H. A. Adams, U. S. N., as bearer of despatches to the Government at Washington."
The point of interest in this intelligence is the fact that Com. Perry concluded a Treaty of Amity and Friendship with the Empire of Japan, at Kennewagawa, near the city of Yeddo, on the 28th of March, 1854. The long doubtful attempt has been entirely successful, and to the United States belongs the honor of making the first international treaty with Japan.
It will be recollected that in July of last year, Com. Perry, with two steam frigates and two sloops of war, paid a visit to Japan as bearer of a letter to the Emperor from the President of the United States, asking them to relax the restrictive policy which has so long closed that Empire to foreign intercourse. Having overcome the reluctance of the Japanese to hold intercourse with them by a firm but altogether peaceful course of proceeding, induced them to

receive some presents and the letter from the President of
the United States, Com. Perry took his departure with the
assurance to the Japanese officials that he should return in
the spring for an answer.

Having visited Loo Choo and China in the autumn and
winter of 1853, the squadron, as spring approached, made
their rendezvous at the Loo Choo group in February and
thence sailed for Japan. . . .

On arriving at Yeddo Bay, Com. Perry was informed by
the Japanese that they were disposed to give the President's
letter a most favorable consideration. . . .

After frequent meetings between Com. Perry on the part
of the United States and the High Commissioners deputed
by the Emperor on the part of the Japanese, the terms were
agreed upon, and the Treaty finally concluded on the 28th
of March. . . .

The Russian fleet, consisting of a schooner, frigate,
sloop-of-war and steam ship, has been at Nangasaki all winter importuning Japan for a treaty, but left in the month of
February, unable to effect their object.

Now it was done.   Perry had opened Japan (if by threats,
by mild threats), and America could look forward to a lucra-
tive trade with the Far East.   The gentlemen of the New York
*Tribune* and *Herald* were among the first to congratulate the
United States on its achievement.   Mr. James Gordon Bennett
declaimed in his *Herald* on June thirteenth:

The success which has attended Commodore Perry's expedition to Japan will by this time have silenced the most
inveterate of the croakers who so confidently predicted that
the Commodore would effect nothing, and that Japan would
remain for many a year to come as secluded and as bar-
barously guarded from the eyes of the world as it has been
for the last thousand years.   This result has long been probable.   From the moment the Emperor consented to hold
intercourse with our envoy, the chances of failure were very

slender. . . . Intercourse with Japan will in reality do more for the people of that empire than for us. To us it will give commercial facilities and maritime advantages; they will derive from the event not only these identical benefits in a much larger degree, but the much greater ones of Christianity, civilization, and ultimately, some notion of political liberty. . . .

For it is hardly possible to set a limit on a horizon to the vista of consequences which this single event opens to our view. . . .

The period for opening actual commercial intercourse with Japan will shortly arrive; and those whose ingenuity and thrift land them first at Matsmai or Sho-di-ma may reap golden harvests. Lines of steamers may be expected to ply between China and San Francisco, touching at the Loo Choo Islands and Japan, and thus the peoples of two continents will for the first time be brought into rapid contact, and close intimacy. We rejoice to think that in conferring this singular boon on his own countrymen and the Japanese, the framer of Perry's instructions has not been animated by any selfish feeling, or narrow prejudice, and that if the boon conferred by that treaty was not extended to all other nations besides the United States, the fault did not lie with us. England and France will lose no time in making the application required by Japanese pride, and before ten years, the Pacific Ocean will in all probability be covered by as many steamers as now float on the Atlantic.

And on the fourteenth, Mr. Horace Greeley nobly seconded those inspiring thoughts:

. . . The straight-forward, determined policy adopted by Commodore Perry, at the outset, is now producing its results, and, contrary to the expectations of nine-tenths of the civilized world—even those who were friendly to the Expedition—Japan has been induced to come forth from the seclusion of centuries. . . .

This memorable success is undoubtedly due to the line of conduct adopted by Commodore Perry—a mixture of prudence, caution and inflexible determination, which led him surely, step by step, to the end he had in view.

. . . To the latter alone belongs the glory of having broken down the barriers which for two and a half centuries, have separated Japan from the world—and all this without the firing of a single gun, or the utterance of a single menace.

## IV

# THE OCEAN TELEGRAPH

(New York *Herald*)

---

Beginning in 1854, a company headed by Cyrus Field and Peter Cooper succeeded after four years in linking Great Britain and the United States by cable. A few weeks after its establishment, the line failed. The Civil War interfered at this point and work was suspended. In 1866, eight years after the first message was sent, Field and his associates laid a permanent cable, which worked.

Previous to the laying of the cable, New York (and, vicariously, the nation at large) was witness to an amusing battle among the newspapers. From Colonial times the importance of foreign news was recognized. Until the cable was successful, this news had to be transmitted by ship, at first in ninety-day passages of the slowest sailing vessels, later by the steam greyhounds. And because the news was important, and because no enterprise could be shown until the exchanges and dispatches had actually reached the shores of the continent, there existed a great rivalry. Newspapers bought and maintained fast dispatch boats, to meet the Atlantic ships a hundred or so miles offshore and rush the tidings they bore into harbor. At Halifax, carrier pigeons were used to speed digests of the news to the nearest telegraph lines. Editors bribed flyboys to steal copies of rival papers, and rushed extras into the streets as quickly as the actual owners of the news.

Mr. Field's cable changed all this. The sphere of enterprise in presenting foreign news was further limited—with dispatches arriving at all newspaper offices at the same time, speed in the composing room told the tale. The reception of the cable in 1858 follows an order familiar to newspaper readers: hysteria first, hesitancy second, and doubt third.

The sensation of Queen Victoria's message to President Buchanan is well told (as is the skepticism of the man in the street) in the New York *Herald* for August 17, 1858:

## THE OCEAN TELEGRAPH

### Another Great Problem Solved

### Tremendous Sensation Throughout the City

### Some of Our People Going Off Half Cocked

### But the Telegraph is a Sure Thing

### Everybody Crazy With Joy

### Now's the Time for a Universal Jubilee
&c.                    &c.                    &c.

The Atlantic Telegraph is at work! That is a great point achieved. The Queen's message has come. That fact settles the important question whether or not the line would work. . . .

The announcement in the afternoon that the "Queen's message is expected" put most everybody on tiptoe for the long expected document. Not a few, however, received the news with suspicion justly entertained from the enterprising false alarms in which the newsboys have pleased to indulge for the past week, with the innocent design of making quick sales and large profits with the evening editions as "Extras; got the Queen's message." But as the evening advanced and word passed from mouth to mouth, and became the town talk in the hotels, barrooms, theatres and other public places, people began to think there must be some fire in company with so much smoke, and the circle of believers increased. It was amusing to hear remarks of both the enthusiastic and the sceptical as the "reception of the Queen's message" was announced as the reason for the thunder of booming cannon early in the evening. "Pshaw, it's another hoax", or "It's only the Niagara coming up", or "It's only a little practicing with the Empire pocket-piece", or "I'm glad it's come at last"; "I wonder what it is?"; "What does the Queen say about the Cable?"; "What is old Buck's answer?"; "Is it really a fact that the message is come?"; "Is it on the newspaper bulletins?" and a thousand other similar inquiries and exclamations met the ear at every step. The croakers were about as usual, and conversations like the following were not infrequent:

"Now, honestly, is the message really sent over the cable?"

"Yes, it certainly is."

"Well, what is the purport of it?"

"Her Majesty simply congratulates the President on the successful laying of the cable, in which she has taken a deep interest."

"Pshaw, is that all?"

"Yes, isn't that enough?"

"No."

"What more could you expect?"

"Why, some noble sentiment worthy of the magnitude of the result."

"But the message is straight to the point. She speaks her heartfelt sentiments without doubt."

"Oh, humbug; everybody knew she felt a deep interest, and expected some manner of expressing it worthy of going down to posterity. I believe the whole d——n thing is a hoax."

But the croakers couldn't cry down the fact which kept gaining credence all the time, that a message had been received over the Atlantic Cable; so the guns kept booming, the stage drivers shouted it out, the conductors on the cars told the pretty girls of it, the newsboys made money out of it, and everybody talked about it, while not a few made a rush for the telegraph and newspaper offices to assure themselves of the truth. . . .

The *Herald* of the following day devoted several columns to the joy of the populace, and to the laudatory placards in store windows, which contained such sentiments as:

LIGHTNING
CAUGHT AND TAMED BY
FRANKLIN

TAUGHT TO READ AND WRITE AND GO ON
ERRANDS BY
MORSE;

STARTED IN FOREIGN TRADE BY
FIELD, COOPER & CO.,
WITH
JOHNNY BULL
AND
BROTHER JONATHAN
AS
SILENT PARTNERS

The New York *Evening Post,* on August twenty-sixth, presented to its readers an item headlined "FIRST NEWS DISPATCH BY THE ATLANTIC CABLE." Part of it read:

Trinity Bay, Aug. 25

The following news has just been received from Valencia, and from its general interest, I have forwarded it to the press for publication.     DE SANTI

Valencia, Aug. 25

A treaty of peace has been concluded with China, by which England and France obtain all their demands, including the establishment of embassies at Pekin, and indemnification for the expenses of war.

Later Indian news are to hand, the dates from Bombay being to the 19th of July. The accounts represent that the mutiny was being rapidly quelled. . . .

The above dispatch was received at Trinity Bay at about nine o'clock last night and would have been here in ample season for publication in the morning papers had not the lines in Nova Scotia closed at nine o'clock.

We understand that after the cable is opened for business, all the land lines will remain open night and day, and the speedy laying of the cable from Placentia Bay, N. F., to Sydney, N. S., or to Portland, Me., will obviate much of the delay and uncertainty in transacting business between New York and Trinity Bay.

The cable then fell silent. Engineers on both sides of the ocean tinkered with it, succeeded in sending messages one way on some days, realized that somewhere along the miles of its length, buried in the ooze at the bottom of the Atlantic, there was a fault. Less than a month after its opening—on September sixth—the first hesitant doubt was voiced by the *Evening Post:*

## CAN THE ATLANTIC TELEGRAPH BE MADE MORE USEFUL?

It is rather unfortunate that, during the whole week that was spent by our City Fathers in celebrating the electrical union of the Old World with the New, we have not been favored with a single instance of its practical usefulness. Not a single public dispatch has traversed the wire for some ten days or more. The difficulties in operating the line still prove insurmountable, and the public is obliged to submit with what patience it may to a most offensive silence, just as it supposed it was coming into a new faculty of speech. It is expected that the machinery in use by the company will be perfected, and the requisite rapidity and distinctiveness of communication established within a few weeks or days. We fear these expectations will not be fully realized, for reasons which we propose to submit, we hope with becoming diffidence, but in the desire that they may prepare the readers' minds to consider the only remedy which has seemed to us as likely to prove effective. . . .

[The editor expounded here a technical theory.]

Having given our explanation of the difficulty, we now propose what we are disposed to believe is the only remedy. Unfortunately it is a remedy that cannot be adapted to the present cable, at least without taking it to pieces. It is to cover the wires, at distances of from thirty to fifty miles throughout the entire length, with bands of hardened steel, perfectly magnetized, to act as relay commutators. . . .

This may be a rather discouraging view to take of the prospects of the instrument already made by the company; but if they will satisfy themselves, as they can by experiment, in a very short time, that the theory is a correct one, if it be correct, the time they will save in getting to work will soon pay the additional expense of laying a new and properly-fashioned cable. . . . In laying a new cable with the improvement, it would be wise to consider the practicability of laying the line directly from New York to the Western Islands and thence to the nearest part of land on the continent of Europe. The advantage derived from the supposed plateau between Newfoundland and Ireland is now deemed by them most conversant with the subject rather fanciful, and the entire forgetfulness of Mr. Maury, the author of the plateau theory in the late celebration, tends to show that the Telegraph Company are pretty well satisfied that it would, so far as the unevenness of the ocean bed is concerned, be about as crazy to lay a telegraph cable in any other direction as that which they adopted.

One week later, in the same newspaper, the bubble of exuberance was finally pricked by this realistic and disgruntled editorial:

## WHAT IS THE MATTER WITH THE ATLANTIC CABLE?

The Managers of the Atlantic Telegraph Company are evidently at their wits' end. They have been disappointed in all their calculations about operating the cable, and there is less prospect now than there was two weeks ago of its being turned to any practical use. Various explanations are offered for the delay in opening the line, of which but two are from official sources. Mr. Field conjectures that it is the change of the shore end at Valencia, while it is insisted upon by others that nothing can be done without a resort to Hughes' recording instrument. We fear that neither of these explanations will be found sufficient; and for reasons which we presented at some length a few days since. . . .

The Atlantic Telegraph Company promised to open the cable for public business on the first of September. Why, then, do the operators at Trinity Bay disdain to furnish the American public with explanations of the difficulties experienced in working the cable? A frank statement of the facts would relieve the Directors from undeserved imputation, satisfy the public, and enable scientific and practical men to aid the operators in discovering the true solution of the difficulties.

# NOON FINANCIAL

The "irrepressible conflict" was initiated
at Harper's Ferry, and though there, for
the time suppressed, yet no man is able
to say when or where it will begin again,
or where it will end.

—Richmond *Daily Enquirer*

# INSURRECTION AT HARPER'S FERRY

(New York *Tribune*)

---

When John Brown crossed the bridge into Harper's Ferry he solidified into a single violent action the combined editorial invective of thirty years. Slavery was no new issue on the October day that saw the seizure of the United States Arsenal and the absurdly gallant stand of the insurrectionists against the troops and the militia. Northern pens had been hurling threats of eternal damnation at the South since Garrison's beginnings in the Thirties, and the South had returned a curse for a curse, an adjective for an adjective. Then in an unexpected twinkling Brown gave this exchange body and fearful meaning. At the head of his little band of blind men he created one of the great stories of the century—and gave a greater one a push toward its enactment.

At Harper's Ferry, Brown was already a familiar figure to the judges of the nation's news. His name had become known in the stories of the Kansas war, where he was a Free Stater equal in ferocity to the most ruffianly of the "Border Ruffians." But somehow (perhaps because his Harper's Ferry venture was so shocking in its unexpectedness) he was not made into the extraordinarily colorful copy he actually was until after he had died. With a little more perspective he might have been— before the hangman ended him—the dramatic figure we now know. Today, after seventy-five years, he is a man of coincidence and paradox. A descendant of New England Puritans to whom there had been but one Book in all mankind's history, he crusaded with ready weapons and with the more frightful passages of Holy Scripture engraved upon his heart. He was a warped servant of God, who in the same voice cried out for the blood of his opponents and for Jehovah to justify his acts. Historians and biographers quarrel over him—but they all agree that he crusaded in the firmest conviction that he was right.

For a time in Kansas, John Brown fought the quiet fight for freedom; then, enraged by outrages and legends of outrages, he gathered an assault party, including several of his sons, and traveled to a ford of Pottawattomie Creek, named Dutch Henry's Crossing for a notorious Border Ruffian. What he himself did there will forever be obscured by controversy. But no obscurity shrouds what happened there—it was starkly told in the Leavenworth *Kansas Weekly Herald,* for June 7, 1856:

On Saturday, the 24th [of May], between the hours of one and two o'clock in the morning, some twenty-one or two men arrived with Sharpe's rifles and sabres, called at Mr. Doyle's house, in the vicinity of Shermansville and Osawatomie and inquired for Mr. Doyle. His eldest son, a young man of about 20 years, came out of the house and inquired what they desired? The reply was that they wanted him and his father. The father immediately got out of bed and went to the door in company with a younger son, a mere boy, and made the same inquiry his son did. The party immediately rushed upon them and closed the door, shutting them outside the house, and one man dressed in full uniform stepped forward, and laying his hand on the shoulder of Mr. Doyle, said he was his friend; that he arrested him in the name of the "Northern Army".

They then dragged all of them to a ravine nearby, and cut

their ears and noses off. The father saw their object was
to kill them, and appealed to them to save the lives of his
two sons; that as for him he was old and could not live
much longer; but for Heaven sake the lives of his two sons,
that they might support their old mother and little sisters.
They heeded not appeals, but fell upon these defenceless
men and cut them to pieces with their sabres. One of the
devils, after running a sabre through the father, cut his
head nearly off with the same weapon. . . .

They then proceeded up to a Mr. Allen Wilkenson's, not
far distant, and asked him to come outdoors; he refused
and they immediately broke down the door, pulled him out of
bed and carried him a short distance from the house, and
butchered him as they had poor Doyle and his two sons.
They then proceeded a short distance further, to the house
of a German, well-known as "Dutch Henry", who is a very
strong pro-slavery man. They called for him but he was
not at home. His brother, William Sherman, was in the
house, and was interrogated as follows:

"How long have you been in the Territory?" "Only a
few days."

"Are you a pro-slavery man?" "No."

"Are you a free state man?" "No."

"Do you belong to the Northern Army?" "No."

"Then, damn you, you are our prisoner!" and they seized
him and carried him off.

The next morning he was found by some neighbors in
the bushes, dead, with his head horribly mangled.

The week that followed saw the hounds of the Kansas and
Missouri press in full bay against Brown and his men. On
June tenth, the Atchison *Squatter Sovereign* warned "Whilst
these rebellious subjects confined themselves to the resistance
of the law, in their attempts to make arrests and execute
processes in their hands, the pro-slavery party in the territory
was determined to stand by the law, and aid the officers in

executing processes and the courts in administering justice. And that, we have no doubt, is still the determination of every pro-slavery man, but there is a time for all things. . . . If civil war is to be the result in such a conflict, there cannot be and will not be any neutrals recognized."

The leader of the execution party was named in the story of the event published in the St. Louis *Morning Herald*, "besides the murders at Ossawatomie, by the noted Brown, others have been attempted in the neighborhood." Congress deplored Brown's act. He was launched as a man of violence.

Kansas was a name common in the daily news for a long time. Harper's Ferry, on the other hand, was no more than the name of a Virginia village on the Baltimore and Ohio Railroad. And Brown, lurching along his chosen path, immortally linked the two. He laid his plans on a farm near the scene of his greatest exploit, and on October 16, 1859, the culmination of his preparations startled every editor within telegraphic hearing.

This is the way the *Southern Argus,* of Norfolk, gave the first news of the raid:

## NEGRO INSURRECTION

### At Harper's Ferry

### Headed by the Abolitionists

### The Armory Seized—Trains Stopped

### Cars Fired Into—One Man Killed

Frederick, Oct. 17—Information has been received here this morning of a formidable negro insurrection at Harper's

Ferry. An armed band of abolitionists have full possession of Harper's Ferry and the United States arsenal.

The express train East was fired into twice, and one of the hands, a negro, was killed whilst trying to get the train through the town.

They have arrested two men who came in with a load of wheat and took their wagon and loaded it with rifles and sent them into Maryland. They are led by two hundred and fifty whites and a gang of negroes fighting for their freedom. They gave Conductor Phelps notice that they would not allow any more trains to pass.

The telegraph wires are cut East and West of Harper's Ferry. This intelligence was brought by the train from the West. Great excitement here.

The *Argus* made this announcement on the nineteenth; simultaneously, the New York *Tribune* went to press with a complete account of the action, naming Brown as the leader:

The night passed without any serious alarms, but not without excitement. The marines were marched over immediately after their arrival, when Col. Lee stationed them within the Armory grounds, so as to completely surround the engine-house. Occasionally shots were fired by country volunteers, but what for was not ascertained. There was only one return fire from the insurgents.

The broken telegraph was soon repaired, through the exertions of Superintendents Westervelt and Talcott, who accompanied the expedition. The announcement that communication was opened with Baltimore gave the Press representatives abundant employment. There was no bed to be had, and daylight was awaited with anxiety. Its earliest glimpses were availed of to survey the scene.

A visit to the different localities in which the corpses of the insurrectionists were lying stark and bloody, a peep close or far off according to the courage of the observer at the Malakoff of the insurgents, was the established order of sight-seeing, varied with a discussion of all sorts of terrible rumors.

The building in which the insurgents had made their stand was the fire-engine house, and no doubt the most defensible building in the armory. It has dead brick walls on three sides, and on the fourth, large doors with window sashes above, some eight feet from the ground.

A dead stillness surrounded the buildings, and except that now and then a man might be seen peeping from the nearly closed door, and a gun's nose slightly protruding, there was no sign of life, much less of hostility, given.

Various opinions were given as to the number of persons within, and the amount of resistance they would be able to offer.

The cannon could not be used without endangering the safety of Col. Washington, Mr. Dangerfield, Mr. Ball and other citizens, whom they still held prisoners. The doors and walls of the building had been pierced for rifles, but it was evident that from these holes no range could be had, and that without opening the door they would be shooting in the dark. Many thought that the murder of the prisoners held was determined upon and that a fight to the death would be the ending of their desperate attempt.

Whilst the people thus looked and speculated, the door was opened and one of the men came out with a flag of truce, and delivered what was supposed to be the terms of capitulation. The continued preparations for assault showed that they were not accepted. Shortly after 7 o'clock, Lieut. [J.] E. B. Stuart, of the 1st Cavalry, who was acting as aid for Col. Lee, advanced to parley with the besieged, Samuel Strider, esq., an old and respectable citizen, bearing a flag of truce. They were received at the door by Captain Brown. Lieut. Stuart demanded an unconditional surrender, only promising them protection from immediate violence and a trial by law. Captain Brown refused all terms but those previously demanded, which were substantially, "That they should be permitted to march out with their men and arms, taking their prisoners with them; that they should proceed unpursued to the second toll-gate when they would free their prisoners; the soldiers would then be permitted to pursue them and they would fight if they could not escape."

Of course this was refused, and Lieut. Stuart pressed upon Brown his desperate position, and urged a surrender. The expostulation, though beyond ear shot, was evidently very earnest, and the coolness of the Lieutenant, and the courage of his aged flag bearer, won warm praise. At this moment the interest of the scene was most intense. The volunteers were arranged all around the building, cutting off an escape in every direction. The marines, divided into two squads, were ready for a dash at the door.

Finally Lieut. Stuart, having exhausted all argument with the determined Captain Brown, walked slowly from the door.

Immediately the signal for attack was given, and the marines, headed by Col. Harris and Lieut. Green, advanced in two lines on each side of the door. Two powerful fellows sprung between the lines, and with heavy sledge hammers attempted to batter down the door.

The doors swung and swayed, but appeared to be secured with a rope, the spring of which deadened the effect of the blows. Failing this, they took hold of a ladder, some forty feet long, and, advancing at a run, brought it with tremendous effect against the door.

At the second blow it gave way, one leaf falling inward in a slanting position. The marines immediately advanced to the breach, Major Russell and Lieut. Green leading. A marine in front fell.

The firing from the interior was rapid and sharp. They fired with deliberate aim, and for a moment the resistance was serious and desperate enough to excite the spectators to something like a pitch of frenzy. The next moment the marines poured in, the firing ceased, and the work was done; while cheers rang from every side, the general feeling being that the marines had done their part admirably.

When the insurgents were brought out, some dead and others wounded, they were greeted with execrations, and only the precautions that had been taken saved them from immediate execution. The crowd, nearly every man of which carried a gun, swayed with tumultuous excitement, and cries of "Shoot them! Shoot them!" rang from every side. The appearance of the liberated prisoners, all of whom, through the steadiness of the marines, escaped injury, changed the current of feeling, and prolonged cheers took the place of howls and execrations.

In the assault Private Ruffert of the marines received a ball in the stomach, and was believed to be fatally wounded. Another received a slight flesh wound.

The lawn in front of the engine-house after the assault presented a dreadful sight. Lying on it were two bodies of men killed on the previous day, and found inside the house; three wounded men, one of them just at the last gasp of life, and two others groaning in pain. One of the dead was Brown's son. Oteway, the wounded man, and his son Watson, were lying on the grass, the father presenting a gory spectacle. He had a severe bayonet wound in his side, and his face and hair were clotted with blood. . . .

A short time after Captain Brown was brought out, he revived and talked earnestly to those about him, defending his course and avowing that he had only done what was right. . . . He seemed fully convinced that he was badly treated and had a right to complain. Although at first considered dying, an examination of his wounds proved that they were not necessarily fatal. He expressed a desire to live and be tried by his country. In his pockets nearly $300 were found in gold. Several important papers, found in his possession, were taken charge of by Col. Lee, on behalf of the Government.

Readers of the New York *Herald* were warned that morning, in an editorial "The Virginia Abolition Insurrection—Its Causes and Possible Consequences":

Our readers will perceive, from the intelligence on the subject which we publish this morning, that the first startling reports of an abolition conspiracy and insurrection at Harper's Ferry, Virginia, were substantially correct. The plot, the outbreak and its suppression, within a few hours have become matters of history. The conspiracy, it appears, was the work of that notorious Kansas free state abolition madman, known as Ossawottomie Brown, and comprehended the madman's idea of the extinction of slavery in Virginia and Maryland by force of arms, beginning with the seizure of the United States arsenal at Harper's Ferry as the shortest method of procuring the weapons of war. . . .

We have thus before us some of the ripening fruits of that mischievous re-opening of the slavery agitation in 1854, commenced by Douglas and Pierce as Presidential candidates for the decisive vote of the South in the Cincinnati Convention. There would have been no border war between Southern Pro-Slavery adventurers and Northern emigrant aid societies had there been no invitations to them to fight out the slavery issue, face to face, on the soil of Kansas. And this man Brown was only a discharged guerrilla free state soldier from the border ruffian scenes of that bloody Territory. Flushed with the success of the work for freedom there, and rendered daring, reckless and an abolition monomaniac by the scenes of violence and blood through which he had passed, he believed the time at hand for carrying the Kansas war for freedom into the heart of the Southern states. He has met with the fate which he courted; but his death and the punishment of all his criminal associates will be as a feather in the balance against the mischievous consequences which will follow from the rekindling of the slavery excitement in the South. . . .

Thinking readers no doubt were interested in the "causes and possible consequences" of John Brown's raid, but a newspaper has comparatively few thinking readers. There was more interest, North and South, in what had happened. Brown was a familiar name, but the adventures of Kansas that had made it so were three years gone, and memory is a fickle thing. What was this monomaniac like? What did he say? What had his men done?

The readers were told. Those who could remember would remark later upon the coincidence that brought J. E. B. Stuart (already opposed to Brown in Kansas) and Robert E. Lee together with him at Harper's Ferry. Stuart was to become the greatest of the Confederate cavalry generals; Lee was to see the United States sponsor Brown's cause, and was to fight against it, and at last was to be revered for one of the most gallant defeats in history. Further, Brown was to die on a scaffold beneath which, in the uniform of a Virginia soldier, stood an actor named Booth. The Norfolk *Southern Argus,* on the morning of October twentieth, added to this mountain of coincidence by presenting a picture of Brown for which it was "indebted to his old pro-slavery antagonist, Capt. H. Clay Pate":

> Brown is nearly seventy years old. He commanded at "Black Jack" (Kansas Territory) June 2d, 1856, when he treacherously took Capt. Pate prisoner, although a flag of truce was waving over Capt. Pate's head.
>
> He was defeated at Ossawottomie 3d Sept. 1856, by Capt. Reid's command. After that he headed a band of horse-thieves.
>
> About the 25th May, 1856, Brown and his sons assassinated five men in the night on Pottowottomie Creek (three Doyles—father and two sons—Wm. Sherman, and Wilkerson, a member of the Legislature) at their homes—all pro-slavery, but unoffending, citizens.
>
> Last Spring Brown made an "irrepressible" foray into Missouri, and carried away seventeen negroes. He was accompanied by Dr. Day, who was caught and recently escaped from jail at St. Joseph. Brown landed his negroes safely in

Canada and got his reward from the abolition societies.

Brown has been a good deal in the South. It is said that he is the last survivor of Murrell's celebrated gang of counterfeiters.

He had eleven sons, who all shared in his enterprises. He has always heretofore escaped unhurt.

In his principles he always professed to be "for war" and to be a strict disciple of the "irrepressible conflict" school.

We hope he will soon recover from his wounds, that the gallows may not be cheated of its fit ornament.

There was a friendlier portrait in the Richmond *Enquirer's* story of the twenty-second:

After some little delay we were introduced in the room where Brown and Stevens lay. We found the former to be a six-footer, although as he lay he had the appearance of being some six inches shorter than that. He has a rather peculiar shaped head, long gray hair, which at this time was matted, the sabre cut in his head having caused blood to flow freely, to the complete disfigurement of his face, which, like his hands, was begrimed with dirt, evidently the result of continued exposure to the smoke of powder. His eyes are of a pale blue, or perhaps a sharp gray—much such an eye as I remember his brother filibusterer, Walker, to have. During his conversation hereinafter reported, no sign of weakness was exhibited. In the midst of his enemies, whose homes he had invaded, wounded and a prisoner; surrounded by a small army of officials and a more desperate army of angry men; with the gallows staring him full in the face, he lay on the floor and in reply to every question gave answers that betokened the spirit that animated him. The language of Governor Wise well expresses his boldness, when he said, "He is the gamest man I ever saw." I believe the worthy Executive had hardly expected to see a man so act in such a trying moment.

The reporter chose wisely when he used the word act in connection with Brown's demeanor. The crusader well knew, as he lay on the floor surrounded by his enemies, that what he said would be copy for the papers, North and South and West. For years he had dedicated his life to this crusade, faithful to it when his family suffered penury, when his sons died violently and too young, when his own daily existence was one of endless guerrilla warfare, pursuit and escape. Now he had at his command the columns of every newspaper to which telegraph wires ran. He had only to speak, and the message he gave would be read in a few hours by the thousands who had been unmoved by his Kansas struggles and his pathetic lectures. He spoke; the reporter for the *Enquirer* recorded what he said:

> The parties present in the room during the conversation were Senator Mason, Hons. Messrs. Faulkner, and Vallandigham, Dr. Biggs, Lieut. Stuart, 1st Cavalry, U. S. A., two New York reporters and the writer. There were a few other persons came in at times, to see what was going on. A preliminary conversation was had, which amounted to no more than inquiries about Brown's condition for talking, and his reply was he would rather like it. His answers at the time when I commenced the full report are all included in what I give.
>
> Sen. Mason—How do you justify your acts?
>
> Brown—I think, my friend, you are guilty of a great wrong against God and mankind. I say that without wishing to be offensive. It would be perfectly right for any one to interfere with you, so far as to free those you wilfully and wickedly hold in bondage. I do not say this insultingly.
>
> Mr. Mason—I understand that.
>
> Brown—I think I did right, and that others will do right who interfere with you at any time, and at all times. I hold that the golden rule, do unto others as you would that others should do unto you, applies to all who would help others who would gain their liberty.

Lieut. Stuart—But you don't believe in the Bible?

Brown—Certainly I do. . . .

Mr. Vallandigham—Where did your men come from? Did some of them come from Ohio!

Brown—Some of them.

Mr. V.—From the Western reserve? Of course none came from Southern Ohio?

Brown—Oh, yes! I believe one came from Steubenville —down not far from Wheeling.

Bystander—The New York "Herald" of yesterday, in speaking of this affair, mentions a letter in which he [Gerrit Smith] says: "that it is folly to attempt to strike the shackles off the slaves by the force of moral suasion or legal agitation", and predicts that the next movement, made in the direction of negro emancipation, will be an insurrection in the South.

Brown—I have not seen a New York "Herald" for some days past, but I presume from your remarks about the gist of the letter that I should concur with it. I agree with Mr. Smith that moral suasion is hopeless. I don't think the people of the slave States will ever consider the subject of slavery in its true light until some other argument is resorted to than moral suasion.

Mr. Vallandigham—Did you expect a general rising of the slaves in case of your success?

Brown—No, sir; nor did I wish it. I expected to gather strength from time to time; then I could set them free.

Mr. V.—Did you expect to hold possession here till then?

Brown—Well, probably I had quite a different idea. I do not know that I ought to reveal my plans. I am here a prisoner and wounded, because I foolishly allowed myself to be so. You overrate your strength when you suppose I would have been taken if I had not allowed it. I was too tardy after commencing the open attack in delaying my movements through Monday night and up to the time I was attacked by the Government troops. It was all occasioned by my desire to spare the feelings of my prisoners and their families, and the community at large.

Questions were now put by almost everyone in the room, as follows——

Q.—Where did you get arms?

Brown—I bought them.

Q.—In what State?

Brown—That I would not tell.

Q.—How many guns?

Brown—Two hundred of Sharp's rifles and two hundred revolvers—what is called the Massachusetts Arms Company's revolvers—a little under the navy size.

Q.—Why did you not take that swivel you left in the house?

Brown—I had no occasion for it. It was given to me a year or two ago.

Q.—In Kansas?

Brown—No! I had nothing given to me in Kansas.

Q.—By whom, in what State?

Brown—I decline to answer that. It is not properly a swivel—it is a very large rifle on a pivot. The ball is larger than a musket ball; it is intended for a slug.

Mr. Brown made a statement intended for the reporters of the Baltimore *American,* Cincinnati *Gazette* and New York *Herald,* who were present, as follows:

"If you do not want to converse any more I will remark to these reporting gentlemen that I claim to be here in carrying out a measure I believe to be perfectly justifiable, and not to act the part of an incendiary or ruffian; but, on the contrary, to aid those suffering under a great wrong. I wish to say further that you had better, all of you people of the South, prepare yourselves for a settlement of this question. It must come up for settlement sooner than you are prepared for it, and the sooner you commence that preparation the better for you. You may dispose of me very easily; I am nearly disposed of now; but this question is still to be settled—the negro question, I mean. The end is not yet. These wounds were inflicted upon me, both the sabre cut on my head and the bayonet stabs in the different parts of my body, some minutes after I had ceased firing, and had consented to surrender for. the benefit of others, and not for my own benefit."

[Several persons present denied this statement.]

Brown resumed—"I believe the Major here (pointing to Lieut. Stuart) would not have been alive but for me. I might have killed him just as easy as I could kill a mosquito, when he came in, but I supposed he came in only to receive our surrender. There had been long and loud calls of surrender from us—as loud as men could yell—but in the confusion and excitement, I suppose we were not heard. I do not believe the Major, or any one else, wanted to butcher us after we had surrendered."

An officer present here stated that special orders had been given to the Marines not to shoot anybody, but when they were fired on by Brown's men and one of them had been killed, and another wounded, they were obliged to return the compliment.

Brown insisted, with some warmth, that the Marines fired first.

An Officer—Why did you not surrender before the attack?

Brown—I did not think it was my duty or interest to do so. We assured our prisoners that we did not wish to hurt them, and that they should be set at liberty. I exercised my best judgment, not believing the people would wantonly sacrifice their own fellow citizens. When we offered to let them go upon condition of being allowed to change our position about a quarter of a mile, the prisoners agreed by vote among themselves to pass across the bridge with us. We took them, in the first place, as hostages, and to keep them from doing any harm. We did kill some when defending ourselves, but I saw no one fire except directly in self-defense. Our orders were strict not to harm anyone not in arms against us.

Q.—Well, Brown, suppose you had any negroes in the United States, what would you do with them?

Brown (in a loud tone and with emphasis)—Set them free, sir!

Q.—Your intention was to carry them off and free them?

Brown—Not at all.

Bystander—To set them free would sacrifice the life of every man in this community.

Brown—I do not think so.

Bystander—I think you are fanatical.

Brown—And I think you are fanatical. "Whom the gods would destroy, they first make mad."

Q.—Was your only object to free the negro?

Brown—Absolutely our only object.

Bystander—But you went and took Colonel Washington's silver and watch.

Brown—Oh, yes! We intended freely to have appropriated the property of the slave-holders to carry out our object. It was for that. Only that; we had no design to enrich ourselves with any plunder whatever.

Q.—Did you know Sherred in Kansas? I understand you killed him.

Brown—I killed no man except in fair fight. I fought at Black Jack and at Ossawottomie, and if I killed anybody it was at one of those places.

In a matter of weeks, Brown had been convicted and hanged. There were many dramatic moments in his trial, at Charlestown (now Charles Town, West Virginia), but none to equal that described in the New York *Tribune:*

A recess was taken up for half an hour, when the jury came in with the verdict.

There was intense excitement.

Brown sat up in bed, while the verdict was rendered.

The Jury found him guilty of treason, advising and conspiring with slaves and others to rebel, and for murder in the first degree.

Brown lay down quickly and said nothing.

There was no demonstration of any kind.

This was on November first. Two weeks had elapsed since the raid. Four more were to pass until the *Tribune* again, describing Charlestown as being under the strictest military discipline "as if the town were under a state of siege," reported somewhat irreverently that "the old man was swung off at 11:15 precisely, he having remained firm and dignified to the last." The New York *Herald* was more reverent and more descriptive:

> The prisoner walked up the steps firmly and was the first man on the gallows. Capt. Avis, the jailer, and Sheriff Campbell stood by his side, and after shaking hands, and bidding an affectionate adieu, he thanked them for their kindness, when the cap was put over his face and the rope about his neck. Avis asked him to step forward on the trap. He replied: "You must lead me; I cannot see." The rope was adjusted, and the military order given, "Not ready yet." The soldiers marched, countermarched, and took position as if an enemy were in sight, and were thus occupied for nearly ten minutes, the prisoner standing all the time. Avis inquired if he was not tired. Brown said, "No, not tired; but don't keep me waiting longer than is necessary."
>
> While on the scaffold, Sheriff Campbell asked him if he would take a handkerchief in his hand to drop as a signal when he was ready. He replied, "No, I do not want it—but do not detain me any longer than is absolutely necessary."

And so he died. The *Tribune* (the "black Republican *Tribune*" to the *Southern Argus* and other papers) declared on the morning of December third, the day after the execution:

> . . . His errors are the errors of a fanatic, not the crimes of a felon. It were absurd to apply to him opprobrious epithets or wholesale denunciations. The essence of crime is the pursuit of selfish gratification in disregard of others' good;

and that is the precise opposite of Old Brown's impulse and deed. He periled and sacrificed not merely his own life— that were, perhaps, a moderate stake—but the lives of his beloved sons, the earthly happiness of his family and theirs, to benefit a despised and downtrodden race—to deliver from bitter bondage and degradation those whom he had never seen. Unwise, the world will pronounce him—reckless of artificial yet palpable obligations he certainly was—but his very errors were heroic—the faults of a bold, impulsive, truthful nature, impatient of wrong and only too conscious that "resistance to tyrants is obedience to God." Let whoever would first cast a stone ask himself whether his own noblest act was equal in grandeur and nobility to that for which John Brown pays the penalty of a death on the gallows.

## II

# LATER FROM TRUXILLO

(New Orleans *Picayune*)

---

While at Harper's Ferry the hangman's hand was removing a White Knight from the confused checkerboard of states, another crusader was continuing to seek the checkmate only to die without achieving it. But for nearly a year, the Black Knight moved over the colored squares, blundering toward his annihilation on the side of a cause forever doomed when John Brown's body fell to the limit of the rope. Not until September of 1860 did William Walker move carelessly; when he did and scorned the protection of the country that had opposed his every action, it was a firing squad that placed him back in the box.

Walker knew as much or more newspaper fame than Brown. He taught uncounted thousands the meaning of the word filibuster; he aroused the governments of the United States and of Europe; he went into the hot countries at the head of an army of fifty-eight men and catapulted himself by sheer military prowess into the presidency of Nicaragua. Here again, in consideration of the career of William Walker, the coincidence of Old Brown recurs: on opposing sides, each strove to minimize the effect of the other's achievements and almost to the day their individual maneuvers contradicted each other. Their names are too seldom linked; they belong together as definitely as any two opposing forces in our history.

They developed from entirely dissimilar beginnings. Brown came of Puritan stock and was a pioneer of the buckskin breeches type. Walker studied in the law and in medicine and, before going to California to be at first a barrister and then an editor, had traveled to Paris. But when in 1855 they started upon their separate journeys, they began careers in parallel. Walker set out for Nicaragua in that year, with his pocket-sized army; Brown went to Kansas. On the day that saw the corpses of the Ossawattomie dead lying butchered in the rising Kansas sun, Walker was considering the legalization of slavery in the country he had seized. On the day that Brown hovered about the red battleground of Kansas, engaged in perpetual guerrilla warfare, Walker's plan had crystallized into decree, nullifying the constitution that outlawed slavery. And on the day that Brown was mounting the scaffold to jerk a little in pathetic climax to the tremendous violence of his life, Walker in New Orleans was assembling his last, fatal expedition.

Walker's arrival in Nicaragua, primarily as a mercenary for the Castellon government, was the beginning (to him) of a union of Central American states. It has been said that he planned to conquer vast territory for ultimate annexation by the United States, but if this were so, Honduran bullets foiled him. His beginnings, then, were purely those of a hired soldier, dedicated to the overthrow of the Chamorra regime, legally in power.

His fame spread and recruits flocked to his banner: reckless Texans and Kentuckians largely, hoping for a good fight and a little plunder. By 1856 he had become President of Nicaragua; by 1857 the wheel of politics and war had turned and he was ousted. The United States at every opportunity opposed his efforts to conquer Central America; he was tried thrice for violation of the neutrality laws, and in every case acquitted. He was a figure of glamour to the newspaper reader and a menace to the officials of organized governments. But he tripped, as Brown had tripped. A British officer was the one who took him captive, when his military skill failed at last to overcome the sheer weight of his opponent's numbers.

New Orleans had known Walker better, perhaps, than any other city. There he had plotted his expeditions, there he had recruited many of his *Filibusteros,* there he had bought and outfitted his small ships. And so, to New Orleans, came the first reports of his downfall. There was a rumor in the beginning, and then a fact, in the columns of the New Orleans *Picayune* of September 18, 1860:

*(By the Balize Line)*

S. W. PASS—The British steamer *Gladiator,* from Truxillo via Ruatan, has just arrived and is on her way up to the city.

The *Gladiator* has on board all the men that remain from Gen. Walker's late unfortunate expedition into Honduras.

Gen. Walker was shot on the 12th inst. at Truxillo.

Col. Rudler, his second in command, was still a prisoner in the castle when the *Gladiator* left.

The detailed report of the party on the *Gladiator* adds but little to the information we already have. Gen. Walker was shot at 8 o'clock on the morning of the 12th, and buried the same day in the public burial ground.

Col. Rudler, Walker's second in command, has been sentenced to four years' confinement in the State Prison at Comayagua.

The rest of the party, about seventy in number, were all permitted to return to the United States.

Of Walker's capture, on the Rio Negro, we have the following additional from an authoritative source. The party sent up the river was under the command of Capt. Salmon of the *Icarus*. On making his appearance, he asked for Gen. Walker. Gen. Walker then stepped forward and said he was the man.

Capt. Salmon then said, "I demand that you surrender to me immediately." Gen. Walker replied, "To whom do I surrender?" Capt. Salmon said, "To an officer of Her Majesty's Government." Gen. Walker then said again, "Do I understand you to say that I surrender to a representative of Her Brittanic Majesty's Government?" Capt. Salmon replied, "Yes." Gen. Walker then drew his sword and formally surrendered, and was taken on board the *Icarus*.

Throughout his career, Walker was regarded variously by the editors of the United States. The principles for which he stood made an editorial line as sharply defined as that which the Messrs. Mason and Dixon ran in 1767. Now he was dead, and the press of the North and South continued to regard him as they always had. The *Picayune* said:

The career of General Walker, whose sad fate has just been announced, has been an extraordinary one. His foray into Lower California first brought him into public notice as a man of great daring, of high powers of endurance and possessing the gift to an extraordinary degree of winning and attaching followers to his person and fortunes.

That unfortunate expedition seems to have given direction to his whole subsequent life. His sudden irruption into Nicaragua; his gradual acquisition of the entire authority of government of that State; his bold administration of its affairs after he was elected to the Presidency; the long and bloody struggle against the combined Central American governments, ending in his discomfiture and return to the United States, are too well known to need repetition. Though driven out of Nicaragua by the union of Central Americans and the interference of our own Federal authorities, he never lost sight of the dream of his life. To weave anew plans for a return to power in Nicaragua, he devoted all his energies. Though they were repeatedly broken asunder at the moment they promised success, he never despaired, but set again about their reconstruction; and at last, after men supposed he had lost the power for reorganization, he suddenly appears on the Honduran coast, captures its principal town, and is apparently on the high road to success, when, if late reports are true, his expedition fails, and the tragic drama closes with the loss of his life.

But the New York *Herald* could not see Walker as a man of destiny. Two days after the *Picayune* paid him a final tribute, the *Herald* said:

Walker came forward in 1855 as a leader. The magnitude of the resources which his appearance in Nicaragua called into active play awakened the attention of the world, and alarmed the cabinets of Europe. But Walker had not the genius to perceive nor the wisdom to combine the vast intellectual and material elements that spontaneously offered themselves to his guidance. None of the leaders in the old school of Quitman filibusterers joined him, for they soon saw that between Walker and themselves there were immense differences in aim and policy. . . . His recent expeditions have been petty affairs and his fate will awaken little sympathy anywhere.

The South had an answer to this. New Orleans particularly would not stand by and watch one of its gallant figures belittled. A fortnight later, the New Orleans *Delta* published its "Posthumous Opinions of General William Walker":

There are already vultures to peck at the dead lion. The dull hoof of the ass is ever ready to spurn the fallen giant. Since the melancholy catastrophe of his last expedition at Truxillo, Gen. Walker's name has not been spared. Why should it be? He stipulated for no terms with public opinion. He craved no mercy at its hands. He asked for no suspension even of its angry verdict. No man is qualified to act the hero unless he is ready to meet the doom of the martyr; and no man was ever readier to do this than he who, the other day, with such calm sublimity of courage, attested with his death the sincerity with which he had consecrated his life to a noble scheme of regeneration. Those whose craven hearts and narrow souls cannot know and feel that it is better to attempt great works at all, will be able to see nothing to admire in Gen. Walker's life, and only something to contemn in his death. Be it so!

But a more active spirit of unfriendliness than this was to have been expected; and proofs of such a spirit we have seen exhibited in more than one quarter. We will pass over the many unfeeling diatribes on the character and career of Walker, contained in Abolition newspapers which have made his death an occasion for effusing their venom against the South, and we will . . . turn to another view of the subject. Here is a graceful tribute traced by the hand of one who knew Gen. Walker, and who knew how to appreciate him as a gifted woman can always appreciate genius and heroism:

*Editors, Delta:* I have been reading a paragraph from the New York *Herald,* wherein the allusion to the late General William Walker is in that slighting tone which jars painfully on my Southern nerves, more especially as my friend is now in his lone Honduranean grave, and has no further chance of *living down* the injustice done his memory by those who could never understand the nature of that which was his high and spiritualized ambition.

It was the misfortune of many who write and prate about Walker never to have known him. And it is the misfortune of us, his friends, to feel that whatever we may do or say, we cannot impress upon the narrow-minded, the prejudiced, the custom-fettered and conventionally-blind, the picture of a man so intuitively impressed with the consciousness of his "mission," as, while maintaining all the respect due to the laws of men and nations, to bend them into subservience to a "higher law." Walker was essentially a Regenerator. Let the term "filibuster" die out in sacred silence on his grave. The coarse, the sensual, the wantonly aggressive, had but little part in him. A man of few passions (and they only the best and purest), he nourished a secret philanthropy and cherished a secret, religiously-conscientious dream, the golden aura of which was the elevating into dignity and prosperity, the rich and beautiful but degraded States of Central America; the solid nucleus proved to be a grave dug by strategem and treachery on the lone Honduranean coast, far from help and friends, where no tell-tale winds could carry away the victim's proud defiance of perjured faith and outraged justice.

## III

# ARRIVAL OF THE PONY

(San Francisco *Alta Californian*)

The Western Pony Express was inaugurated on an April morning, when in St. Joseph, Missouri, a lean rider slouched to the side of his horse, climbed easily into the saddle, grinned down at the spectators and vanished beyond the town's limits at a gallop. But this rider, although he was a trail-blazer, was by no means a pioneer. The express rider had been used in America from its earliest beginnings, whenever tidings had to be borne swiftly from place to place. We have seen him galloping over the Revolutionary countryside, bearing dispatches from General Washington in the field. And between the Revolution and the beginnings of the Pony Express of the Central Overland and Pikes Peak Express Company, many newspapers made use of riders. Presidential messages were hurried northward from Washington, so that readers of the Philadelphia and New York papers could get them more promptly than three days after their delivery. Even after 1844, when Professor Morse proved to the skeptical that he could transmit intelligence over a wire, the riders were necessary. The Baltimore *Sun,* during the Mexican War, maintained an expensive relay of sixty fine horses, used to speed news from the front via New Orleans to Baltimore. Such stories as this, printed in the *Sun* for October 4, 1847, were not uncommon:

## FROM GEN. SCOTT'S ARMY
## BATTLE OF CHAPULTAPEC

Our "pony" team, as if in anticipation of the great excitement prevailing in the city on Saturday evening, came flying up to the stopping post with the most thrilling and important intelligence yet received from the seat of war, fully twenty-four hours in advance of locomotives, steamboats and even the telegraph.

The news brought by them being twenty-four hours in advance of the mail, and of such an exciting and thrilling interest, we put to press at a late hour on Saturday night, an "Extra Sun" with full details, which were sought after by thousands of our citizens during yesterday morning.

The *Sun's* pony gave good service. Gradually he was replaced by the widening telegraph lines. But as late as 1860, the copper strands had not yet penetrated to the Pacific Coast. California was a world away. The pony came forward again and for a year and a half (until electricity made his furious pace no faster than a laggard schoolboy's) California read the news he carried, and the papers found frequent use for the headline: "ARRIVAL OF THE PONY."

In 1860, the California telegraph extended from San Francisco as far as Carson City. On March thirty-first, the *Territorial Enterprise* of the latter place spoke of the forthcoming pony:

This enterprise is the first acknowledgement of the superiority of the central route, promising the results we have been so long contending for. We look upon it as the pioneer of the great highway of nations. First on the programme is the "Pony Express," communication between San Francisco and New York, nine days. That is annihilating space that but a few years since took months to travel. By spring, the wants of the business that led to the establishment of this line will be supplied by the telegraph. The next move on the programme will be the establishment of a stage line, making the time from the Missouri River to Carson City in ten or twelve days; and last, the great crowning feature of all, will be the Pacific Railroad. The merits of the great overland central route, from now and forevermore, will receive the attention they deserve.

Two weeks later—on April sixteenth—the first pony arrived and impelled the editor of the San Francisco *Herald* to write:

The Pony Express has performed a feat which excites the wonder and admiration of all. We are in receipt of letters only fourteen days from Washington City—an air line distance of over three thousand five hundred miles—showing a speed of two hundred and fifty miles a day, obtained by steamboat, railroad, magnetic telegraph and horse flesh. A dispatch from Washington, dated March 30th, informs us that the Pacific Railroad Bill, the same mooted last year, would be called up in the Senate a week from the date above mentioned. It provides for the transportation of the mails, troops, seamen, munitions of war, army and navy supplies, and all other Government services by railroad from the Mississippi River to San Francisco.

More prosaic then, more romantic now, was the announcement in the confused advertising columns of the same edition:

### PONY EXPRESS
### EIGHT DAYS
### FROM SAN FRANCISCO TO NEW YORK

The Pony Express of the Central Overland California and Pikes Peak Express Company will leave San Francisco for New York and intermediate points on FRIDAY, the 20th day of April, 1860, and on every FRIDAY thereafter at four o'clock P. M.

Schedule time from San Francisco to New York for telegraphic dispatches, Eight Days; for Letters, Twelve Days.
                    WM. M. FINNEY, General Agent.

N. B.—The public will understand that by Telegraphing to Carson City, twenty-seven and a half hours later intelligence can be sent to St. Joseph, Mo., than by letter from San Francisco.

So the pony rode. From April, 1860, to October, 1861, the riders were the heroes of the West. But when they passed with the first inept clackings of a telegraph sounder, they went almost unlamented. There was nothing said of the romance of their brief span in the light of fame. Standards have changed: California in 1861 thought the telegraph the most romantic of all possible communications, and not until seventy-five years later is the Pony Express accorded the full measure of its glamour. But while we could wish that the editors had bowed more gracefully to the departing Pony, we can sympathize with the realism with which the *Alta Californian* cheered the telegraph:

> The overland telegraph is completed. San Francisco is in instant communication with New York and the other great cities of the Atlantic seaboard. It is a great change for us. A few years ago we received intelligence from the other side only semi-monthly by steamer, and generally from 25 to 30 days old, at that. Then followed the semi-weekly mail, by the overland route, which brought us news twice a week, on the average 18 or 20 days old. And last came the Pony, sweeping across the Continent by the Central route, in everlasting gallop, with dates varying from 14 to 4 days after its departure. . . .

From his owners, the Pony received his epitaph, here reprinted from the San Francisco *Herald:*

NOTICE

By Orders from the East Coast

the

PONY EXPRESS

WILL BE DISCONTINUED

The Last Pony Coming This Way Left Atchison, Kansas, Yesterday

WELLS, FARGO & CO., Agents.

# WALL STREET CLOSE

" . . . after he returned from the confer-
ence and the arrangement for the surrender, he spoke briefly and told them he
had made as good a fight as he could,
and now he had made as honorable a
capitulation as possible under the circumstances. Then, bursting into tears,
he slowly rode off to his tent. . . . "
—New York *Times*

# I

# THE WONDERFUL NAVAL VICTORY

(Richmond *Dispatch*)

———————

It is unlikely that we shall ever know again so complete a newspaperman's war as the one the states fought over slavery. There, for four years, was a spectacle made to measure for the reporter. In New York and elsewhere, newspapers were beginning to reap great harvests from enterprise, and with their surpluses they could afford to cover the war the way we now cover a three-alarm fire. The press, led by the mighty New York *Herald* with its sixty-odd correspondents, told its public every slight fact about the progress of the struggle. Because the day of the cavalry charge and open movement had not yet passed, the correspondents could stand at vantage points and watch the war in its actual theater, instead of in dispatches and on maps at headquarters far behind the lines. And finally, this war more than any other was of great interest to nearly every citizen: it was fought at home, it was fought over an issue in which every man had a side, and it was fought colorfully.

It is not possible to select any single story and say, "This was the most important newspaper story of the war." Historically, there were three: the *Monitor* and *Virginia,* Lee's surrender and Lincoln's assassination. But we cannot be sure that others did not, at the moment of their first publication, overshadow at least the first two of these. Therefore, for the purposes of this book, we take history's word for what was important in the War of the Rebellion.

The engagement between the *Monitor* and the *Virginia* was that rarity among battles: a victory for both sides.

The two vessels involved were purely experimental. The Confederates salvaged a Union frigate called the *Merrimac*, which had been sunk at its Norfolk dock. They sheathed its sides in cast-iron plates and mounted at portholes the heaviest guns the hull would support. When they had finished, they had what they called the ironclad *Virginia:* a boat with a speed of about five knots and so ungainly that she had to be guided with a towline when she sailed out for her first trip. The Union adversary, on the other hand, was faster, more maneuverable and less vulnerable. Built by John Ericsson at the Greenpoint yards, in New York, she was a ship with a deck riding only a few inches above the water, and with only one target—a cylinder of iron plates—in the center. This cylinder, mounting two guns, revolved much as a modern gun-turret revolves.

The story of the *Monitor* and the *Virginia* rightfully begins in New York, several days before the battle at Hampton Roads, when the *Monitor* sailed for the South. Her departure was mentioned merely in a list of shipping cleared, and before she arrived on the scene, half the battle of Hampton Roads (and most of its damage) was over.

The *Virginia*, then, had a clear field for her first day's assault. In the Norfolk *Day Book* for March 11, 1862, there appeared a conception of the feeling her appearance inspired in the breasts of the Union tars:

. . . It is said that the Captain of the *Congress*, on seeing the *Virginia* bear down towards his ship on Saturday, mustered his men, and addressed them thus: "My hearties, you see before you the great Southern bugaboo, got up to fright us out of our wits. Stand to your guns, and let me assure you that one good broadside from our gallant frigate, and she is ours! . . ."

The *Day Book* also presented in the same edition, a complete account of the "bugaboo's" achievements later that day:

On the morning of the 8th, the steam frigate "Virginia," Flag Officer Franklin Buchanan, Commanding, left her moorings at the Dock-Yard, and attended by the steam-tugs "Beaufort," Lieut. Commanding Parker, and the "Raleigh," Lieut. Commanding Alexander, steamed down the harbor.

It was a gallant sight to see the iron-clad Leviathan gliding noiselessly through the water, flying the red pennon of her commander at the fore flag-staff, and the gay Confederate ensign aft.

Not the least impressive thought which she suggested, was that her gallant crew, under a commander and officers worthy to direct their destiny and defend the flag she bore, went thus boldly with smiles and huzzahs to solve a new problem in maritime warfare—to make the "trial trip" of the "Virginia" the trial of battle.

Nor could any man behold the little tugs with their gay ensigns at peak and masthead, their battle flags set, steaming in her wake, without an emotion of admiration for the brave men they thus bore, and a prayer for their deliverance.

In the wake of all came the Port Admiral with a staff of naval officers.

Thus down the harbor, past the wharves, thronged with eager citizens, past the batteries, whose parapets were dark with soldiers, steamed the squadron.

Through the two barricades and then the "Virginia" put her helm astarboard, and took the South channel.

Meantime the morning was still as that of a Sabbath. The two frigates lay with their boats at the booms and wash clothes in the rigging. Did they see the long dark hull? Had they made her out? Was it ignorance, apathy, or composure? These were the questions we discussed as we steamed across the flats to the south of the frigate, with the two gallant little gunboats well on our starboard beam heading up for the enemy. Our doubts were solved by the heavy boom of a gun from beyond Sewell's Point. The reverberation rolled across the sun-lit water and died away, but still the clothes hung in the rigging, still the boats lay at the booms. Another gun (twenty minutes past one) broke on the air, and a tug started for Newport News, while at the same time two others left Old Point, taking the channel inside Hampton bar. Steadily, with a grim and ominous silence, the "Virginia" glided through the water, steadily and with defiant valor the "Beaufort" and "Raleigh" followed where she led. At ten minutes to two, a rifle gun from one of these little vessels rang out, then a white puff from her consort. Still the clothes in the rigging, still the boats at the boom. Was this confidence? It could not be ignorance. Did it mean torpedoes, submarine batteries, infernal machines? The gunboats have fired again, and lo! here away to the eastward were the "Roanoke" and "Minnesota" rising like prodigious castles above the placid water, the first under steam, the second in tow. Other puffs of smoke, other sharp reports from the gunboats, but the "Virginia" goes on steadily, silently to do her work. Now the in-shore frigate, the "Cumberland," fires, now the "Virginia" close aboard, now Sewell's Point battery, now the "Minnesota," now the "Roanoke," now the air trembles with the cannonade. Now the "Virginia" delivers both broadsides, now she runs full against the "Cumberland's" starboard bow, now the smoke clears away and she appears to be heading up James River. This at 22 minutes to 2. The "Congress" now lets fall foretopsail, and then the main, and so, with a tug alongside, starts down the North Channel, where the "Minnesota" has grounded, and presently runs plump ashore. Meanwhile the

"Virginia" opens upon the Yankee fort; slowly she steams
back, and the "Cumberland," sunk now to her white streak,
opens upon her again. A gallant man fought that ship—a
man worthy to have maintained a better cause. Gun after
gun he fired; lower and lower sunk his ship; his last discharge comes from his pivot gun, the ship lurches to starboard, now to port, his flag streams out wildly, and now the
"Cumberland" goes down on her beam ends, at once a monu-
ment and an epitaph of the gallant men who fought her. The
"Virginia" stops. Is she aground? And the gunboats "Raleigh" and "Beaufort"? Glorious Parker! Glorious Alexander! There they are on the quarters of the "Congress"
hammering away, and creeping up closer and closer all the
time. At ten minutes to 4 the "Congress" struck. Parker
hauled down the ensign, ran up his own battle flag in its
place; there the heroic Tayloe, who fought the "Fanny" at
Roanoke Island and Elizabeth City, got his wound—there
the gallant young Hutter fell, all shot by the dastards who
fired from the ship and shore when the white flag was flying
at the main and mizzen of the "Congress".

Here too, and in the same way, Flag-Officer Buchanan,
and Flag-Lieut. Minor were wounded. Now, the James
River gunboats, whose dark smoke had been seen against
the blue distance ever since 3 o'clock, came dashing along
past the shore batteries. Tucker, the courtly and chivalrous,
leading the van with the "Jamestown", Lieut.-Commanding
Barney, close aboard, and the little "Teaser", Lieut. Webb,
in her wake—like a bowlegged bull-dog in chase of the long,
lean, stag hounds. It was a gallant dash, and once past the
batteries, the two heavy vessels took position in the line of
battle, while the "Teaser" dashed at the "Minnesota", looking no larger than a coke-boat. And right well she maintained the honor of her flag and the appropriateness of her
name. Now the "Roanoke" puts her helm up and declines
the battle. Now the "Virginia" is thundering away again.
The "Teaser" is still closer in. We are closer in—sizz!
comes a shell ahead; presently another, astern; finally, a
third, with a clear, sharp whizz, just overhead, to the great

delight of the Commodore, who appreciated the compliment of these good shots, which were the last of six directed shots at the "Harmony". Now the schooner "Reindeer" comes foaming along, cut out from under the shore batteries, she reports, and is sent up in charge of acting Master Gibbs. And next the gallant "Beaufort" runs down. Parker stops and brings on board the great piece of bunting we saw hauled down just now. He brings also some thirty prisoners, and some wounded men—men wounded under that white flag yonder desecrated by the Yankees. One of these lies stretched out, decently covered over, gasping out his life on the deck—a Yankee shot through the head, all bloody and ghastly, killed by the inhuman fire of his own people. Another, pale and stern, the Captain of the "Beaufort's" gun, lies there too, a noble specimen of a man who has since gone where the weary are at rest. A gallant man, a brave seaman! We shake hands with Parker, he gets back to his vessel slightly wounded, as is Alexander also, and steams back gallantly to the fight. The "Patrick Henry", the "Jamestown", the "Teaser", the "Beaufort", the "Raleigh", and the grand old "Virginia" are all thundering away. We steam down and speak the first. We hear a report of casualties; we shake hands with friends; we shove off, cheer and steam towards the Swash channel. Presently, through the thickening gloom, we see a red glare; it grows larger and brighter and fuller, and redder. It creeps higher and higher, and now gun after gun booming on the still night, as the fire reaches them; the batteries of the "Congress" are discharged across the water in harmless thunder. It was a grand sight to see; and by the light of the burning ship we made our way back to Norfolk. At half-past 11, the act of retribution was complete, for at that hour, with a great noise, she blew up.

Too jubilantly, as it was not yet time for jubilation, the Richmond *Dispatch* cheered the victory, in an editorial "THE WONDERFUL NAVAL VICTORY." Even as the editorial was printed, news columns were given over to the arrival of the *Monitor* and the great naval stalemate of March ninth:

We have scarcely recovered from the astonishment with which the whole town was thunderstruck at the astounding news on Sunday. The annals of naval warfare contain no parallel to this extraordinary achievement. It stands alone unprecedented, and at a single blow has revolutionized the whole system of naval warfare. That a single vessel, and that not of a large size, could be so constructed and so controlled as to demolish three of the largest and most powerful men-of-war in the world, is a prodigy which we can scarcely credit even now. And yet it is so. The Virginia, aided by two or three side-wheel steamers and gun-boats, has sent to the bottom three war-ships, which were the pride of the United States and the wonder of the world. Hampton Roads, where hostile fleets and transports have so long rode in safety and defiance, is now a more unsafe place for the strongest Federal ship than the mid-ocean in a tornado. The "perfect failure", as the Yankees pronounced the Virginia, has proved the most brilliant success of naval architecture; and her heroic commander, his officers and men, as well as their comrades of the other vessels, have covered themselves with glory.

The readers of the New York *Herald,* who on the tenth had been dismayed to learn of the loss of their three ships, were cheered when on the morning of the eleventh there appeared the sequel:

The day closed, indeed, with sadness in the hearts of our officers, besides having the fact resting on their minds that the hostile machine that had just made such murderous work had only retired apparently to recruit itself, and then return to complete the destruction she had so auspiciously commenced, having the floating vessels here at her mercy. While despondency settled on many brows, and conjectures were rife as to where the Merrimac would direct her attention the next day, a gleam of hope arose. At eight o'clock in the evening a bright, movable light was discovered seaward coming from the direction of Cape Charles light. It being known that the Ericsson Battery had left New York a few days previous, surmises were rife that this light might proceed from the deck. The best night telescopes were brought into requisition, and in less than half an hour after it first hove in sight the fact was circulated that the Ericsson Battery was coming up the Roads. The news spread like wildfire; the ramparts in the fort were soon lined with troops. At nine o'clock the Monitor anchored off Fortress Monroe. Lieutenant Commanding Worden immediately reported to Flag Officer Marston, and subsequently to General Wood. It was at once determined by those officers to send the battery to Newport's News, to protect that port, also to defend the Minnesota, which was still on shore. Before she started on her mission an additional supply of ammunition was placed on board, and at half-past eleven o'clock the Monitor went on her mission, to await the appearance of things the following day. The arrival of the Monitor was, indeed, providential.

This day (Sunday) the day broke fair. As the sun broke on the horizon a slight haze was visible on the water, which prevented an extended vision. At half past six o'clock A. M. this haze cleared away. Looking towards Sewell's Point there appeared the Merrimac, and the rebel steamers Yorktown and Patrick Henry. They were stationary—the Merrimac to the right of the others, blowing off steam. Their appearance was the cause for a second alarm. The rebel craft seemed deliberating what to do—whether to move on to attempt the destruction of the Minnesota, which was yet aground, or move on to the Union fleet anchored near the Rip Raps. The appearance of the Merrimac on this second visit caused great precipitation in the removal of our transport fleet to a safe harbor a mile or two up the

Chesapeake Bay. At seven A. M. a plan seemed to have been adopted, and the Merrimac steamed in the direction of the Minnesota, which was still aground. The Yorktown and Jamestown were crowded with troops, and steamed slowly after the Merrimac. The plan of the latter seemed to be to destroy the Minnesota, and then proceed to shell out the Union camp at Newport's News and land and take possession of the Union camp with their own troops. The Merrimac steamed along with boldness until she was within three miles of the Minnesota, when the Monitor essayed from behind the latter and proceeded towards the Merrimac. At first the rebel craft seemed nonplussed, and hesitated, no doubt in wonderment, at the queer looking machine approaching her. The Merrimac then closed the distance between her and the Monitor until they were within a mile of each other. Both batteries stopped. The Merrimac fired a shot at the Minnesota, to which no reply was made. The rebel craft then fired at the Monitor; the latter replied, hitting the Merrimac near the water line. The Merrimac then commenced firing very rapidly, first from her stern gun at the Monitor, and then her broadside guns, occasionally firing a shot at the Minnesota. The fight went on in this way for an hour or two, both vessels exchanging shots pretty freely. Sometimes the Merrimac would retire followed by the Ericsson, and *vice versa*. While the fight between the batteries was going on, one hundred solid nine inch shot were sent up from Fortress Monroe on the steamer Rancocas to the Minnesota. At a quarter past ten o'clock the Merrimac and Monitor had come into pretty close quarters, the former giving the latter two broadsides in succession. It was promptly replied to by the Monitor. The firing was so rapid that both craft were obscured in columns of white smoke for a moment or more. The ramparts of the fort, the rigging of the vessels in port, the houses and the bend were all crowded with sailors, soldiers and civilians. When the rapid firing alluded to took place, these spectators were singularly silent, as if doubtful as to the result. Their impatience was soon removed by the full figure of the Monitor, with the Stars and Stripes flying at her stern, steaming around the Merrimac, moving with the ease of a duck on the water. The distance between the vessels was forty feet. In this circuit, the Monitor's guns were not idle, as she fired shot after shot into her antagonist, two of which, it is alleged, penetrated the Merrimac's sides.

At eleven A. M. the Minnesota opened fire, and assisted the Monitor in engaging the Merrimac. She fired nine-inch solid shot with good accuracy, but with apparently little effect. The Merrimac returned the fire, firing shell, one of which struck and exploded the boiler of the gunboat Dragon, which was alongside the Minnesota endeavoring to get her off. By this unfortunate affair, Jos. McDonald, sailor, was seriously scalded. For the next hour the battle raged fiercely between the Merrimac on the rebel side and the Union vessels, the Monitor, Minnesota and Whitehall, but with no particular result.

The Minnesota being the best mark for the Merrimac, the latter fired at her frequently, alternately giving the Monitor a shot. The Merrimac made several attempts to run at full speed past the Monitor to attack and run down the Minnesota. All these attempts were parried, as it were, by the Monitor. In one of those attempts by the Merrimac she ran her plough or ram with full force against the side of the Monitor; but it only had the effect of careening the latter vessel in the slightest degree. The rebel boats Yorktown and Patrick Henry kept at a safe distance from the Monitor. The former vessel, at the beginning of the fight, had the temerity to come within respectable range of the Monitor. The latter fired one shot at her, entering her pilot house, carrying it away, and, no doubt, killing a number of rebels. She retired out of range.

The fight raged hotly on both sides, the opposing batteries moving around each other with the skill, ease and dexterity of expert pugilists. The Merrimac, though the strongest, did not move with the dexterity of her antagonist; hence the Monitor had the advantage of taking choice of position. At a quarter before twelve o'clock, noon, Lieutenant Hepburn, the signal officer on the ramparts at Fortress Monroe, reported to General Wool that the Monitor had pierced the sides of the Merrimac, and in a few minutes the latter was in full retreat, heading for Sewell's Point, and chased for a few minutes by the Monitor. The Merrimac had evidently suffered to some extent, and it was thought at one time that she was sinking. After she got safely under the guns of the rebel battery at Sewell's Point, she stopped and signalled for help from her consorts, who were beating a retreat. Subsequently two tugboats, or gunboats, went alongside and took her in tow, and proceeded to Norfolk. This ended the engagement.

The Merrimac evidently came out in the morning without the expectation of meeting any obstacle more than on the preceding day, and no doubt the presence of the Monitor, when it struck her view, was sudden and wholly unexpected.

The Monitor was handled with unsurpassed skill, decision and coolness, for which all praise should be given her officers. She has come up to the expectations that were formed of her, and has proved herself impregnable to the heaviest shot at close quarters.

Lieutenant Worden, who handled the Monitor so skilfully, is in Washington, in the hands of a surgeon. He was in the pilot house of the Monitor when the Merrimac directed a whole broadside at it, and received his injuries from the minute fragments of powder which were driven through the lookout holes. Lieutenant Worden was stunned by the concussion, and was carried away. On recovering, he asked, "Have I saved the Minnesota?" The reply was, "Yes, and whipped the Merrimac." To which he answered, "Then I don't care what becomes of me."

The injuries of Lieutenant Worden are not supposed to be dangerous.

On examining the Monitor after the engagement, though shell after shell had exploded on her decks and solid shot struck the tower, yet no perceptible damage had been done to the vessel, nor injury to the crew, with the exception already mentioned. One of the crew of the Monitor was asked how the boys felt during the engagement.  He replied, "Oh, first rate; the shot and shell from the Merrimac sounded like hailstones on our decks."


## II

# THE GLORIOUS CONSUMMATION

(New York *World*)

---

Lee knew his predicament.  So, we suppose, did the editors of the few remaining newspapers near the scene of the Appomattox campaign, those editors who pleaded in their papers for "clean rags, for which we will pay the highest market price," so that they might continue to print the most cheerful news they could find—such news as this, in the Richmond *Examiner* for March 1, 1865:

### NORTH GEORGIA

The West Point road is reported to be completed within nine miles of Atlanta.  Dalton is the only fortified post now occupied by the enemy in North Georgia, and his force there is reported to consist of only two or three brigades. This shows of what value is "Yankee Conquest" and by what frail tenure he holds the country he has overrun, where he is only able to place here and there a straggling garrison.

And on March thirtieth, barely ten days before they all came true, the editor printed mocking predictions:

It is evident that the month of April will witness a decisive turn, given one way or another, to GRANT's grand converging campaign.  A little month—we have but to sustain our army and keep our banner flying for one month, and the mighty, dead lift effort of the Federal power will have been made, and will have failed, as usual. Our enemies cannot wait; they are in a hurry for success at once; because they are but too well aware that they are in the midst of the last campaign they can by any means pretend to undertake against the Confederacy. Therefore their exertions will be superhuman in this coming month. SHERMAN advancing northward to the Danville railroad; THOMAS and STONE-MAN coming down from the valleys of East Tennessee upon Lynchburg, with the design of stretching a hand to SHERI-DAN somewhere about Burkeville, while GRANT continues to hold LEE as he says, "by the throat", ready to receive the surrender of the city when it shall be starved into submission, and also to intercept the "flight" of General LEE, who, according to the best Yankee authority, is thinking of nothing but showing a clean pair of heels—this is the programme; it must be fulfilled in every part, or it all falls to the ground together. In the enemy's country they obviously think the plan cannot by possibility fail this time. Richmond, as they assure one another, is in a perfect chaos of anarchy and despair. The "chiefs of the slave-holders' Rebellion" have given up the cause, and ten days, or at the most, twenty, are allowed for the final consummation.

Ten days *were* enough for the final consummation. By April ninth, Lee was telling his troops what had happened to them, and riding off to his tent, in tears. Here was the great story of the war itself, so tremendous that none could imagine it being overshadowed by a greater in less than a week.

At the time of the surrender, thousands of dollars already had been spent by the New York press in its intense rivalry for news. Bennett, of the *Herald,* lavish in money as well as in phrase, had covered the war with a correspondent in every headquarters and a *Herald* wagon creaking along in every advance. The others could not match him, but they spent up to their limits. It remained for the New York *World* to print the best and most exciting story of the struggle between the two titans. On the morning of the fourteenth there appeared an account of Lee's efforts to escape that nearly filled the first page. The reporter ignored telegraph tolls and wrote:

### The Hounds and the Hares

On that morning of Monday which beheld the occupation of Petersburg and Richmond by Union troops, the two grand armies of the Potomac and the James began a pursuit which will be remembered as the swiftest, the most unrelenting, and the most successful in history.

Lifted and thrown by the tremendous onsets of Saturday and Sunday from the earthworks he had occupied for years, Lee, uniting his forces near Chesterfield Court House, westward and midway between the two cities he had deserted, pushed straight on for the Appomattox. Crossing the river at Devil's bend, he struck the Richmond and Danville Railroad at Amelia Court House on Wednesday; and began to strain every sinew of his command to escape down that road via Burke's station to Danville, before Grant could head him off.

Grant was too quick for him. The flight of the Army of Northern Virginia had not begun before the hounds—swift legions with steel fangs and baying cannon—were on its track. Arising from only a few hours' rest after victory, Sheridan, with his troopers, started westward on Monday, below the Appomattox, along the river road. Down from the James swept the army under Ord, and rendezvousing with the Army of the Potomac at Sutherland's station, fifteen miles west of Petersburg, crossed the route of its march, pursuing the line of the Petersburg and Lynchburg Railroad to Burkesville. The Army of the Potomac, following mainly in the track of Sheridan, aimed at the Richmond and Danville road, in the vicinity of Jetersville, six miles below Amelia Court House.

## A Race for Life

One glance at a good map will show what a pretty race it was. Three days and nights, hurrying, hurrying, the two great armies, scarcely fifteen miles apart, thundered in through villages and valleys, over hills and streams, toward a common goal. That goal—the Richmond and Danville railroad—which should strike it first? Should we come upon it to find that the prey had passed; to get a glimpse of its vanishing flanks; to send after it a farewell cannon shot or two; to sit ourselves down forthwith, wiping our wet foreheads and thanking God and Grant that at least we had got Petersburg and Richmond? Or should we, *could* we, have the gladness of meeting the hunted thing face to face out of its dens, giving it a shot between its scared eyes, worrying it, torturing it into giving up its fearful ghost at last?

The last vindictive thought inspired the men not only to endurance, but to a kind of frenzy. They marched as victors should; they sang and cheered along the roads like demons. Spanning the days with feet that never seemed to tire, their swift tramp sounded also far into sleepless nights. Dark divisions that sank to slumber in some forest in the evening at ten, awoke with the drum at two, to eat a meal as hasty as a bird's, and then to start, with bands playing, flags waving, and shouts that might have roused the tardy sun, upon the roads again. All the hardships and inconveniences of other marches were turned to joys in these. Wading rivers became a glorious *divertissement*. The soldiers went into the water up to their waists, joking, laughing, and emerged shaking themselves and rolling upon the banks like a happy drove of Newfoundlands.

Villagers, astonished and curious, asked what "you all" were going so fast for?

"We're the devil after Lee!" cried a soldier.

"O, we're after Lee,
Infantree and cavalree

and we're bound to smash him up before the morning."

After Lee! After Lee! General Grant, General Meade,

General everybody who appeared in sight of the tugging columns, received an ovation.

"Hard work, General; but, if you want us to go, we will go," said a red-faced soldier to General Grant, as he was riding by one afternoon near sunset.

"Keep going for a while yet, then, boys," said the General.

"We will! We will! If you'll promise us a sight of Lee," and the air rang with cheers. . . .

[A somewhat technical description of the maneuvers of Wednesday has been here deleted. The reporter described how Sheridan, traveling at top speed, succeeded in beating Lee's advance guard to the Richmond Railroad, and how Lee, learning of this, started a new march—from Amelia Court House to Farmville on the Appomattox. Impressed with the speed of Lee's army, the reporter described the attack on its rear guard by the Union Second Corps, at Deatonville, and of the series of harassing attacks upon Ewell's force by the Sixth Corps and the Sheridan, Custer and Merritt cavalry divisions.]

### Corraling a Hare

At this moment the rebel General Ewell, who had heard since 12 o'clock the thunders of the retreating conflict on his left, sat, during a momentary halt, beneath a tree, writing a dispatch which reads as follows:

General Lee: For God's sake, and humanity's sake, surrender your army. You are outnumbered and beaten. To continue the contest longer is to court nothing but slaughter and ruin.

Ewell.

Scarcely had it been signed when the rattle of carbines and the racket of musketry, from flank and front and rear, aroused the despondent rebel to "continue the contest" a little longer, for the sake of his own honor. Forming his lines on the banks of a difficult creek, he made at first a fierce resistance. The Sixth corps—Seymour and Wheaton's divisions—charged across with cheers, piercing his insufficient front. The cavalry, rushing in by squadron, doubled up his right flank. The artillery of the Second corps plowed through his left and center. One half hour, and it was all over with General Ewell. White flags leaped up along his lines, thick as ladies' handkerchiefs in Broadway windows on a procession day. The battle was over; the game was caught. Ewell, with his staff, his whole remaining corps, including Generals Curtis Lee, Ramseur, DeBarr, Kershaw, Button and Corse, fourteen pieces of field artillery with caissons, three hundred wagons, seventy ambulances, a large quantity of medical stores, were captured. The Sixth corps, in this admirable assault, is said to have lost nearly a thousand killed and wounded.

General Sheridan was in command of the Sixth corps and cavalry during the fight. The character and issue of that fight, as also the chase of the forenoon preceding it, show how almost utterly broken down and demoralized the Army of Northern Virginia had come to be. On every mile of the pursuit all kinds of abandoned material of war were picked up, until they became an incumbrance to our march. Artillery, caissons, wagons and ambulances, with dead or broken down mules still hanging to the traces, lay overturned in gullies. Cooking utensils, mess furniture, even the officers' baggage, had been thus left, from very dire necessity, behind. While too—as the occasional fierce resistance of the foe to our advance showed—neither the pride nor the established bravery of Lee's once invincible troops were quite erased, it is plain that they fought without hope. It was the desperate, brief defiance of the wolf to the hounds. It gave their main army breathing spells, momentary but vain respite from the bolts of an awful pursuit, that sometimes brought our men in sight of the supply trains, not yet abandoned, which the rebels still pushed on before. Stragglers fell out along their line of march, sick in body, sick at heart, begging for something to eat.

"Something to eat? Why don't you forage on the country, as we have to do?" demanded our men.

"We have no time," they say, "no time to cook, to eat or sleep. Nothing but marching, marching, marching. We are tired."

## The Game at Bay

In the midst of disaster, Lee had not utterly despaired. He had not yet, it appears, given up hope of reaching Danville. It has been shown how, on this same Thursday, while the Second corps pressed upon his rear, and while Sheridan and the Sixth corps destroyed his flanking column under Ewell, the main body of his forces, pushing down at railroad speed between the Army of the Potomac and the Appomattox toward the Southside railroad crossing at High Bridge, came upon the detachment of cavalry and infantry sent out in the morning by General Ord. This detachment, although fighting bravely, was completely used up by overwhelming numbers. Colonel Washburn, its commander, was mortally wounded. The lieutenant-colonel of the Fourth Massachusetts was also wounded. Nearly all the infantry were captured, and fifty were killed while attempting to escape by swimming a stream. General Reed, who was sent out to withdraw the detachment from its dangerous position, arrived in time to engage in the fight, and to be mortally wounded in the neck.

General Ord hastened up the Twenty-fourth corps, too late to relieve his own unfortunate advance, but early enough to check Lee's in the vicinity of Rice's Station. Foster's division, which was first, found itself outflanked on the left. Turner's division thrown in on the left and a detachment of cavalry still beyond, at last sufficed to cover the hostile front. Skirmishing, but no important fighting, ensued, and continued during the day; the enemy gradually retreating to the river, toward which the Second corps had also pressed them above, beyond Sailor's crest. A series of brilliant charges toward nightfall by the last named corps gave us nineteen pieces of artillery and two hundred wagons, and drove them still further on into the strong fortifications which guard the High Bridge.

During the night Lee was very busy. Crossing a portion of his troops over High Bridge, he prepared his trains and the remainder for the retreat, to which, on the following (Friday) morning, he was compelled by the charges of half an army. Setting fire to the High Bridge, and falling slowly back along the lower side of the Appomattox, he parked his trains and assumed a new position just beyond the pleasant village of Farmville. Here, until night, he held us at bay. From here he directed his last unavailing efforts to pierce our lines, to get around our left flank, to escape to Danville. The Army of the Potomac kept a front of steel before him, losing, in the contest, one of its noblest officers, General Thomas A. Smythe, of the Second corps. The Army of the James, stealthily marching below, and possessing Prince Edward's Court House, shut off escape in that direction. Moving up from Prince Edward's Court House to the left, General Ord took position in conjunction with the Second corps in the afternoon, effecting an almost complete surround of the devoted rebel army.

At night General Grant, entering Farmville, sent his first note to General Lee, asking the surrender of his forces. On this day as before we had effected large captures of prisoners, stragglers, and material. The *debris* of the rebel retreat lay in every road and gully, and on the banks of every stream. The universal statement of prisoners was that the rebel army was falling to pieces from sheer exhaustion. General Grant, too prudent before to arrogate his right to a triumph not yet wholly won, and too generous to insult a great antagonist by a demand that would have been a boast so long as his foe had a chance of success, now chose to "Shift from himself the responsibility of any further effusion of blood" by a request so firm and so chivalrous in its wording that Lee himself was deeply touched by it.

### AGAIN ON THE SCENT

Still hoping, still laboring, with sleepless energy, and relying somewhat, perhaps, upon a possible relaxation of the pressure about him under the belief that he would comply with Grant's desire, General Lee may have endeavored to sustain the last impression by his dispatch, sent in reply:

"Though not entirely of the opinion you express of the hopelessness of further resistance on the part of the Army of Northern Virginia, I reciprocate your desire to avoid useless effusion of blood, and therefore, before considering your proposition, ask the terms you will offer on condition of surrender"

He commenced Friday night, getting his trains and his army across the Appomattox, partially burning the bridges behind him.   Such a movement did not escape the keen vigilance of Grant.   Ere the dawn of Saturday, while the rebel commander doubling again in his tracks, had begun a northwesterly march, striking the Petersburg and Lynchburg pike leading to Appomattox Court House, the Union armies were following close on his flank and rear.   Meade, with the Second, Sixth and Fifth corps, pursued along the pike and along the south bank of the Appomattox.   Sheridan marched straight for Appomattox Court House, in a line as direct as possible, between the river and the Lynchburg Railroad. Ord, with the Army of the James, still kept on like a wary hound below, making for Appomattox Court House via Pamplin's Station.

And now again, the fury and terror of the march.

All day long, plunging, stumbling, dropping its hundreds of stragglers, and wagons and worn out animals by the way; sore of foot, desperate at heart, but still held in some sort together by the stern, magnificent will of a single man, the hunted army of Virginia kept up its superb retreat.

All day long the Nemesis pursued—dark columns, high of heart, fleet of foot, swinging up into the line occasionally to scourge with musketry and cannon the sullen rear of the foe. Its banners fluttered gayly in the breeze; at times reviving strains of martial music thrilled along the ranks.

As before, the enemy showed his teeth. The Second corps, striving in the advance beyond Appomattox mountain, found a rebel corps in line at noon. Miles' division, in the advance, charged, suffered severely, and was driven back. The remaining divisions came up and dislodged the foe, effecting, as usual, large captures. Lee had set fire to many of his abandoned wagons, but our men were often upon them before they were destroyed, thus fulfilling the maxim of Napoleon, "Keep your sword close to the enemy's loins." Meade, with the Second and Sixth corps, kept on in rear, while Sheridan, with his cavalry—the Fifth corps following in his wake and the Twenty-fourth corps struggling up from below—strove hard for Appomattox Court House in advance.

## PUSHED TO THE WALL

That (Saturday) evening Custer's division of cavalry quickly followed by Merritt's, had succeeded in reaching Appomattox Court House, working around to the very front and advance guard of the rebel army, which they engaged. A savage conflict, lasting about two hours, resulted in a victory that gave us a thousand prisoners, thirty-six colors, and twenty-two pieces of artillery. Custer had also captured on his way five trains of cars near the station. Lee's army, after this repulse, stood still, marshalled near Appomattox Court House.

The shadows of evening fall; the sounds of battle cease; a hundred thousand yellow camp fires mock the stars. Not all their light combined is bright enough to show the watchful eyes of Lee what fate is gathering round him. He knows that Meade, with the Second and Sixth corps, is behind him, and to the east of him. He knows—for he has been made to feel—that Sheridan is before him. But he does not know that the Fifth corps, after a terrible, swift march, has arrived to join Sheridan; that the Twenty-fourth and Twenty-fifth corps are coming up from below, and will be ready to co-operate before the morning. He does not know, in fact, that while the night speeds on his army is surrounded!

He sits alone—this man of iron who, with a sinking cause and a starving army, had kept both alive so long. His head—that grand head of which a perfect portrait is before me now—rests on a hand so strong, so true—ah! would to God, I heard some say, it had not been a rebel's! So noble a form—noble even in its attitude of despondency—might become a king. As he sits there within the lamplight, brooding over the snares about him, he slowly changes a foot and clenches a hand under the impulse of a thought, and "somewhat grimly smiles". Beneath that smile, memory and hope, cohabiting together, have conceived a new resolve!

## The Last Turn

This is hardly the time or the place in which to do justice to the character of Robert E. Lee. Yet one element of it was certainly indicated by what occurred next morning, if it had not been sufficiently shown before. Pride *might* have impelled Lee, on that morning, to make the last attempt which he did make to escape from the toils; but pride alone might have hesitated to assume the responsibility of sacrificing more lives in an effort so forlorn. It is not too much to say, after having become somewhat acquainted with his nature through those who know him best, that the strong allegiance to principle which alone impelled him to "take up arms amid a sea of troubles" in behalf of a faulty cause, alone impelled him to make a last, vain, bloody struggle against a sea of troubles at the end. It will not fail to be recorded that Robert E. Lee, before his surrender, ran a good race, and fought a gallant fight.

He had some hope, it seems, of breaking through our lines. His resolve of the night before was to make the attempt against Sheridan in his front, who, he imagined, from the fact that he had met nothing but cavalry the night before, would have nothing but cavalry to oppose him in the morning. Burning his wagons, spiking and burning his artillery, sacrificing even his own private baggage to assist in lightening the burdens of his army, he made, early on Sunday morning, a tremendous dash down the Appomattox Court House Road, against the sleepless "man of the sabers". The musketry of the Fifth corps, joining with the carbines of the cavalry in a hoarse and savage reply that sent his men back like horses on their haunches, told him, at last, that "all was over and done".

# NIGHT FINAL

FORD'S NEW THEATRE, Tenth Street
Above Pennsylvania
There Will Be No Performance at This
Theatre Tonight
—Washington *Evening Star*
April 15, 1865

# A CRIME WITHOUT A NAME

(Philadelphia *Public Ledger*)

---

The nation was glutted with sensation. For four years it had gorged itself upon the thrilling names of Lee and Grant and Beauty Stuart and Stonewall Jackson. It had read of the battles at Vicksburg and the Wilderness, Antietam and Chancellorsville. Now it was spent and passionless, and for a while it would rather read quiet and innocent fiction or amusing editorials without the sting of hatred in them.

The cessation of startling news after the surrender of Lee lasted six days—from April 9 to April 15, 1865. And then there were fulfilled the disregarded prophecies in two obscure items, which had appeared a month and four months before. The first of these, an advertisement, was printed by the Selma, Alabama, *Dispatch:*

One Million Dollars Wanted. to have Peace by the First of March. If the citizens of the Confederacy will furnish me with the cash, or good securities for the sum of one million dollars, I will cause the lives of Abraham Lincoln, Willian H. Seward and Andrew Johnson to be taken by the First of March next. This will give us peace, and satisfy the world that cruel tyrants cannot live in a land of liberty. If this is not accomplished, nothing will be claimed beyond the sum of fifty thousand dollars in advance, which is supposed to be necessary to reach and slaughter the three villains. I will give myself one thousand dollars towards this patriotic purpose. Every one wishing to contribute will address Box X, Conaba, Alabama. December 1, 1864.

The second, closer to home and a surer possibility, found its way into the columns of the Philadelphia *North American* for March 8, 1865:

A DESIGN TO ASSASSINATE THE PRESIDENT
    Washington—A man named Clements has been turned over to the civil authorities by the military, against whom the evidence is positive that he had all his plans arranged for the assassination of the President on Inauguration Day. He is in jail here.
    Clements and another person came from Alexandria, Virginia, on Saturday. They were both extremely disorderly, and seemed to have been drinking freely. Clements, in particular, was very abusive, and said, using gross and profane language, that he came here to assassinate the President, that he was late by about one-half an hour, and that his Saviour would never forgive him for failing to do so; that he would do it that night, namely the fifth of March, and that he came expressly to do it, and he would do it before he left town.

So much for the prophecies. The editors had read them, and, in the press of the next minute's news, forgotten them. The war rolled toward its end as they were being printed. Time, which creates news but is never governed by it, brought April. Washington found on its doorsteps on the morning of the fourteenth, a copy of the *National Daily Intelligencer* containing, among other things, an advertisement of Miss Laura Keene's last appearance in *Our American Cousin*. And in the evening Washington again found a paper on its doorsteps— this time the *Evening Star*—announcing:

    Lieutenant General Grant, President and Mrs. Lincoln have secured the state box at Ford's Theatre tonight, to witness Miss Laura Keene's *American Cousin*.

Among the readers of this item was a guest of the National Hotel, black-eyed, black-haired, blackly impelled. John Wilkes Booth, who had carried in his heart a frightful design, also attended Ford's Theatre that night; but he saw nothing of the performance. Instead he created perhaps the biggest single story of the nineteenth century. The shooting of Lincoln had every needed element for the great news story: it was shocking, not alone because the President was shot, but because the reasons for such an act, with the ending of the Civil War, seemed removed. It was exciting, because hundreds saw the assassin fire and flee, and saw his victim slumped in infinite pathos in his chair. It was properly important—a leading American actor shooting the President at the performance of a first-rank star's play. And, finally, it was a sustained story, for Booth was not caught until the sensation had begun to die.

The shot heard by the audience at Ford's—at first believed to be part of the play—started a chain of telegrams baffling even to editors who had been made resourceful in the crucible of war. Mere minutes after the shot was fired (and before, it is safe to say, Booth had crossed the Anacostia Bridge, a few miles away), reporters were frantically scribbling dispatches, to infect their superiors with their own gasping excitement. So unexpected was the event that a newspaper like the New York *Tribune* presented everything it had obtained over the wire, in the precise order of its reception:

HIGHLY IMPORTANT!
The President Shot!
Secretary Seward Attacked

First Dispatch
Washington, April 14, 1865.

*To the Associated Press:*
The President was shot in a theatre tonight and perhaps mortally wounded.

### Second Dispatch

To Editors: Our Washington agent orders the dispatch about the President "stopped." Nothing is said about the truth or falsity of the report.

### Third Dispatch

*Special to the New York Tribune:*

The President was just shot at Ford's Theatre. The ball entered his neck. It is not known whether the wound is mortal. Intense excitement.

### Fourth Dispatch

*Special to the New York Tribune:*

The President expired at a quarter to twelve.

### Fifth Dispatch

Washington, April 15, 12:30 a. m.

*To the Associated Press:*

The President was shot in a theatre tonight and perhaps mortally wounded.

The President is not expected to live through the night. He was shot at a theatre.

Secretary Seward was also assassinated.

No arteries were cut.

Particulars soon.

### The Particulars

Washington, April 14—President Lincoln and his wife, together with other friends, this evening visited Ford's Theatre for the purpose of witnessing the performance of the "American Cousin."

It was announced in the papers that General Grant would also be present, but that gentleman instead took the late train of cars for New Jersey.

The theatre was densely crowded and everybody seemed delighted with the scene before them.

During the third act, and while there was a temporary pause for one of the actors to enter, the sharp report of a pistol was heard, which merely attracted attention, but suggested nothing serious, until a man rushed to the front of the President's box, waving a long dagger in his right hand and exclaiming, *"Sic Semper Tyrannis!"* and immediately leaped from the box, which was of the second tier, to the stage beneath, thus making his escape amid the bewilderment of the audience, from the rear of the theatre, and, mounting a horse, fled.

The screams of Mrs. Lincoln first disclosed the fact to the audience that the President had been shot, then all present rose to their feet, rushing toward the stage, many exclaiming, "Hang him! hang him!"

There was a rush toward the Presidential box, when cries were heard, "Stand back!" "Give him air!" "Has any one stimulants?"

On a hasty examination, it was found that the President had been shot through the head above and back of the temporal bone, and that some of the brain was oozing out.

He was removed to a private house opposite to the theatre, and the Surgeon General of the Army and other Surgeons were sent for to attend his condition.

On an examination of the private box, blood was discovered on the back of the cushioned rocking chair on which the President had been sitting, also on the partition and on the floor. A common single-barrelled pocket pistol was found on the carpet.

A military guard was placed in front of the private residence to which the President had been conveyed.

An immense crowd gathered in front of it, all deeply anxious to learn the condition of the President. It had been previously announced that the wound was mortal, but all hoped otherwise. The shock to the community was terrible.

At midnight, the Cabinet, with Messrs. Sumner, Colfax and Farnsworth, Judge Carter, Governor Oglesby, General Meigs, Colonel Hay, and a few personal friends, with Surgeon General Barnes and his medical associates, were around his bedside. . . .

The parting of his family with the dying President is too sad for description.

The President and Mrs. Lincoln did not start to the theatre till fifteen minutes after eight o'clock. Speaker Colfax was at the White House at the time and the President stated to him that he was going, although Mrs. Lincoln had not been well, because the papers had advertised that General Grant and they were to be present, and as General Grant had gone North, he did not wish the audience to be disappointed.

## Attempted Assassination of Secretary Seward

When the excitement at the theatre was at its wildest height, reports were circulated that Secretary Seward had also been assassinated. On reaching this gentleman's residence, a crowd and military guard were found at the door, and on entering, it was ascertained that the reports were based upon truth; everybody there was so excited that scarcely an intelligible account could be gathered, but the facts are substantially as follows:

At ten o'clock P. M. a man rang the bell, and the call having been answered by a colored servant, he said he had come from Doctor Verdi, Secretary Seward's family physician, with a prescription, at the same time holding in his hand a small piece of folded paper, and saying, in answer to a refusal, that he must see the Secretary, as he was entrusted with a particular direction concerning the medicine. He still insisted on going up, although repeatedly informed that no one could enter the chamber. The man pushed the servant aside and walked quickly to the Secretary's room and was there met by Mr. Frederick W. Seward, of whom he demanded to see the Secretary, making the same representations which he did to the servant. What further passed in the way of colloquy is not known, but the man struck him in the head with a *billy*, severely injuring the skull and felling him almost senseless. The assassin then rushed into the chamber and attacked Major Seward, Paymaster in the United States Army, and Mr. Hansell, a Messenger of the

State Department and two male nurses, disabling them all. He then rushed upon the Secretary who was lying in bed in the same room, and inflicted three stabs in the neck, but severing, it is hoped, no arteries.

The assassin then rushed downstairs, mounted his horse at the door and rode off before an alarm could be sounded and in the same manner as the assassin of the President. . . .

Eight hours after the crime and while thousands in the city were unaware of its commission, the *Intelligencer* in Washington sent to press its edition naming

## THE MURDERER OF THE PRESIDENT

Developments have rendered it certain that the hand that robbed our President of life was that of John Wilkes Booth, an actor. Since his arrival in this city he is said to have declared that he traveled three days and nights in order to reach here in time. His identification as the man who leaped from the box is complete; and his hat, which was secured, has been identified as that worn by the man who hired the horse which bore him from the spot. The pistol by which his deadly purpose was accomplished was found in the theatre and a spur that fell from his boot was picked up on the stage. A bowie knife, supposed to be the one he brandished, was found on F Street between Ninth and Tenth. The horse he rode was hired at Pumphrey's stable; on entering the theatre he left it in charge of a boy at the alley in the rear of the theatre. This boy subsequently gave it in charge to another. Both of the boys are now under arrest.

The words used by Booth on jumping from the box were, as nearly as we can ascertain, *"Sic Semper Tyrannis*—Virginia is avenged!"* . . .

About eleven o'clock last night two men crossed the Anacostia Bridge, one of whom gave his name as Booth and the other as Smith. The latter is believed to be John Suratt.

Last night a riderless horse was found, which has been identified by the proprietor of one of the stables previously mentioned as having been hired from his establishment. Accounts are conflicting as to whether Booth crossed the bridge on horseback or on foot; but as it is believed he rode across, it is presumed that he exchanged his horse.

From information in possession of the authorities, it is evident that the scope of the plot was intended to be much more comprehensive. The Vice President and other prominent members of the Administration were particularly inquired for by the suspected parties, and their precise localities accurately obtained; but, Providentially, in their cases the scheme miscarried.

In three minutes after the death wound was inflicted on the President, Superintendent Richards telegraphed to all parts of the city news of the murder and instructions to be followed for the capture of the assassins.

A boat was at once sent down the Potomac to notify the gunboats on the river of the awful crime, in order that all possible means shall be taken for the arrest of the perpetrators. The most ample precautions have been taken and it is not believed the culprits will long succeed in evading the overtaking arm of justice.

Among the circumstances tending to fix participancy in the crimes on Booth were letters found in his trunk, one of which—apparently from a lady—supplicated him to desist from the perilous undertaking in which he was about to embark, stating that the time was inauspicious, the mine not yet ready to be sprung.

The Philadelphia *Public Ledger* recalled this Booth to its readers, in a story printed on the seventeenth:

Booth is a fine looking fellow, about twenty-five years of age. He is of medium height, fine-featured, black haired and black-eyed. As an actor he was wretched, and it was a matter of great mortification to him that he had not been able to win reputation as an actor. The pistol with which he shot the President was a single-barrelled, silver mounted Derringer.

And, on the same day, what had transpired in the

## INVESTIGATION OF THE MURDER

Superintendent Richards, upon examination of the theatre private box in which Mr. Lincoln was shot, says that the shot was fired by Booth through the door of the box. Booth first opened the door, and getting range of the President, closed the door and placed the pistol against it and fired. Then, rushing into the box, he cut with a large dirk Major Rathburn, who was the only male in the box with the President. It is believed that Booth took Rathburn for General Grant. Rathburn was cut severely on the arm, but the injury inflicted is not serious.

James B. Stewart, lawyer, sat near the stage, and as Booth regained his foot, Mr. Stewart started to catch him. After some difficulty, Stewart reached the stage and ran after Booth. He believes that if the actors had not, unintentionally, of course, got in his way, he would have succeeded in overtaking the assassin, but Booth, having often played in Ford's theatre, was well acquainted with the stage, and in his flight ran behind the scenes so expertly that he reached the back door and mounted his horse just as Mr. Stewart succeeded in gaining the threshold of the door.

On the seventeenth, belatedly, the *Public Ledger* presented the story told by the star of the play Lincoln had been watching. The reporter wrote that Miss Laura Keene was

behind the scenes on the northern side of the theatre, while the President's box was on the southern side. She was expecting the ingress of Mr. Spear. Mr. Booth pushed his way suddenly through the side scene. She for a second looked at him, and she heard the cry that the President was shot. She then knew something was occurring, as women were screaming, men hallooing, and children crying as if a fire panic had taken place. Miss Keene went to the front of the stage and addressing the bewildered audience, said, "For God's sake, have presence of mind and all keep your places, and all will be well." Miss Keene, after momentarily arresting the panic and the consternation in the audience, heard the cry of Miss Harris, saying, "Miss Keene, bring some water." Miss Keene made her way to the President's box. There she saw Mrs. Lincoln in the agony of a devoted wife, uttering the most piteous cries. Miss Keene attempted to pacify her.

This book—and others as large—could be filled with reprints of the action and thought of the American people, learning of its loss. The Richmond *Whig* called the crime "the heaviest blot which has ever fallen upon the people of the South"; New York correspondents wrote of the "bereavement that shuts out all other thought from the public mind"—the New York representative of the Philadelphia *Public Ledger* added a cynical admonition, "It is to be hoped that our politicians will be sufficiently restrained by the National grief to defer their visits to President Johnson. The most of them seem to be impressed with the belief that their advice is absolutely necessary to enable him to administer the Government." In Washington, the *Intelligencer* said that "everything about the Mansion wears the most solemn aspect and there is scarcely a dry eye among all the vast concourse who enter to gaze upon the lifeless form," and the Richmond *Whig*, a few days after the assassination, regretted that no public demonstration of grief would be possible "because it is the desire of the military authorities [the Union army then occupied the city] that there shall be no assembly of the people in this city for the present." The *Whig* added that it had "heard expressions of grief on all sides, condemning and deploring the awful deed in unmeasured terms."

This account of Philadelphia's feelings, reprinted from the *Public Ledger,* is typical:

After a week of rejoicing bordering on frenzy; after the hosannas of praise in behalf of our victorious armies; and while the whole city was ablaze with excitement over the approaching illumination to commemorate the nation's deliverance, came the news of the nation's loss. The sad story was known to but few persons on Friday night. Outside of the newspaper offices it did not spread very far, but with the break of day the newsboys' cry awoke the people to a knowledge of the tragedy. It was with difficulty that men could be made to believe the story. That such an event could occur at the capital of the nation was hard to comprehend, and men and women took counsel together at early dawn, and with tearful eyes and saddened countenances prayed that there might be some mistake. Soon the people found their way to the heart of the city to learn the full extent of the tragedy. Work was suspended in workshop and factory; counting houses and brokers' offices were closed; merchants closed their stores, and everybody crowded to the newspaper offices, to catch the first announcement of a possible improvement in the President's condition.

Past political differences were forgotten in the universal sorrow, and men discussed the event as a national humiliation and shame. Sadness was visible in every face. When the Official Gazette put at rest all hopes by announcing the death of Mr. Lincoln, the grief of the people was manifest in all directions. Strong and brave men wept as they read the news, and the gleam of rage was seen to sparkle in the eyes of the more excitable. Within an hour after the announcement of Mr. Lincoln's death, Chestnut Street was draped in mourning. Heavy masses of black were suspended from every building. The newspaper offices set the example. On the upper part of Chestnut Street, the white marble buildings, hung in black, presented a neat appearance.

The crowd remained upon the street until after nightfall. The great anxiety appeared to be to learn whether the assassin had been captured. . . .

Many of the city churches were heavily draped in mourning, though the black, in most of them, was tastefully arranged. . . .

John Wilkes Booth, at an early period of his life adopted the stage. Some of the citizens of Philadelphia may remember him as one of the stock company at the Arch Street Theatre. He did not make any figure at all during the engagements.

In the midst of this apparently universal wailing, there could be heard expressions of joy. Not all men thought Lincoln had been martyred. Some said as much, and the accounts of what happened to them pepper the pages of the Eastern press. Among the acts of violence reported were:

*(In San Francisco):*

Several men have been lynched in several places for expressions of joy at the assassination. General McDowell has issued an order for the instant arrest of any person expressing approval of Lincoln's death and for the suppression of any journal so offending.

*(In Maryland):*

Joseph Shaw, editor of the Westminster (Carroll County) *Democrat,* whose paper was mobbed, and material destroyed the night after the murder of the President, on account of the disloyal statements expressed by the editor, and who was also warned away by the people, returned yesterday to Westminster. Last night he was again waited on by a delegation of citizens, who knocked at his door. He appeared and fired into the crowd, wounding a young man named Henry Bell. Upon this, the enraged citizens killed Shaw on the spot.

*(In New England):*

George Stone was tarred and feathered at Swampscott last week, for cheering at the death of the President; and Major Otis Wright, of Lowell, narrowly escaped hanging for expressing joy at Mr. Lincoln's death. Fifteen minutes were given for him to leave the city, never to return.

*(In Philadelphia):*

Several men who were alleged to have used language indicative of pleasure at the Nation's calamity were mobbed and only saved from violence by the exertion of the policemen. A conductor on the Tenth and Eleventh Street Railway got himself into trouble by expressing his belief that the Nation had not suffered any loss. He was at once discharged from the employ of the company.

While most men mourned and a few rejoiced, the hunt—spurred by rewards totaling one hundred thousand dollars—was being pushed for Booth and his fellow plotters. The authorities trying to track down the assassin were handicapped in many ways. They had poor transport and communication. They were innocently betrayed by the well-meaning thousands who had seen and recognized the assassin: in New York, heading for the Canadian border; on the eastern shore of Maryland, awaiting a ship that would carry him into safe exile; in the South, where he was reaping rich rewards for his villainy. By the twentieth not a newspaper reader in America did not know that Booth was an actor (and a poor one, which was something of a libel); that he had been injured in his leap to the stage; and that he was being aided by a number of accomplices and accessories.

At this time, it was the practice for newspapers to print the accounts of important happenings involving the government in the form of Official Gazettes. Many of these came from the pen of Edwin M. Stanton, Secretary of War. During the war, he had written dozens of articles that were rushed to the presses, but he never wrote a more welcome one than this dispatch sent to Major General Dix, in New York on April twenty-seventh:

> J. Wilkes Booth and Herrold were chased from the swamp in St. Mary's County, Maryland, and pursued yesterday morning to Garrett's farm, near Port Royal, on the Rappahannock, by Colonel Baker's forces.
> The barn in which they took refuge was fired.
> Booth, in making his escape, was shot through the head and killed, lingering about three hours, and Herrold was taken alive.
> Booth's body and Herrold are now here.

So died Booth. For two weeks he had been the target of editorial pens and the missiles they had hurled at him included nearly every epithet in the language. Hunted, as he says in his diary "like a dog" for a crime he felt merited the world's approval, he was come upon in a barn, and shot, and given a brandy-soaked rag to suck in his last pain-racked hours. His obituary appears in the New York *World* for April twenty-ninth, under the signature of George Alfred Townsend.

Although Townsend's lead implies that all his information was given to him by the hunters, the story itself argues strongly that he was in at the kill. Once he wrote ". . . leaving one soldier to guard the old man—and the soldier was very glad of the job"; and again, "A bold clarion call came from within, so strong as to be heard at the house door"; and once again, " . . . still invisible, as we were to him." Whether he was present or not, Townsend wrote with a certain understanding of Booth. His story started in the office of Lafayette Baker, chief of the United States Secret Service, whence, following the capture

of Doctor Mudd, who treated Booth for his broken leg, Baker
sent to Lookout Point, Maryland, a telegrapher and two detectives. One of the detectives returned immediately, bringing
with him a negro who had seen Booth and his accomplice,
David Herold. Baker ordered twenty-five troopers, under command of E. J. Conger and Lieutenant L. B. Baker, his former lieutenant colonel and his cousin respectively, to pursue the
search in the vicinity of Point Royal. Townsend's story described in full detail the early stages of the chase, in which the
troopers obtained their first legitimate lead from the news that
a Confederate officer, returning from service under Moseby,
had assisted Booth in crossing the Potomac. The cavalrymen
went to the inn at which this officer was stopping, obtained
confirmation of Booth's whereabouts from him, and:

> Taking this captain along for a guide, the worn-out horse-
> men retraced, although some of the men were so haggard and
> wasted with travel that they had to be kicked into intelligence
> before they could climb to their saddles. The objects of the
> chase thus at hand, the detectives, full of sanguine purpose,
> hurried the cortege so well along that by 2 o'clock early
> morning, all halted at Garrett's gate.
> In the dead stillness, Baker dismounted and forced the
> outer gate; Conger kept close behind him and the horsemen
> followed cautiously. They made no noise in the soft clay,
> nor broke the all forboding silence anywhere, till the second
> gate swung open gratingly; yet even then no hoarse nor
> shrill response came back, save the distant croakings, as of
> frogs or owls, and the whiz of some passing night-hawk.
> So they surrounded the pleasant old homestead, each horse-
> man carbine in poise, adjusted under the grove of locusts,
> so as enclose the dwelling with a circle of fire. After a pause,
> Baker rode to the kitchen door on the side, and dismounting,
> rapped and hallooed lustily. An old man, in drawers and
> night-shirt, hastily undrew the bolts and stood on the thresh-
> old, peering into the darkness.

Baker seized him by the throat at once and held a pistol to his ear. "Who—who is it that calls me?" cried the old man. "Where are the men who stay with you?" challenged Baker. "If you prevaricate, you are a dead man!" The old fellow, who proved to be the head of the family, was so overawed and paralyzed that he stammered and shook and said not a word. "Go light a candle," cried Baker sternly, "and be quick about it." The trembling old man obeyed, and in a moment the imperfect rays flared upon his whitening hair and bluishly pallid face. Then the question was repeated, backed up by the glimmering pistol. "Where are these men?" The old man held to the wall and his knees smote each other. "They are gone," he said. "We haven't got them in the house—I assure you they are gone." Here there were sounds and whisperings in the main building adjoining, and the lieutenant strode toward the door. A ludicrous instant intervened. The old man's modesty outran his terror. "Don't go in there," he said feebly. "There are women undressed in there."

In the interim, Conger had also entered, and while the household and its invaders were thus in tableaux, a young man appeared as if he had risen from the ground. The muzzles of everybody turned on him in a second; but while he blanched, he did not lose loquacity. "Father," he said, "we had better tell the truth about the whole matter. Those men whom you seek, gentlemen, are in the barn, I know. They went there to sleep." Leaving one soldier to guard the old man—and the soldier was very glad of the job, as it relieved him of personal hazard in the approaching combat—all the rest, with cocked pistols at the young man's head, followed on to the barn. It lay a hundred yards from the house, the front barndoor facing the west gable, and was an old and spacious structure, with floors only a trifle above the ground level.

The troops, dismounted, were stationed at regular intervals around it and ten yards distant at every point, four special guards placed to command the door and all with weapons in supple preparation, while Baker and Conger went directly to the door. It had a padlock on it and the key of this Baker secured at once. In the interval of silence that ensued, the rustling of planks and straw was heard inside, as of persons rising from sleep.

At the same moment, Baker hailed: "To the persons in this barn. I have a proposal to make; we are about to send into you the son of the man in whose custody you are found. Either surrender him your arms and then give yourselves up, or we'll set fire to the place. We mean to take you both, or have a bonfire and a shooting match."

No answer came to this of any kind. The lad, John M. Garrett, who was in deadly fear, was here pushed through the door by a sudden opening of it, and immediately Lieutenant Baker locked the door on the outside. The boy was heard to state his appeal in an undertone. Booth replied:

"Damn you. Get out of here. You have betrayed me."

At the same time he placed his hand in his pocket as for a pistol. A remonstrance followed, but the boy slipped out and over the reopened portal, reporting that his errand had failed, and that he dared not enter again. All this time, the candle brought from the house to the barn was burning close beside the two detectives, rendering it easy for any one within to have shot them dead. This observed, the light was cautiously removed, and everybody took care to keep out of its reflection. By this time the crisis of the position was at hand; the cavalry exhibited some variable inclinations, some to run away, others to shoot Booth without a warrant, but all excited and fitfully silent. At the house nearby, the female folk were seen collected in the doorway, and the necessities of the case provoked prompt conclusions. The boy was placed at a remote point and the summons repeated by Baker:

"You must surrender inside there. Give up your arms and appear. There is no chance for escape. We give you five minutes to make up your mind."

A bold, clarion call came from within, so strong as to be heard at the house door:

"Who are you and what do you want with us?"

Baker again urged: "We want you to give up your arms and become our prisoners."

"But who are you?" hallooed the same strong voice.

Baker—That makes no difference. We know who you are and we want you. We have here fifty men, armed with carbines and pistols. You cannot escape.

There was a long pause and then Booth said: "Captain, this is a very bad case, I swear. Perhaps I am being taken by my own friends." No reply from the detectives.

Booth—Well, give us a little time to consider.

Baker—Very well. Take time.

Here ensued a long and eventful pause. What thronging memories it brought to Booth we can only guess. In this little interval he made the resolve to die; but he was cool and steady to the end. Baker, after a lapse, hailed for the last time: "Well, we have waited long enough. Surrender your arms and come out, or we'll fire the barn."

Booth answered thus: "I am but a cripple, a one-legged man. Withdraw your forces one hundred yards from the door and I will come. Give me a chance for my life, Captain. I will never be taken alive."

Baker—We did not come here to fight, but to capture you. I say again, appear, or we fire the barn.

Then, with a long breath, which could be heard outside, Booth cried, in sudden calmness, still invisible as we were to him: "Well, then, my brave boys, prepare a stretcher for me."

There was a pause, repeated, broken by low discussions within between Booth and his associate, the former saying, as if in answer to some remonstrance or appeal, "Get away from me. You are a damned coward, and mean to leave me in my distress, but go, go. I don't want you to stay. I won't have you stay." Then he shouted aloud:

"There's a man inside who wants to surrender."

Baker—Let him come, if he will bring his arms.

Here Herold, rattling at the door, said, "Let me out; open the door. I want to surrender."

Baker—Hand out your arms, then.

Herold—I have not got any.

This was said in a whining tone and with an almost visible shiver. Booth cried aloud at this hesitation, "He hasn't got any arms; they are mine and I have kept them."

Baker—Well, he carried the carbine, and he must bring it out.

Booth—On the word and honor of a gentleman, he has no arms with him. They are mine and I have got them.

At this time, Herold was quite up to the door, within whispering distance of Baker. The latter told him to put out his hands to be handcuffed, at the same time drawing open the door a little distance. Herold thrust forward his hands, when Baker, seizing him, jerked him into the night and straightway delivered him over to a deputation of cavalrymen. The fellow began to talk of his innocence and plead so noisily that Conger threatened to gag him unless he ceased. Then Booth made his last appeal, in the same clear, unbroken voice:

"Captain, give me a chance. Draw off your men and I will fight them singly. I could have killed you six times tonight, but I believe you to be a brave man and would not murder you. Give a lame man a show."

It was too late for parley. All this time, Booth's voice had sounded from the middle of the barn.

Ere he ceased speaking, Colonel Conger, slipping around to the rear, drew some loose straws through a crack, and lit a match upon them. They were dry and blazed up in an instant, carrying a sheet of smoke and flame through the parted planks and heaving in a twinkling a world of light and heat upon the magazine within. The blaze lit up the black recesses of the great barn until every wasp's nest and cobweb in the roof was luminous, flinging streaks of red and violet across the tumbled farm gear in the corner, ploughs, harrows, hoes, rakes, sugar mills, and making every separate grain in the high bin adjacent gleam like a mote of precious gold. They tinged the beams, the upright columns, the barricades, where clover and timothy, piled high, held toward the hot incendiary their separate straws for the funeral pile.

They bathed the murderer's retreat in a beautiful illumination, and while in bold outline his figure stood revealed, they rose like an impenetrable wall to guard from sight the hated enemy who lit them. Behind the blaze, with his eye to a crack, Conger saw Wilkes Booth standing upright on a crutch. He likens him in this instant to his brother, Edwin, whom he says he so much resembled that he half-believed, for the moment, the whole pursuit to have been a mistake. At the gleam of the fire Wilkes dropped his crutch and his carbine, and on both hands crept up to the spot to espy the incendiary and shoot him dead. His eyes were lustrous like fever, and swelled and rolled in terrible beauty, while his teeth were fixed and he peered with vengeance in his look; the fire that made him visible concealed his enemy. A second he turned glaring at the fire, as if to leap upon it and extinguish it, but it had made such headway that this was a futile impulse and he dismissed it. As calmly as upon a battle-field a veteran stands amidst a hail of ball and shell and plunging iron, Booth turned at a man's stride and pushed for the door, carbine in poise, and the last resolve of death, which we name despair, set on his high bloodless forehead.

As so he dashed, intent to expire not unaccompanied, a disobedient sergeant, at an eye-hole, drew upon him the fatal bead. The barn was all glorious with conflagration and in the beautiful ruin this outlawed man strode like all we know of wicked valor, stern in the face of death. A shock, a shout, a gathering up of his splendid figure as if to overtip the stature God gave him, and John Wilkes Booth fell headlong to the floor, lying there in a heap, a little life remaining.

"He has shot himself," cried Baker, unaware of the source of the report, and rushing in, he grasped his arms to guard against any feint or strategy. A moment convinced him that further struggle with the prone flesh was useless. Booth did not move, nor breathe nor gasp. Conger and two sergeants now entered and taking up the body they bore it in haste from the advancing flames and laid it without upon the grass, all fresh with heavenly dew.

"Water," cried Conger, "bring water."

When this was dashed into his face, he revived a little and stirred his lips. Baker put his ear close down and heard him say:

"Tell mother—I die—for my country."

They lifted him again, the fire encroaching in hotness upon them, and placed him on the porch before the dwelling.

A mattress was brought down, on which they placed him and propped his head and gave him water and brandy. The women of the household, joined meantime by another son, who had been found in one of the corn cribs, watching, so he said, to see that Booth and Herold did not steal the horses, were nervous, but prompt to do the dying man all kindness, although waved sternly back by the detectives. They dipped a rag in brandy and water, and this being put between Booth's lips, he sucked it greedily. When he was able to articulate again, he muttered to Mr. Baker the same words, with an addenda: "Tell mother I died for my country. I thought I did for the best." Baker repeated this saying at the same time, "Booth, do I repeat it correctly?"

Booth nodded his head. By this time the grayness of dawn was approaching; moving figures inquisitively coming near were to be seen distinctly, and the cocks began to crow gutterally, though the barn was by this time a hulk of blaze and ashes, sending toward the zenith a spiral line of dense smoke. The women became importunate at this time that the troops might be ordered to extinguish the fire, which was spreading toward their precious corn cribs. Not even death could banish the call of interest. Soldiers were sent to put out the fire and Booth, relieved of the bustle around him, drew near to death apace. Twice he was heard to say, "Kill me, kill me." His lips often moved, but could complete no appreciable sound. He made once a motion which the quick eye of Conger took to mean that his throat pained him. Conger put his finger there, when the dying man attempted to cough, but only caused the blood at his perforated neck to flow more lively. He bled very little, although shot quite through, beneath and behind the ears, his collar being severed on both sides.

A soldier had been meanwhile dispatched for a doctor, but the route and return was quite six miles, and the sinner was sinking fast. Still, the women made efforts to get to see him, but were always rebuffed, and all the brandy they could find was demanded by the assassin, who motioned for strong drink every two minutes. He made frequent desires to be turned over, not by speech but by gesture, and he was alternately placed upon his back, belly and side. His tremendous vitality evidenced itself almost miraculously. Now and then his heart would cease to throb and his pulses would be as cold as a dead man's. Directly life would begin anew, the face would flush up effulgently, the eyes open and brighten, and soon relapsing, stillness reasserted, would again be dispossessed by the same magnificent triumph of man over mortality. Finally, the fussy little doctor arrived, in time to be useless. He probed the wound to see if the ball were not in it, and shook his head sagely and talked learnedly.

Just at his coming, Booth had asked to have his hands raised and shown him. They were so paralyzed that he did not know their location. When they were displayed he muttered, with a sad lethargy, "Useless, useless." These were the last words he ever uttered. As he began to die the sun rose and threw beams into all the treetops. It was of a man's height when the struggles of death twitched and lingered in the fading bravo's face. His jaw drew spasmodically and obliquely downward; his eyeballs rolled toward his feet and began to swell; lividness, like a horrible shadow, fastened upon him, and with a sort of gurgle and sudden check, he stretched his feet and drew his head back and gave up the ghost.

They sewed him up in a saddle blanket. This was his shroud; too like a soldier's. Herold meantime had been tied to a tree but was now released for the march. Colonel Conger pushed on immediately for Washington; the cortege was to follow. Booth's only arms were his carbine, knife and two revolvers. They found about him bills of exchange, Canada money, and a diary. A venerable old negro living in the vicinity had the misfortune to possess a horse. This horse was a relic of former generations, and showed by his protruding ribs the general leanness of the land. He moved in an eccentric amble, and when put upon his speed was generally run backward. To this old negro's horse was harnessed a very shaky and absurd wagon, which rattled like approaching dissolution and each part of it ran without any connection or correspondence with any other part. It had no tailboard and the shafts were sharp as famine; and into this mimicry of a vehicle the murderer was to be sent to the Potomac River, while the man he had murdered was moving in state across the mourning continent. The old negro geared up his wagon by means of a set of fossil harness, and when it was backed up to Garrett's porch, they laid within it the discolored corpse. The corpse was tied with ropes around the legs and made fast to the wagon's sides. Herold's legs were tied to stirrups, and he was placed in the center of four murderous looking cavalrymen. The two sons of Garrett were also taken along, despite the sobs and petitions of the old folks and women, but the rebel captain, who had given Booth a lift, got off amidst the night's agitations, and was not re-arrested. So moved the cavalcade of retribution, with death in its midst, along the road toward Port Royal.

When the wagon started, Booth's wound, until now scarcely dribbling, began to run anew. It fell through the crack of the wagon and fell dripping on the axle and spotting the road with terrible wafers. It stained the planks and soaked the blankets; and the old negro, at a stoppage, dabbled his hands in it by mistake: he drew back instantly, with a shudder and stifled expletive. "Gor-r-r dat'll never come off in de world; it's murderer's blood." He wrung his hands, and looked imploringly at the officers and shuddered again. "Gor-r-r, I wouldn't have dat on me fur tousand, tousand dollars." The progress of the team was slow, with frequent dangers of shipwreck altogether; but toward noon the cortege filed through Port Royal, where the citizens came out to ask the matter, and why a man's body covered with somber blankets, was going by with so great escort. They were told it was a wounded Confederate, and so held their tongues. The little ferry, again in requisition, took them over by squads, and they pushed from Port Conway to Belle Plain, which they reached in the middle of the afternoon. All the way the blood dribbled from the corpse, in a slow sanguine exudation. The old negro was niggardly dismissed with two paper dollars; the dead man untied and cast upon the vessel's deck, steam gotten up in a little while, and the broad shores of the Potomac saw this skeleton ship flit by, as the bloody sun threw gashed and blots of unhealthy light along the silver surface.

All the way associated with the carcass went Herold, shuddering in so grim companionship and in the awakened fears of his own approaching ordeal, beyond which it loomed already, the gossamer fabric of a scaffold. He tried to talk for his own exoneration, saying he had ridden, as was his wont, beyond the East Branch, and returning, found Booth wounded, who begged him to be his companion. Of his crime he knew nothing, so help him God, &c. But no one listened to him. All interest in crime, courage and retribution centered in the dead flesh at his feet. At Washington, high and low turned out to look on Booth. Only a few were permitted to see his corpse for the purpose of identification. It was fairly preserved, though on one side of the face distorted and looking blue like death, and wildly bandit-like, as if beaten by avenging wounds.

Yesterday, the Secretary of War, without instruction of any kind, committed to Colonel Lafayette C. Baker, of the secret service, the stark corpse of Wilkes Booth. The secret service never fulfilled its volition more secretively. "What have you done with the body?" I said to Baker. "That is known," he answered, "to only one man living besides myself. It is gone. I will not tell you where. The only man who knows is sworn to silence. Never till the Great Trumpeter comes shall the grave of Booth be discovered." And this is true. Last night, the 27th of April, a small row boat received the carcass of the murderer; two men were in it; they carried the body off into the darkness; and out of that darkness it will never return. In the darkness, like his great crime, may it remain forever, impalpable, invisible, non-descript, condemned to that worse than damnation, annihilation. The river-bottom may ooze about it, laden with great shot and drowned manacles. The earth may have opened, to give it that silence and forgiveness which men will never give its memory. The fishes may swim around it, or the daisies grow white above it, but we shall never know. Mysterious, incomprehensible, unattainable, like the times through which we live and think upon as if we only dreamed them in perturbing fever, the assassin of a nation's head rests somewhere in the elements, and that is all; but if the indignant seas or the profaned turf shall ever vomit this corpse from their recesses, and it receives humane or Christian burial from some one who does not recognize it, let the last words those decaying lips ever uttered be carved above them with a dagger, to tell the history of a young and once promising life—*useless! useless!*

The postcript to the story of Booth may be found summed up in the New York *Herald* headline in its edition of July 8, 1865:

## EXECUTION

### Expiating the Great Crime

### Hanging of Mrs. Suratt, Payne, Harold and Atzerott

### Full and Complete Details of the Affair

### Efforts to Defer the Execution of Mrs. Suratt

### A Writ of Habeas Corpus Issued for Her But It is Disregarded by President Johnson's Orders

### How the Prisoners Passed Their Last Night

Mrs. Suratt and Payne Preserve Their Stolid Indifference
to the End

---

Terror and Agitation of Atzerott and Harold

---

HOW THEY DIED

---

TERRIBLE STRUGGLES OF PAYNE

---

THE FINAL SCENE OF THEIR BURIAL

---

SKETCHES OF THE CRIMINALS

---

&c. &c. &c.

## II

# THE MEMBER FROM SITKA

(New York *Evening Post*)

---

For the sum of seven million two hundred thousand dollars, the United States in March, 1867, contracted to purchase from the Imperial Russian Government a huge and worthless land near the Arctic Circle. Today we know this land as Alaska. William H. Seward, who engineered the purchase in his capacity of Secretary of State, was roundly censured for his foolhardiness in buying a tract of ice for so preposterous a sum as seven millions of dollars. (From 1880 to 1935, the gold yield of Alaska was approximately four hundred million dollars.)

When the midnight ceremony at which the treaty of purchase was signed was revealed, the editors cut loose. The New York *Evening Post* refused to take the matter at all seriously, commenting on April 1, 1867:

All the Yankees do not live in America. If a Connecticut clockmaker should sell you a worthless clock at a high price and persuade you that he had done you a favor, that would be called a Yankee trick; but if a Russian Emperor sells you a piece of worthless land at a high price, and makes it a matter of special favor, what is that? . . .

The first question which occurs to a sane man, not crazed with greed of land, is, "What can we do with it?" Will the newly acquired coast be erected into a territory? Shall we have a member from Sitka in the next Congress, accompanied by a sworn interpreter, and drawing two or three hundred thousand dollars per annum for mileage, to the great distress of Mr. Horace Greeley? Will the sixty thousand inhabitants, of whom fifty thousand are Esquimaux, be called upon to elect a territorial legislature, and to frame and adopt a code of laws? and what kind of a code will they construct?

The outspoken James Gordon Bennett, however, considered the facts of the case more carefully, and wrought his consideration into these words, in his *Herald* for the same date:

From the details in yesterday's HERALD it appears that on Friday night last a treaty was concluded between the Russian minister at Washington on behalf of the Czar and the Secretary of State on behalf of the United States, in which the Russian Government agrees to convey to the United States all its possessions on the American continent known as Russian America, in consideration of the payment thereof of seven millions of dollars. . . .

Seven millions for Russian America? Is the country worth the money? It covers an area of 481,278 square miles, equal to that of all the country east of the Allegheny mountains, from Maine to Mississippi inclusive, an area from which we could cut out ten States of the size of New York and still have a considerable remnant left. This Russian corner of America is watered by a river, the Kvichpak, which upon the map cuts as respectable a figure as the Mississippi. It is a tremendous river. As for the agricultural and manufacturing resources of this glorious acquisition, we cannot say much, when it is considered that, excepting a mere strip of the coast, from fifty-four forty up to sixty, the whole of the purchase lies above the sixtieth degree of north latitude, or in the latitude of Greenland. The products of the country, in fact, are snow, ice and icebergs, Esquimaux men and dogs, white bears, reindeer, furs, hides, oil and ivory. The annual exports, under Russia, are as follows:

| | |
|---|---|
| Whale, seal and walrus oil............(No report) | |
| Skins of seals.................................... | $10,000 |
| Fur-bearing sea otter skins................. | 1,000 |
| Beaver skins, fine quality..................... | 12,000 |
| Land otter, white and blue fox and stone marten skins........................... | 2,500 |
| Walrus, or sea horse teeth.................. | 20,000 |

Now this, it must be confessed, is a rather scanty agricultural, manufacturing and commercial exhibit for a region of nearly five hundred thousand square miles in extent. In this view, "in point of fact," so far is this new purchase from being worth seven millions of dollars that it may be pronounced, barring the fish, oil and beaver skins, utterly worthless and good for nothing. Seven millions of dollars for such a country, looking only at its products, is unquestionably a high price, compared with the splendid Louisiana purchase from the first Napoleon for fifteen millions of dollars.

Politically considered, however, this cession of Russian America becomes a matter of great importance. It indicates the extent to which Russia is ready to carry out her *entente cordiale* with the United States. It involves a delicate hint from the Czar to England and France that they have no business on this continent; it places the British possessions on the Pacific Coast in the uncomfortable position of a hostile Cockney with a watchful Yankee on each side of him, and it involves a warning that his best policy will be to sell out and leave the Pacific seaboard from Mexico to Behring Straits in the unbroken possession of Brother Jonathan. We know that Mr. Seward has always had a weakness for the annexation of Canada, and this treaty which he has concluded with Russia is only a flank movement for this great object. It is a step gained, a foothold secured for closer and more decisive operations.

III

# THE LAST ACT IN THE GREAT FARCE

(New York Evening Post)

The Congress had little liking and less respect for the President who succeeded Lincoln. Andrew Johnson quarreled endlessly with the lawmakers, in the confusion of emotions resulting from the conquest of the South. Finally, the President dismissed Stanton, his Secretary of War, and Congress seized upon the action as ample excuse for an impeachment trial. The New York *Herald,* on March 3, 1868, remarked of this maneuver:

. . . The Senate had received a communication from the President announcing the removal of Stanton and the appointment of General Lorenzo Thomas as Secretary of War *ad interim,* and after considering it, they resolved, and, as it had been reported by a party vote "that under the constitution and laws of the United States the President has no power to remove the Secretary of War and designate any

other officer to perform the duties of the office *ad interim.*"
This judgment having been pronounced in advance by the
Senate, the trial of Andrew Johnson by that body under
charges from the House of having disregarded his oath of
office and violated the constitution and laws would seem to
be a mere mockery. . . . So paltry, however, in the light of
common sense appear these "high crimes and misdemeanors"
upon which Mr. Johnson is arraigned that we cannot imagine
how justice can strain them to his removal even in a two-
thirds radical Senate. . . . The mountain is in labor, however, and we expect the grand result will be another little
mouse.

The ironical Washington *National Intelligencer,* for March
thirteenth, ridiculed the entire proceeding in this editorial:

## FATALITY OF CRIME

. . . Thus, the impeachment is a necessity. If President
Johnson be suffered to remain in office, the dreaded judgment of the Supreme Court will go into effect, the Constitution of the United States will be put in force all over the
United States, and all legislation, whether of party cau-
cuses, negro conventions or of Congress, which conflicts
with its expounded convictions, must be annulled, chains be
broken and citizens set free. But that would not be all.
Congress must then purge itself by the instant repeal of all
revolutionary legislation, or confess itself, before a jeering
world and an indignant people, the most shameless, the most
cruel and the most unconscionable oppressor that ever abused
a Constitution or defrauded a constituency. . . .

They *must* remove President Johnson from office. Well
do some of the less circumspect of their speakers and writers
disclose without decency the deep and pervading sense of
the party necessity: *"Unless we destroy constitutional government in this country, we shall certainly be outvoted by
the Conservatives next fall."* . . . They "must" remove the

President. Let them make the effort. Let them persevere in the effort. Let them record their everlasting dishonor over a whole summer's farcical and false prosecution and a noble and candid defense; but they cannot remove the people's chief Magistrate without cause as long as they allow him a trial.

The "Last Act in the Great Farce" was reported by the New York *Herald* for May twenty-seventh, in a story beginning:

Wash. May 26, 1868—The country will be relieved on learning that the impeachment, after a hard struggle, died today. With some kicks and splurges and with one desperate effort to retain its lease on life, it yielded up the ghost, to be buried, it is hoped, as soon as possible. . . .

IV

# DRIVING THE LAST SPIKE

(San Francisco *Bulletin*)

---

ODE

On the Completion of the Pacific Railroad

I.

Hark! the sound
Comes through the air, and o'er the ground
Clang of bells and cannon's roar.
From Eastern strand and Western shore
Peals ring out,
Millions shout
The work is done.

## II.

Work is done!
And echoing sound returns—is one
East and West, which once were twain
And echoing answer speaks again
The marriage vow,
Uttered now
Binds bride and groom.

## III.

From gloomy gorge and beetling brow
While rocking engines, whirling wheel,
And rattling car, the tremor feel,
Spans the land,
Iron band
And thews of brass.

## IV.

Over land
And mountain peak and golden sand,
Across Sierra's glittering snows
Where lightning music comes and goes
Joy to tell,
Gun and bell
Proclaim abroad.

## V.

North and South,
Hand to hand and heart to mouth
Infant lisp and manhood's voice:
Let every listening heart rejoice,
Hail and tell
All is well
The Nation's one.

## VI.

Lightning's play
On cable's span, proclaim the day
To Europe and to Asia far
The rising of the western star
Across the sea
They and we
Together joined.

## VII.

O'er the world
With lightning speed the news is hurled:
"The East and West are bound with bands
The occident with father-lands."
Iron rail
Never fail
In peace or war.

## VIII.

Hail! and praise!
That our eyes have seen the days
When thews of iron span the land
From East and West—join hand in hand
Hosannas sing,
Voices ring:
Glory to God—Amen!

San Francisco *Bulletin*
May 10, 1869

The completion of the transcontinental railroad was a signal
for celebration wherever lived men who knew the lust for
travel.  Gathered at Promontory Point, in Utah, on the May
day that saw the last spike driven, were reporters from many
newspapers. The San Francisco *Bulletin's* young man "flashed"
his office with this message:

Promontory Summit, May 10, 1869—12 o'clock M—The
great work is done. The last tie is laid. The last rail is
joined. The last spike is driven on the Great Pathway from
East to West and the high road of commerce and travel is
finished.

On the tenth, eleventh and thirteenth, the *Bulletin* printed
columns of description of the ceremonies in Utah. The following is a composite from stories appearing on the three
days:

. . . Some 3,000 gentlemen—professionals, capitalists,
graders, etc., were on the ground; also some 20 ladies, relatives to officers and friends of the company's, with the
Chinese, who ought not to be forgotten on this day. Some
3,000 people were present at the ceremony, in which the
interest of the whole American people is centered and which
affects all thoughtful minds in Europe and America.

Shortly before noon two trains, one from the West drawn
by a Central Pacific engine, No. 60, handsomely decorated,
and one from the East, drawn by engine No. 119, of the
Union Pacific Railroad, moved to the spot and the Chinese
on the Central Pacific side placed the last few ties in position. The last rails but one were placed and spiked. The
spikes at the closing rail, except the end ones, were driven
by H. Nottingham, President, Michigan, Central and Lake
Shore Railroad, and Railroad Commissioner H. Hayne, of
Nevada. Other spikes were driven by Sherman, of San
Francisco and other friends of the road. The crowd
thronged the spot when the moment for completing the work
had arrived. Gen. Casement addressed them in a few words,
asking for space that all might see the interesting sight.

Messrs. Stowbridge and Reed, the two Superintendents
of Construction, then took up the California laurel tie, and
placed it under the closing joints.

Edgar Mills, of Sacramento, as President of the occasion, called the assembled people to order.

The Rev. Dr. Todd, of Pittsfield, offered a short and very appropriate prayer. The tie under the last joint being in position, the end of the rails were adjusted, the right, looking west, by the Union Pacific Railroad men, and the left by the Central Pacific Railroad men.

The next ceremony was the presentation, in the name of California, of the golden spike by Dr. Harkness with an address. . . .

Governor Stanford responded to the speeches.

"Now, Gentlemen, with your assistance, we will proceed to lay the last tie, the last rail, and drive the last spike."

After Governor Stanford concluded, the electric wire was attached to the hammer held by Governor Stanford and standing at one side, and Dr. Durant at the other, at a given signal, both struck two light blows. The first blow given by Governor Stanford made it known to the East as well as in the West. . . . The next business was the reading of the following telegram, to the President of the United States:

To His Excellency, General U. S. Grant, President of the United States:—We have the honor to report the last rail laid—the last spike driven. The Pacific Railroad is finished.

LELAND STANFORD
President, Central Pacific Railroad

THOMAS DURANT
Vice President, Union Pacific Railroad

This concluded the regular order of business and the photographers began their work while the crowd stood still. Major Russell, of New York, A. A. Hart, of Sacramento, and C. R. Savage of Saint Louis had instruments on the ground, and when these attempts to perpetuate the scene were over, cheering commenced for the united roads. . . .

When this had ceased, the participants retired to the festive board, spread in one of the magnificent cars brought from the Union Pacific Railroad. The two locomotives moved up until their pilots rubbed together, symbolic of the friendly salutes of their respective owners. . . .

The operators on the western line had only one wire and it was overloaded with work. The instrument never ceased for a minute from early forenoon to 3 in the afternoon, taking specials. The eastern wire was also kept going all day. Some newspapers had three men on the ground, and it was all I could do to keep myself from being choked out. . . .

At 7 o'clock, except for a few business cars, two telegraph offices and some restaurant tents, the summit was deserted. As soon as the ceremony was over and the locomotives of the respective companies had met at the junction, the California tie was taken up again and pine wood, with common spikes, substituted. That was immediately attacked by hundreds of jack-knives and soon reduced to a mere stick. The ever-watchful Chinamen then took up the remains, sawed into small pieces and distributed it among them. The Chinese really laid the last rail and drove the last spike.

The first passenger train from the East passed over at 9:30 this morning.

Thus passed off, in a comparatively quiet and unostentatious manner the greatest event which has happened on this coast since the finding of gold at Sutter's Mill. . . . Twelve years ago this spring, Wells, Fargo & Company commenced running their line of stages. Yesterday they ran their last trip; the last coach was driven by one of the oldest drivers, Kenny, who joined them in the autumn of 1857. Now, the coaches have gone as the Pony Express went, and as the one coach became four, so in another 12 years, the one line of rails will be quadruple, and then barely satisfy the demands of freight shippers and travelers.

In its local story, the *Bulletin* described San Francisco's actions thus:

As soon as the despatches were received in this city today, that the golden spike would soon be driven in the last rail of the Pacific Railroad, Mr. Greenwood, Superintendent of the Fire Alarm Telegraph, cleared the striking apparatus of the bell at the Central Office and left it subject to the control of the operator at the end of the road.   It had been arranged that each blow with the sledge should be designated by a stroke of the bell here.   About half past 11 A. M. he received a despatch stating that the preparatory ceremonies were going on; that a prayer was being offered and that the spike would soon be driven.   At 11:44:37 seconds A. M., mean time, the first blow was struck, and instantly the great bell here pealed out its loud clamor and the gun at Fort Point, fired by the same current, bellowed its thunder out over the broad foldings of the Golden Gate.   Seven strokes of the bell followed, each marking a blow of the sledge, and as the operator East was telegraphing that all was finished, two additional strokes were given; nine in all.   Similar signals were made at St. Louis, Chicago, New York and other Eastern cities, announcing the final completion of the great national work.

The frenzied joy with which this news was received may be compared with the hysteria that later greeted Lindbergh's passage to Paris. In Chicago, whose celebration was the largest in the country, the *Republican* reported on the eleventh, that:

. . . The people in the streets set up one general shout of rejoicing; voices mingled with the clangor of bells—every fire bell in the city sounding the notice—and noise of bells mingled with the shrieks of locomotives, and the shrieks of these with their piercing, shrill notes, of the tugs and steamers on the river, and these with the hoarse bellowing of the cannon giving forth the welcome tidings, made a noise and clangor enough to satisfy the most exacting.

And editorially, the same paper gave thanks:

... While all have just reason to rejoice at the completion of the most wonderful undertaking of the nineteenth century, no single city has such cause for jubilation as Chicago. This great mart is the mighty heart of the interior commercial system of the Union, where center the long railroad arteries which are to pour the prodigious currents of trade and growth, stirring up continually with the thrill of new motives and world-wide purpose. ...

The telegraph long ago brought us together in heart. The iron rail yesterday brings us hand to hand with our brethren of the Pacific, and Chicago, the central city and *entrepot* of the continent, yesterday stretched out her railway system to both seaboards.

Although on May eighteenth the Sacramento *Daily Bulletin* reported that letters to New York had reached there in eight days, it was not until July twenty-fourth that the first through car from the Pacific coast reached New York. The *World* told of this event next morning in an inside-page story headed "UNPRECEDENTED RAILROAD DESPATCH":

Yesterday morning the Pullman sleeping car "Wahsatch" arrived at the Hudson River Railroad Depot about 8 o'clock. It was expected by seven in the morning, but an hour's delay in Albany prevented the train's arrival on time. There were thirty passengers who made the through trip, among whom were ten children, and during the entire journey there was nothing occurred to mar the pleasure of the company. Two officials of the French Government, who were among the party, started yesterday for Havre in the French steamer, and, if they have a safe passage at the usual speed, they will have made a journey from the Pacific coast to Paris in seventeen days.

The Pullman car left Sacramento at half past six Saturday morning, July 17. The passengers dined that day at Cisco, on the top of the Sierra Nevada mountains, and stopped for supper at Wadsworth, Nevada. Running all night they arrived for breakfast at Elko, Sunday morning; dined that day at Orine, and supped at Terris. Breakfast was served Monday morning at Promontory Point, Utah, dinner at Deseret, and supper at Wahsatch. Tuesday morning breakfast at Rawlings, dinner at Laramie, and supper at Cheyenne. On Wednesday morning the party breakfasted at North Platte, dinner was had at Grand Island, and supper at Missouri Valley. Thursday breakfast was taken at Cedar Rapids, Iowa, dinner at Dixon, Ill., supper at Niles, Mich. Friday the car got into Detroit at 3:35 A. M., crossed the river on the ferry boat, and the party took breakfast at London, Canada West, and arrived at Niagara at noon, and at Rochester for supper. Saturday morning the company took breakfast in New York City, after having traversed 3,167 miles.

The passengers complain of the difficulty of obtaining good water, otherwise they were well furnished with the best of food. They saw no Indians and were as unmolested and untroubled as though sitting in their own homes.

At Promontory Point no connection was made and thereby fifteen hours were lost. On arriving at Fremont the car took the branch road called the Sioux City and Pacific Road, and ran to California Junction. There it crossed the Missouri River in a ferry boat and ran to Missouri Valley Junction, when a connection was made with the Chicago and North Western Railroad. Considering the failures in making connections, and the fact that the trains averaged but twenty-six miles an hour, it will be seen that there is a prospect of making a through trip in about four days.

Mr. Pullman joined the California party at Chicago and came into the city and immediately went to Long Branch. The passengers expressed themselves well pleased with the trip and the accomodations afforded them, and feel a pardonable pride in being the first to make a trip from the Pacific to the Atlantic without change of cars. Over the plains, thousands of prairie dogs chased the train, and many elk and deer were seen, but no buffaloes. The passengers did not look at all jaded, and expressed no feeling of fatigue. All along the route the voyagers were cheered by the people who had gathered to see the car come in. . . .

On the Wednesday previous to the departure of the train from Sacramento, the sale of tickets was advertised and before night all had been sold.

The car is beautifully fitted up. Carpeted with elegant Brussels, the ceiling is frescoed in lavender, crimson and gold, and the side windows are all of heavy plate glass. There are twenty-five sofas in the car, which can be converted into berths, and sliding doors form them into separate apartments, so that they are as snug as staterooms. Over these sofas are suspended berths which can be folded up and thus form a portion of the roof of the car. The car is in good condition and the return trip will be made on Saturday night.

Here a new era in railroad travel begins. Twenty years ago, 118 days were necessary to compass the trip, by doubling the Horn. Now, from ocean to ocean, a little over six days are consumed.

# FIRST SPORTS

Our latest dispatches say that one hundred
thousand people are without homes and
without food in Chicago. . . . Had San
Francisco suffered such a calamity, Chicago, without doubt, would have been
prompt to render assistance. This is
our opportunity. . . .
            —San Francisco *Bulletin*

# I

# FIRE!

(Chicago *Tribune*)

---

Whether Mrs. O'Leary's cow was responsible or not (and the dispute over this legend never has been settled), the Chicago fire ranks as the criterion by which all conflagrations shall be judged. Within a few hours after one great fire had devastated part of the city and exhausted the firemen, the second and annihilating blaze began in an outhouse behind a DeKoven Street home. The San Francisco *Morning Bulletin* for October 9, 1871, published a dramatic dispatch, written and filed while the fate of Chicago was still in doubt:

### Third Dispatch

Chicago, Oct. 9—1:15 A. M.—The fire is still raging and with increased fury. It has spread almost with the velocity of the wind, and has now reached West Monroe street, a distance or more than a mile from where it started, and it covers a breadth of nearly half a mile reaching from the river to Jefferson street. The district already burned over involves an immense number of lumber yards, and the freight depots of the Chicago, St. Louis, and Pittsburgh, Fort Wayne and Chicago roads. The property already destroyed counts up many millions of dollars, and perhaps the half is not told.

The task of arresting it seems fourfold greater than it did one hour ago, and none dare venture the opinion as to when or where it will stop. Brands from the fire were blown across to the east side of the river and set a wooden building

on fire directly adjoining the Chicago gas house.  The
flames spread in every direction, the adjoining buildings
being all of the tinder box kind, the prospect is that the
gas house will be destroyed and the city draped in darkness.
A terrible panic is prevailing throughout the whole city.
Almost everybody (Here the wires gave out.  They are
supposed to have burned down in Chicago.—TELEGRAPH
OPERATOR)

Those who manned the Chicago *Tribune* struggled valiantly
against the enormity of their news, and gave to what readers
were willing to see their tragedy set down in columns this
graphic picture, published October 11, 1871:

During Sunday night, Monday and Tuesday, this city
has been swept by a conflagration which has no parallel in
the annals of history for the quantity of property destroyed,
and the utter and almost irremediable ruin which it wrought.
A fire in a barn on the West Side was the insignificant case
of a conflagration which has swept out of existence hundreds of millions of property, has reduced to poverty thousands who, the day before, were in a state of opulence, has
covered the prairies, now swept by the cold southwest wind,
with thousands of homeless unfortunates, which has stripped
2,600 acres of buildings, which has destroyed public improvements that it has taken years of patient labor to build
up, and which has set back for years the progress of the
city, diminished her population and crushed her resources.
But to a blow, no matter how terrible, Chicago will not
succumb.  Late as it is in the season, general as the ruin is,
the spirit of her citizens has not given way, and before the
smoke has cleared away, and the ruins are cold, they are
beginning to plan for the future.  Though so many have
been deprived of homes and sustenances, aid in money and
provisions is flowing in from all quarters and much of the
present distress will be alleviated before another day has
gone by.

It is at this moment impossible to give a full account of the losses by the fire, or to state the number of total accidents which have occurred. So much confusion prevails, and people are so widely scattered that we are unable for a day to give absolutely accurate information concerning them. We have, however, given a full account of the fire, from the time of its beginning. . . .

### THE WEST SIDE

At 9:30 a small cow barn attached to a house on the corner of DeKoven and Jefferson streets, one block north of Twelfth street, emitted a light, followed by a blaze, and in a moment the building was hopelessly on fire. Before any aid could be extended the fire had communicated to a number of adjoining sheds, barns and dwellings and was rapidly carried north and east, despite the efforts of the firemen. The fire seemed to leap over the engines and commenced far beyond them, and, working to the east and west, either surrounded the apparatus or compelled it to move away; in less than ten minutes the fire embraced the area between Jefferson and Clinton for two blocks north, and rapidly pushed eastward to Canal street.

When the fire first engulfed these blocks and the efforts of the undaunted engineers became palpably abortive to quench a single building, an effort was made to head it off from the north, but so great was the area that it already covered at 10:30 o'clock and so rapidly did it march forward that by the time the engines were at work the flames were ahead of them, and again they moved on north. From the west side of Jefferson street as far as the eye could reach in an easterly direction—and that space was bounded by the river—a perfect sea of leaping flames covered the ground. The wind increased in fierceness as the flames rose, and the flames wailed more hungrily for their prey as the angry gusts impelled them onward. . . . It was now about 1:15 o'clock.

But, while it seemed as if the demon of flame had reached a desert and needs must die, a new danger appeared to threaten the city.   From the South Side, in the neighborhood of Adams street, whereabouts no one on the West Side could guess with any degree of certainty, rose a column of fire, not large, but horribly suggestive.   Such engines as could be moved were called off from the West to protect the South Side's property, and the flames left to die of inanition.

The fire of Saturday burned the region in the West Division from Van Buren street northward to Adams, and all east of Clinton street to the river, Murry Nelson's elevator alone standing.   The light from the burning remnants of these eighteen acres of ruins illumined the heavens on Sunday evening.   Precisely at half-past 9 o'clock, the fire bells sounded an alarm, and a fresh light, distinct from the other only to those living west of the fire, sprung up. . . . The wind carried this fire straight before it, through the next block, and so on northward until it reached Van Buren street, where it struck the south line of the district burnt the night before.   Here this fire ought to have stopped, and here, under ordinary circumstances, it would have stopped.   But the wind, fierce and direct, carried the flames before it, cutting as clean and as well defined a swath as does the reaper in the field, and the fire gradually but rapidly extended laterally. . . .

### The Great Conflagration

At about twenty minutes past midnight the work of destruction began in the South Division.   While the flames were nearing the South Branch at Harrison street as well as sweeping northward to the burnt district of Saturday night and before any communication of fire had been handed to the east side of the river, a blazing messenger sailed on the wings of the hurricane, overleaping a distance of fully a quarter of a mile and lodged against the dry clapboards of a three story tenement house, situated near the gas works. . . . The momentary contact of the fire-brand with the side of the building was sufficient.   The dry siding took fire like a lucifermatch, and before there was time to turn around, the entire structure was enveloped in flame.   At this time the neighborhood known as "Conley's Patch", and the most squalid, poverty-stricken, crime-stained portion of Chicago, contained but few people awake or close at hand, the great part being absent at the scene of the fire across the river, while the women and the children were in bed and asleep. A cry of horror and alarm was at once raised, but not soon enough, it is almost certain, to enable the sleeping inhabitants to save themselves. The frightened wretches came crowding out of the blazing tenements, but sooner than we can write it, all escape from the lower part was cut off, and there is every reason to suppose that from five to ten human beings perished in the flames at this point.

### RIGHT AND LEFT

the fire spread, travelling among the dry tenements, thickly distributed, at a rate of speed faster than a man could walk. Within sixty seconds, the space of one block had been traversed. . . . A lurid mass of flames was hurled bodily across Monroe street toward the north, lapping up the stables of John V. Farwell and Co., and the American Merchants' Union Express Company before more than half a dozen of the hundred-odd magnificent horses could be rescued, the remainder of the noble and valuable animals either burned or suffocated within two minutes. . . .

### FASTER THAN IT COULD BE TRACED

or, at least faster than, from any position of observation, the lookerson could accurately note the precise buildings which were overtaken in their order, the flames now raged toward the river and the lake. The finest of Chicago's business architecture—and this the marvel of all America—was included in the ravages of the fire. At 4 o'clock in the morning the line of flame and ruin in the South Division extended from above Harrison street northward to the main branch of the river, a distance of almost one mile. To the eastward it had reached Dearborn street, having included the Michigan Depot, the mammoth Ogden House, covering an entire block of ground, the new and unoccupied Bigelow House, both of Honore Blocks, Lombard and Reynolds'

Blocks, Farewell Hall, all the line of seven-story marble buildings on LaSalle street, the Chamber of Commerce, Court House, Sherman House, Briggs House, Tremond House, Crosby's Opera House, Wood's Museum, Hooley's Opera House, the Dearborn Theatre, the *Post, Mail, Staats Zeitung, Times, Republican* and *Journal* offices, so that the THE TRIBUNE was the only daily newspaper in Chicago left untouched, McVickers the only theatre and the Palmer House the only first class hotel. . . . People began to lift up their heads and thank God that something was to be left of Chicago, and at half-past 6 o'clock in the morning there was a good reason to believe the conflagration had spent itself. Thankful and contented in this belief, large numbers of tired watchers went to their homes—if they had any—to get a little food and rest. It was as well that they went, for they were spared the fearful renewal which occurred so soon afterward. At about 7 o'clock in the morning a sudden gust of wind,

### A PERFECT WHIRLPOOL

swept and eddied through Dearborn street, beginning at Jackson street where, at that time, the fire had died down to embers. Beds of live coals were caught up bodily by the hurricane and hurled against and upon the wooden structures across the street, and in a moment the fire had gained a foothold and swept on once more to the northward and southward. All that had been left untouched between Jackson and Madison streets and between Dearborn street and the lake shore, was now doomed to destruction, and as the fury of the first hurricane of wind subsided, there came almost a lull, so that the fire began to work southward and westward. . . .

On the corner of State was a wooden building which was too inflammable to be allowed to stand. The proper method of stopping was here adopted and the principal actor in the contest was thereafter a red-capped chap in a square-box wagon in which were also placed several hundred pounds of powder. . . .

SCENE FROM THE TRIBUNE BUILDING

The sight from the windows of THE TRIBUNE Building was one the like of which few have ever seen. At fifteen minutes to 2 o'clock the view was like this: To the southwest rose a cloud of black smoke, which, colored with the lurid glare of the flames which caused it, presented a remarkable picture. Due west another column of smoke and fire rose, while the north was lighted with the flying cinders and destructive brands. In ten minutes more the whole horizon to the west, as far as could be seen from the windows, was a fiery cloud, with flames leaping up along the whole line, just showing their heads and subsiding from view like tongues of snakes. Peal after peal was sounded from the Court House bell. The fire was on LaSalle street, had swept north, and the Chamber of Commerce began to belch forth smoke and flame from windows and ventilators. The east wing of the Court House was alight; then the west wing; the tower was blazing on the South Side, and at 2 o'clock the whole building was in a sheet of flame. The Chamber of Commerce burned with a bright steady flame. The smoke in front grew denser for a minute or two, and then, bursting into a blaze from Monroe to Madison streets, proclaimed that Farwell Hall and the buildings north and south of it were on fire. At 10 minutes past 2 o'clock the Court House tower was a glorious sight. It stood, a glowing, almost dazzling trellis-work, around which was wrapt a sheet—a winding sheet—of flame. At a quarter past two the tower fell, and in two minutes more a crash announced the fall of the building. The windows of the [Tribune] office were hot, and the flames gave a light almost dazzling in its intensity. . . . At 2:30 the fire was halfway down Madison street; the wind blew a hurricane; the fire-brands were hurled along the ground with incredible force against everything that stood in their way. Then the flames shot up in the rear of Reynolds' Block, and THE TRIBUNE Building seemed doomed. An effort was made to save the files and other valuables, which were moved into the composing room, but the building stood like a rock, lashed on two sides by raging waves of flame, and it was abandoned. It was a fire-proof building and there were not a few who expected to see it stand the shock. The greatest possible anxiety was felt for it, as it was the key to the whole block. . . . When the walls of Reynolds' Block fell, and Cobb's Building was no more, the prospects of its standing were good. Several persons went upstairs and found it cool and pleasant—quite a refreshing haven from the hurricane of smoke, dust and cinders that assailed the eyes. . . .

At 7 o'clock Monday morning the whole region designated (city, east of Dearborn street) was considered saved, no fire being visible except a smoldering fire in the barber's shop under the TRIBUNE office, which, being confined in brick walls, was not considered dangerous. Every effort was made to quench it, but the Water Works had gone up, and the absence of water, while it announced how far north the flames had reached, forbade any hopes of quenching the fire below. . . .

### SCENES ON WABASH AVENUE

. . . As the fire commenced spreading up the avenue a wild scene of confusion ensued. The street was crowded with vehicles of all sorts, many drawn by men who found it impossible to procure draught animals. The sidewalks were filled with a hurrying crowd, bearing in their arms and upon their backs and heads articles of clothing, furniture, &c. Ladies dressed in elegant costumes, put on with a view of preserving them, and with costly apparel of all kinds thrown over their arms and shoulders, staggered along under the unwonted burden. Poor women with mattresses on their heads, or weighted down with furniture, tottered with weary steps up the crowded street. Nearly everyone wore a stern expression, and moved on without a word, as if they had braced up their minds to endure the worst without manifesting any emotion. . . . Poor little children shivered in the cold night air and looked with wildly-open eyes upon the scenes they could not comprehend. Ludicrous incidents were of occasional occurrence, lighting up with a sort of horrible humor the terrible realities of the situation. Women would go by with dogs in their arms—their pets being all they had saved from the ruins of their homes. An octogenarian sat in a yard, with a large cat enfolded in his feeble embrace. Men dragging wagons wore green veils over their faces to protect their eyes from the blinding dust. Drunken men staggered among the crowds apparently possessed of the idea that the whole affair was a grand municipal spree, in which they were taking part as a duty that should be discharged by all good citizens. . . .

Truckmen and express drivers were hailed from the steps of houses, or eagerly pursued by the occupants with a view of securing their aid in removing household goods to places of safety. In many cases the appeals were unsuccessful, their services having been previously engaged by other parties; but when they were disengaged, they charged the most exorbitant prices, ranging from $5 to $100 for a load, and turning up their noses at offers of amounts less than they demanded. This class of people made great profit out of the calamities of their fellow citizens. Their pockets may be heavy today, but their consciences, if they have any, should be still heavier. The instances of generosity, however, were far in excess of those of greed and selfishness. . . . Good angels, in the shape of women, distributed food among the sufferers; and spoke kind words to those who appeared to labor under the severest affliction. . . .

### NORTH DIVISION

As early as 3 o'clock in the morning of Monday the people on the North Side, or many of them, began to get a little nervous. . . . By daybreak, the fire, moving northward, had gotten to Rush street bridge, which was crowded with people. In order to prevent this aiding the fire in crossing it, it was turned, but THE ONLY RESULT WAS THE DESTRUCTION OF THE PEOPLE WHO WERE ON IT.

The fire crossed there, without paying any attention to the removal of the bridge, and seizing upon the frame buildings, the ware-houses and the lumber yards, moved rapidly northward toward the Water Works. The people living in that section, and north of there, thought that the best place for them to seek shelter was on the lake shore, and they rushed that way, carrying with them what they could. They very soon found that they were

### Between Two Deaths

the fire on one side of them, and the water on the other, into which the intense heat of the fire was driving them. Many lay there half in the water and half in the sand, with their heads down in order to get as much air as they could. The smoke driving from the shore made it almost impossible to live, but, as they were surrounded on three sides, and there were no boats, they remained where they were and suffered as patiently as possible. . . .

One man was seen marching off with a glass kerosene lamp, and after he had carried it about a block, he met a friend, who asked him what was the use of carrying a thing like that any further. He looked at it, observed that there did not seem to be much use in it and tossed it away. . . .

During Monday night the feeling of uneasiness on the West Side was very great. The high wind was still blowing although it halted for a moment near sunset and there were profound apprehensions that new fires would be set in other places by persons who were desirous of plundering, or who were influenced by a morbid feeling, which occasionally prevails in such cases. Patrols were organized and a pretty decent watch was kept up, which, with the extraordinary precautions taken in putting out fires in the stoves, prevented the occurrence of any calamity. There were continued rumors of arrests, and of the summary punishment of persons who had been caught in the act of arson. . . .

### Incendiaries Killed

The damnably depraved character of some of the ruffians of the city was perfectly illustrated on Monday and the ensuing night by attempts made to promote pillage by fire set by incendiaries in different parts of the city. To the credit of the inhabitants of the city be it said the villains generally met with the fate they deserved. The following are some illustrations, rumored and authentic:

—A boy attempted to help on the conflagration by igniting a clothes line saturated with kerosene and throwing it into a building on Thirty-second street. He received his deserts at the hands of the firemen, who saw the act, and "now sleeps in the valley." . . .

—Bridget Hickey was arrested for setting fire to a barn in the rear of a house on Burnside street. By some mistaken idea of clemency, she was not hanged.

—Two men, who were caught trying to set fire to the Jesuit Church on the West Side, were disposed of without ceremony and the lookerson were pleased to say "Served 'em right." . . .

—At about 11 o'clock yesterday forenoon a man, also residing on Fourth avenue, caught a man in the basement of his house, number unknown, armed with hay and matches. He gave the alarm and the incendiary was caught and stoned and battered to death. He lies on the avenue yet, near Fourteenth street. . . .

—At about 3 o'clock yesterday afternoon, residents on the South Side were alarmed by a cry of fire, which increased when they saw smoke ascending from Mr. Schaffer's store, corner of State and Thirty-first streets. It was evidently the work of an incendiary, and owing to the devilish ingenuity used by the scoundrel who did the work, much difficulty was found in extinguishing the fire. Commissioner Sheridan happened near the place and assisted to put out the blaze. A meeting of over 200 citizens was held immediately and Mr. Sheridan empowered the Chairman to swear in all he thought fit as special policemen. There was indignation enough to have put a summary end to the devil, had he been caught, and a determination to treat all such as dogs unworthy of life. . . .

### ITEMS IN GENERAL

Business men all day yesterday were looking round for the recovery of their safes and what they contained. The banks, or rather their ruins, were surrounded all day. . . .

The readiness and rapidity with which places of shelter
and rations of food have been supplied to the homeless and
hungry are remarkable. The doors of the school-houses and
churches have been thrown wide open in the South and West
Divisions, and yesterday they were thronged with the poor
victims of the fire, some of whom found their way there, and
others were brought by charitable people engaged in the mission of hunting them up. Food in abundance was supplied,
and the watering carts brought water from the lake and distributed it in hose to buckets, when it was conveyed into the
churches and dealt out.

## II

# THE GUILTY MISS ANTHONY

(Boston *Morning Journal*)

---

For more than fifty years of her life, Miss Susan B. Anthony battled intelligently for women's rights. She began her
career as a temperance worker, but attendance at meetings of
organizations devoted to the theory of equal rights for men and
women converted her to the more important cause. She
plagued Congress with petitions and pleas and was a member
of the first delegation of women heard by a Congressional
committee. In 1872 she stalked into a polling place in Rochester, New York, and demanded the right to vote, quoting the
Constitution to support her. The result of this action was a
conviction for having voted illegally, a circumstance which
brought this comment in the Boston *Morning Journal's* editorial columns for June 19, 1873:

A New York jury has most ungallantly found Susan B.
Anthony guilty of "having voted in the last election for the

Congressional candidate for the Twenty-fifth District and for the congressman-at-large." If this was wrong, the next question that arises is, what right had the election officers to take her vote? Somebody ought to prosecute them. In the meantime it may be well understood that Miss Anthony voted merely as a "test case" to know whether she and all women had a right to vote. That is, she sought light from the ballot box and now she gets it from the jury box. It is not exactly what she wanted, "on the contrary, quite the reverse", but she and all other people interested in her enterprise will have at least the satisfaction of knowing that woman suffrage is not to be dragged into vogue under cover of constitutional amendments made for other purposes; but that when the people of the United States get ready for the great reform in question, they will say so plainly and alter their laws accordingly.

Stupid man, opposing this woman's fight, found recourse in his masculinity: many of the speeches delivered by great statesmen against Miss Anthony were too obscene for publication. The following editorial, from the New York *World* of July 30, 1869, is a fair example of the advantages taken of her because of her sex—here, however, a sense of humor on the part of the writer saved his piece from vulgarity.

## VOICES OF THE NIGHT

Miss Anthony and Mrs. Norton, equal sisters in the struggle for women's rights, seem to have made simultaneously one grand discovery which we should be sorry to have to believe in, and which really is no discovery at all, be it correct or incorrect. Miss Anthony avers that she "makes her best speeches on her pillow", and Mrs. Norton that she is "never so happy in her expressions as when she lies awake at night". As an alleged matter of fact, we say this is no discovery at all. Mrs. Caudle claimed to have made it years ago, and her hapless spouse never disputed the claim.

History is full, too, of examples which may be twisted to prove it true. According to ARISTOPHANES, it was by a deadlock in midnight sessions that the ancient female reformers of Athens finally carried their points. And it is certainly significant that MINERVA, the recognized goddess of female wisdom, should have selected the owl as her emblem. But how can MISS ANTHONY know anything positively on the subject? MRS. NORTON, having an audience, even though it be no better audience than a mere man, and a husband at that, may possibly feel assured of her own powers by the effect she produces upon another. But MISS ANTHONY has made public confession that she not only practices nocturnal isolation as a habit, but believes in it as a holy and hygienic duty. How, then, can she assert with such confidence that her lonely efforts, made

> "When none but night
> And her still candle see"

really do transcend her public performances on the platform?

Possibly they may be more entertaining to herself, but that carries no certain guarantee of their potency over other minds and hearts. LANDOR sings in his sweet, high way about ROBERT BROWNING that

> "There is delight in singing though none hear
> Beside the singer"

and this is doubtless true. But such delight is necessarily barren, so far as touches the wide, wide world. And a lady whose mission is to elevate men to a level with women (that contemptible organ of the hidebound past, the *Tribune,* puts it the other way—more's the shame!) should find her highest sphere, not in the evanescent ejaculations of an unfruitful soliloquy, but in the communication to her pillow of thoughts that breathe, and words that burn.

This thing is important, and should be thoroughly settled. If MRS. NORTON and MISS ANTHONY are right, it is clear that one of the consequences of the success of the women's rights movement will be the conversion, for all political purposes, of day into night. When women take human affairs publicly in hand, we shall, of course, insist upon their doing their very best; and if they can only do their very best, as MISS ANTHONY and MRS. NORTON so solemnly declare, after sun-down, our legislative assemblies must follow example of the British Parliament.

It will be a wonderful thing for our Congressmen and Senators (the male sex, we hope, will be allowed a fair share of representative offices) to find the due discharge of their functions constrain them

> "To sit all night till broad daylight
> And go home with the girls in the morning."

Strange forms of parliamentary speech, too, will come then upon us. Both MRS. NORTON and MISS ANTHONY seem to insist upon it that the recumbent attitude which the Romans considered most favorable to digestion is necessary to the full development of the feminine power of persuasion. It will be odd, at first, to hear the honorable Senator from Massachusetts flinging savory parts of speech at the honorable Senatrix "on the Democratic sofa-bedstead." It will be inconvenient in many ways, perhaps, at first. But everything has its compensations. Legislative vigilance will be quickened. "Fat men and such as sleep o' nights" will be discouraged and discountenanced, and intending CAESARS so be kept in awe by Congresses of lean and hungry CASSIUSES. And if the women keep the fair promise of their apostles, and really "do their best," there is no saying but that they may eventually

> "make the face of heaven so fine
> That all the world will be in love with night."

The *World* sang a different tune, when Miss Anthony died in 1906. Prominent among its editorials for March fourteenth was this tribute:

Susan Anthony has died full of years and of such honor as the world at last found itself compelled to pay to womanly courage.

She could not live to see the right to vote granted to the women of America, not even to see a majority of them demanding it. But she far outlived the time when the answer to her arguments took the form of abusive words and pictures and even of mob violence; and she saw extended to her sisters the school suffrage in twenty-four states, full suffrage in four and a partial municipal suffrage in several others.

The story of Miss Anthony's life is the history of the woman's rights movement in this country for more than fifty years. Lucretia Mott, Lydia Maria Child, Abby Kelly Foster, Lucy Stone, Antoinette Blackwell and Elizabeth Cady Stanton answered with her to the early roll-calls of the movement. She survived every member of the famous group. Her span of life was a year less than that of Mrs. Stanton, who died in 1902.

## III

# ABDUCTION OF A CHILD

(Philadelphia *Inquirer*)

It has been more than sixty years since a child disappeared from a quiet Philadelphia suburb, but tomorrow he may be the subject of a story in your favorite newspaper. The headline of such a story will read somewhat like this:

COAST DOCTOR SAYS
HE IS CHARLEY ROSS

If such a story appears, it is almost certain that the coast doctor is in error. Since the July day in 1874 when Charley Ross rode off into oblivion with a man in a wagon, there have been dozens of claimants to his name. Foundlings, orphans and others of obscure beginnings are convinced that the re-

porter for the Philadelphia *Inquirer,* on July 3, 1874, spoke of
them when he wrote:

> Between four and five o'clock on Wednesday afternoon
> two men drove up to a house in Germantown, in front of
> which two children were playing. One of the men got out
> and lifted the two boys into the vehicle, which was then
> driven off. At Palmer and Richmond streets one of the
> children was set down on the pavement and given money
> with which to go and buy shooting crackers, but when he
> started after the toys the men drove off with the other child,
> which has not been since seen or heard of. The detectives
> are looking into the case.

Perhaps the reporter for the *Inquirer* would have been hap-
pier to let the whole matter drop there. He had written his
story as poorly as it is possible to write a story: no names appeared in it, no ages, nothing of the parents of the boy, or
exactly where he lived. But the story was too great to be thus
dismissed by a poor craftsman. The beginnings of a sixty-
year hue and cry were heard; and three days later the *Inquirer*
managed to place before its readers a fuller account of the
case:

> On Wednesday last Charley Brewster Ross, aged 4 years
> and his brother, aged 6 years, sons of Christian K. Ross,
> were playing in a lane in the rear of their residence, Ger-
> mantown, when a wagon containing two men drove up, and
> at their invitation the children got in for the purpose of
> taking a ride. The vehicle was driven off and the oldest boy
> was found the same evening at Palmer and Richmond
> streets, Nineteenth Ward, where he had been put out of the
> carriage, but Charley, the youngest, is still missing. The
> former states that he had been given some money by one of
> the men to buy shooting crackers, and that he started for the

store for that purpose, but when he returned the carriage and his little brother were missing. The parents of the child are almost distracted about him and have offered a reward for his return. No motive can be assigned for the carrying away of the little one, and at the present time the whole affair is wrapped in mystery. Little Charley was dressed in a brown linen suit, with short skirt, a broad brimmed unbleached Panama hat with black ribbon and laced shoes and blue and white striped stockings. He has long flaxen curly hair, hazel eyes, clear skin, round full face, is well formed and without any marks except those made by vaccination on the arm.

This story was headlined briefly "A MYSTERY". And such it still remains. . . .

# FINAL SPORTS

REPORTER—Is it safe to enter the country lying immediately west of the Black Hills?

GENERAL CUSTER—It is somewhat dangerous. The Indians have their right to it; it is not reserved to them, but they have the privilege of going there to hunt at their pleasure.

—New York *Herald*

# I

# BLOODY WORK BY THE INDIANS

(Washington *Evening Star*)

---

The Fourth of July, 1876, was more than an ordinary day of celebration. It was a joyous centennial: an even hundred years before, the Colonies had thrown off the yoke of oppression and injustice and had stood forth before the world as a new nation. Since the day on which a declaration of independence had been "proclaimed . . . in the presence of many thousand spectators, who testified their approbation by repeated acclamations," much had happened in America. The frontiers had been pushed westward, until there remained few of the original wildernesses. Towns had sprouted, railroads had crawled like worms over the countryside, the pioneers had grown up and become oldest inhabitants. The Union had been threatened and in four bloody years had overcome the threat. Peace lay upon the land everywhere but in the Far West, where the Indian was being forced to his last courageous and futile stand.

They prated much of justice in Helena, Montana Territory, on that Fourth of July. The townspeople paraded and fired off "shooting crackers" and six guns. Fat politicians (they have *always* been fat) yelled their patriotic platitudes, empurpling their faces. And far off in the hills, the Sioux under Sitting Bull and Crazy Horse added their savage voices. Nine days before, they had slain Custer and all his men in a

231

ravine, and scalped the bodies and retired to their own celebration.

The spreading of the frontiers had for years been pushing the Indians into smaller and smaller territories. At last, in 1868, the Sioux were given the Black Hills area for their own, forevermore. It was a sound treaty, forced upon a reluctant red man who had been doublecrossed too often by the white. But the white man signed each time in good faith—how could he foresee that the discovery of gold on the Indians' land would make virtual abrogation of the treaty advisable?

The government at Washington proclaimed, on December 6, 1875, that all Indians not on reservations by January thirty-first of the next year would be regarded as hostiles and would be pursued as such. It was in this pursuit that George Custer found his death. He had been hurled out of West Point, before his time was up, to become a Union officer; he had been made a general before he was twenty-five; he had lived his whole life in an atmosphere of warfare, and in June, 1876, he reached its violent end. On that July fourth in Helena, the celebrants were rudely jostled out of their joyous mood by the cries of newsboys, carrying extras of the *Daily Herald:*

By W. H. Norton

Stillwater, M. T.,

July 2, 1876.

Muggins Taylor, scout for General Gibbon, got here last night, direct from Little Big Horn. General Custer found the Indian camp of about 2,000 lodges, on the Little Horn, and immediately attacked the camp. Custer took five companies and charged the thickest portion of the camp. Nothing is known of the operations of this detachment only as they trace it by the dead. Major Reno commanded the other seven companies, and attacked at the lower portion of the camp. The Indians poured in a murderous fire from all directions; besides, the greater portion fought on horseback.

Custer, his two brothers, nephew and brother-in-law were all killed, and not one of his detachment escaped. Two hundred and seven men were buried in one place, and the killed is estimated at 300, with only 31 wounded. The Indians surrounded Reno's command and held them one day in the Hills, deprived of water, until Gibbon's command came in sight, when they broke camp and left. The Seventh fought like tigers, and were overcome by mere brute force. The Indian loss cannot be estimated, as they bore off and cached most of their killed. The remnant of the Seventh Cavalry and Gibbon's command are returning to the mouth of the Little Horn, where the steamboat lies. The Indians got all the arms of the killed soldiers.

There was more of this story to be told. Three days before the Helena *Herald* learned of the disaster on the Little Big Horn, the correspondent for the St. Paul and Minneapolis *Pioneer-Press and Tribune* sat in a tent in the wild country through which Custer's ill-fated cavalry had been traveling and wrote:

## THE TERRIBLE DETAILS

*Special to the Pioneer Press and Tribune*

### SIOUX EXPEDITION
Mouth of the Big Horn, July 1,
Via Bismarck, D. T., July 6.

Long before the arrival of this dispatch you will have heard of the tragedy which has been enacted here. The ghastly details would seem to court oblivion if it were in the nature of things possible to forget or cloak them.

At noon on the 22nd day of June, General Custer, at the head of his fine regiment of twelve veteran companies, left camp at the mouth of the Rosebud, to follow the trail of a very large band of hostile Sioux, leading up the river, and westward in the direction of the Big Horn. The signs indicated that the Indians were making for the eastern branch of the last named river, marked on the map as the Little Big Horn.

At the same time General Terry, with Gibbon's command of five companies of infantry, four of cavalry, and the Gatling battery, started to ascend the Big Horn, aiming to assail the enemy in the rear. The march of the two columns was so planned as to bring Gibbon's command within co-operating distance of the anticipated scene of action by the evening of the twenty-sixth. In this way only could the infantry be made available, as it would not do to encumber Custer's march with foot troops.

On the evening of the 24th, Gibbon's command was landed on the South bank of the Yellowstone, near the mouth of the Big Horn, and on the 25th was pushed twenty-three miles over a country so rugged that the endurance of the men was taxed to the uttermost. The infantry then halted for the night; but the department commander, with the cavalry, advanced twelve miles farther, to the mouth of the Little Big Horn, marching until midnight, in the hope of opening communication with Custer.

The morning of the twenty-sixth brought the intelligence communicated by three badly frightened Crow scouts of the battle of the previous day and its results. The story was not credited, because it was not expected that an attack would be made earlier than the 27th, and chiefly because no one could believe that a force such as Custer commanded could have met with disaster. Still the report was in no manner disregarded. All day long the toilsome march was plied, every eye bent upon a cloud of smoke, resting over the southern horizon, which was hailed as a sign that Custer was successful, and had fired the village. It was only when night was falling that the weary troops lay down upon their arms. The infantry had marched 29 miles.

The march of the next morning revealed at every step some evidence of the conflict which had taken place two days before. At an early hour the head of the column entered a plain half a mile wide, bordering the left bank of the Little Big Horn, where had recently been an immense Indian village, extending three miles along the stream, and where were still standing two funeral lodges, with horses slaughtered around them, and containing the bodies of nine chiefs. The ground was strewn everywhere with carcasses of horses, and cavalry equipments, besides buffalo robes, packages of dried meat, and weapons and utensils belonging to the Indians. On this part of the field was found the clothing of Lieuts. Sturgis and Porter, pierced with bullets, and a blood-stained gauntlet belonging to Col. Fales. Further on were found the bodies of men, among whom were recognized Lieut. Mc-Intosh, the interpreter, from Fort Rice, and Reynolds, the guide.

Just then a breathless scout arrived, with the intelligence that Colonel Reno, with a remnant of the Seventh Cavalry, was entrenched on a bluff near by, waiting for relief. The command pushed rapidly on, and soon came in sight of a group surrounding a cavalry guidon, upon a lofty eminence on the right bank of the river. General Terry forded the stream, accompanied by a small party, and rode to the spot. All the way the slopes were dotted with the bodies of men and horses. The General approached, the men swarmed out of the works and greeted him with hearty and repeated cheers. . . .

In the center of the enclosure was a depression in the surface, in which the wounded were sheltered, covered with canvas. Reno's command had been fighting from Sunday noon of the 25th until the night of the 26th, when General Terry arrived, which caused the Indians to retire. Up to this time Reno and those with him were in complete ignorance of the fate of the other five companies, which had been separated from them early on the 25th, to make an attack under Custer on the village at another point. While preparations were being made for the removal of the wounded, a party was sent on Custer's trail to look for traces of his command. They found awaiting them a sight fit to appall the

stoutest heart. At a point about three miles down the right
bank of the stream, Custer had evidently attempted to ford
and attack the village from the ford. The trail was found to
lead back up the bluff and to the northward, as if the troops
had been repulsed and compelled to retreat, and at the same
time had been cut off from regaining the forces under Reno.
The bluffs along the right bank come sharply down to the
water, and are interspersed by numerous ravines. All along
the slopes and ridges, and in the ravines, lay the dead, arranged in order of battle, lying as they had fought, line behind line, showing where the defensive positions had been
successfully taken up, and held till none were left to fight.
There, huddled in a narrow compass, horses and men were
piled promiscuously. At the highest point of the ridge lay
Custer, surrounded by a chosen band. Here were his two
brothers and his nephew, Mr. Reed, Colonels Yates and
Cooke, and Captain Smith, all lying in a circle of a few
yards, their horses beside them. Here, behind Yates' company, the last stand had been made, and here one after another these last survivors of Custer's five companies had met
their death. The companies had successively thrown themselves across the path of the advancing enemy, and had been
annihilated. Not a man had escaped to tell the tale, but it was
inscribed on the surface of these barren hills in a language
more eloquent than words.

And in Washington, the *Evening Star*—on July tenth—recalled how valorous a warrior Custer had been in the Civil
War, and reprinted this engaging anecdote as a tribute to a
soldier slain:

The Alexandria *Sentinel* prints an incident in the life of
Custer never before published: While Custer was "feeling"
of the enemy's cavalry in the forests of Spottsylvania, a
regiment belonging to Gen. Rosser's (Confederate) brigade
became suddenly engaged with a portion of that of Custer,

at very close quarters, necessitating a charge through a narrow open space, up to the edge of a wood in which Custer's men were posted, and from which, being partly protected by a fence, they delivered a destructive fire, which, with their visible knowledge of the enemy's superior position and strength, made the Virginians falter. Rosser, as was his wont, dashed into the open field to rally them. Of commanding and striking figure, he did not dream that over that line of foes, directing and controlling their fire, flashed an eye like Mars' to command, but impressive as a woman's to the claims of friendship, and which, even in the moment of bloody strife, recognizing him as an old friend of West Point, was beaming upon him in kindness and love!

There was many a horseman wondered, that day, why the enemy's fire so suddenly ceased, when Rosser, recognizing the uselessness of a further attack, withdrew his men. But the next day, as they kept moving by the flank, following the Federal cavalry and the line of the "swing," a farmer, by whose house they passed, handed a Confederate trooper a note addressed to Gen. T. L. Rosser, which had been left with him by a Federal officer. The note was delivered as addressed, and read somewhat thus:

"Dear ——: (The name used was the old familiar nickname of West Point, not now remembered by this writer.) You expose yourself too much, on the field, old fellow. I recognized you yesterday, and with difficulty saved your life, by stopping my fire. Don't do so again, but live to laugh over old times, after the war, with

Your friend,<br>
G. A. CUSTER.

P. S. I whipped Fitz Lee on Wednesday, and intend to give you a good dressing the first chance I get in a fair field."

II

## DEATH OF PRESIDENT BRIGHAM YOUNG

(Deseret *Evening News*)

---

Joseph Smith, the prophet, had a vision in 1823, so he said, in which he was commanded to form the Church of Jesus Christ of Latter Day Saints. Four years later, he announced his discovery of the Book of Mormon, a scripture in golden plates. His sect flourished in Palmyra, New York, and in time moved to the new West, where it was revealed lay the Promised Land.

The history of Joseph's Latter Day Saints is a history of violence. They were driven from Kirkland, Ohio, where they went originally, to Missouri, which in turn drove them out. In 1839, Joseph Smith, and his brother, Hyrum, founded Nauvoo, Illinois, where they remained for several restless years. In 1844, the two brothers were arrested for treason and taken to Carthage, Illinois, and there, according to the Quincy *Herald* for June twenty-ninth, occurred a lynching:

Gov. Ford arrived in this city yesterday morning, much worn down by travel and fatigue, having left Carthage yesterday. It is now certain that only Joseph and Hyrum Smith are killed, and they were murdered in cold blood. It seems that while Gov. Ford was absent from Carthage to Nauvoo, for the purpose of ascertaining satisfactorily the strength of the Mormon force, an excited mob assembled near Carthage, disfigured themselves by painting their faces, and made a rush upon the jail, where Joe and his fellow prisoners were confined. The guard placed by the Governor to protect the jail were overpowered by superior numbers, the door of the jail forced and both shot. Hyrum was instantly killed by a ball which passed through his head. Joe was in the act of raising the window when he was shot both from without and within, and fell out of the window to the ground. Richards, whom we supposed yesterday was dead, escaped unhurt by shutting himself up in a cell in the jail. Mr. Taylor, the editor of the Nauvoo Neighbor, was in the room with the Smiths, and received three balls in his leg and one in his arm. He is not considered dangerous. Three of the assailants were slighty wounded. . . .

The dead bodies of the Smiths were conveyed to Nauvoo by order of the Governor yesterday. It was supposed by many that the Mormons, on seeing them, would break away from all restraints, and commence a war of extermination. But nothing of the kind occurred. They received their murdered friends in sorrow—laid down their arms and remained quiet. Col. Singleton and his company of 60 men are still in Nauvoo and the Mormons submit to their authority.

Two years later, in the Springfield Illinois *State Register* for September 18, 1846, the warfare between the Mormons and their enemies was depicted in its serious stage:

Carthage, Sept. 12, 1846,
11 O'clock P. M.

As I have just one moment to write before the mail closes, I hasten to let you know that the two belligerent parties in this county have gone to work in earnest. On yesterday, the Anti-Mormons marched within two miles of the city, where they intended to encamp for the night. Immediately on their arrival, picket guards were stationed around. A few moments only elapsed, however, until the picket guard of the city and the guard of the Antis had a brush; which brought the whole camp to arms, which resulted in an engagement which lasted three quarters of an hour, in which it is stated that eleven Mormons were killed and some wounded—no loss to the Antis. After this things quieted down for the night, with each party laboring diligently all night in preparation for today. At about one o'clock today (Saturday) while at my dinner in Carthage, a cannonading commenced, which lasted just one hour and a quarter. I immediately started for the scene of action, which ceased before I got there. The Antis had nine wounded and two or three supposed to be mortal. The Mormons had three killed, as far as ascertained; but it is generally believed by them that their loss will be more than this. The engagement took place on the west side of the city, on the La Harpe road, as the Antis were advancing toward the Temple or in that neighborhood. I learn from the Antis that were in the battle that both sides fought manfully. At first the Mormons gave back a little and then took a firmer position, which they held until the firing was over. The Anti-Mormons then retreated to the camp, after firing thirty or forty rounds of cannon on each side. It is said that several houses were demolished by the cannon of the Antis. . . .

And a few days later, in the *Missouri Republican,* of St. Louis, the capitulation of the religious soldiers was reported in a dispatch from Carthage:

The Mormon war is at last ended. On Wednesday evening, the Quincy Committee prevailed on the Mormons to surrender; and yesterday, at three o'clock the Antis marched into, and took possession of, the city of Nauvoo. The Mormons stipulated to leave forthwith, or as fast as they possibly can get away, except a committee of five, who are to remain to dispose of the property yet belonging to the community. No property has or is to be destroyed—although a strong disposition exists with many of the Antis to destroy the Temple. By refraining from violent measures the Antis have saved themselves from a great deal of reproach.

A gentleman, who left Nauvoo yesterday, said the Mormons were leaving as fast as they could get away. Yesterday was a happy day for the citizens of Hancock county, as peace is now permanently restored to it.

The Mormons traveled westward, now under the guardianship of Brigham Young. They decided, when they left Nauvoo, to go to the limits of civilization, where they could pursue their mode of life without interference, and in the summer of 1847, they founded Salt Lake City, in what they called the State of Deserét.

For ten years their activities were arbitrary but not too illegal. The Territory of Utah was organized, with Brigham Young as the first governor. Not until 1857 did the Mormons strike another blow against the sensibilities of their fellows. This was the Mountain Meadow Massacre, described in an extra by the Los Angeles *Star* on October tenth:

> In our last publication, we gave the substance of a rumor which had just then reached us, of the massacre of a large party of immigrants on their way to this State, by Great Salt Lake City. We were unwilling at first to credit the statement, and hoped that rumor had exaggerated the facts, but the report has been confirmed, and the loss of life is even greater than at first reported. This is the foulest massacre which has ever been perpetrated on this route, and one which calls loudly for the active interposition of the Government. Over one hundred persons have fallen by the hands of the merciless destroyers, and we hope that immediate steps will be taken by the authorities to inflict a terrible retribution on those concerned. There is no longer reason to doubt the facts—we have them from different parties, and all agree in placing the number of the slain at over one hundred souls, men, women and children.
>
> The details, as far as yet known, are these: A train of emigrants from Missouri and Arkansas, for this State, were waylayed and cruelly butchered on the route, at a place called Santa Clara Canon, near the rim of the Great Basin, about three hundred miles from Salt Lake City. The scene of the massacre is differently designated, as the Santa Clara Canon, the Mountain Springs, and the Mountain Meadows.

But all agree in locating it near the rim of the Great Basin, and about fifty miles from Cedar City, the most southern of the Mormon settlements. Of a party of about one hundred and thirty persons only fifteen infant children were saved. . . .

Further details of the affair were recorded in the Sacramento *Democratic State Journal* of October fourteenth:

The news published on our first and third pages today, nearly equals in amount, and exceeds in interest, that usually furnished upon the arrival of a steamer from the Atlantic States. A partial synopsis of the intelligence was received by us immediately upon the arrival of the *Senator,* and published in our issue of Monday morning. The details are even more horrible than the brief telegraphic report led us to imagine. We refer, of course, to the massacre of the men, women and children, at the Mountain Meadows, near the rim of the Great Basin. The number of the murdered is set down at over one hundred persons, and although the details furnished are somewhat scanty still, enough can be gathered to allow the imagination to fill up a measure of suffering and merciless treatment sufficient to cause the blood to boil, and the feeling of revenge to rise uppermost in the mind.

The affair happened about the 12th of September, and the butchery continued for nearly or quite two days. The immigrants were hemmed in by the savages, and slain at their leisure, until all were killed, except a few children, who were sold to the Mormons. The cause for all this is stated to be the ill treatment received by the Indians from this same party of immigrants, consisting of the poisoning of an ox, from eating which several of the savages died, and other like occurrences.

The story is related by the Mormons, and it is probable that although they have not made it any worse than the facts warrant, yet they may have changed many important features of the affair to suit their own individual purposes. In fact, the Mormons are suspected of having assisted, directed, or urged the matter, and many circumstances attending the slaughter, or the report of the same, would tend to increase this suspicion. In the first place, it seems improbable that any body of men, such as usually composes a train, would adopt a course of treatment which if it did not bring down upon their own heads the revenge of the Indians, could not fail to cause evil or danger to the trains immediately following. In addition to the poisoning of the ox referred to, they are accused of impregnating with strychnine the wells from which the savages obtain their supplies of water. Such a tale bears a sort of improbability upon its face, and it is difficult of belief. The tale, too, that a train containing forty-five men, capable of bearing arms, should be attacked in that locality, and utterly destroyed, seems hard of belief by any one acquainted with the habits of immigrants and the character of the Indians found upon the Plains. In our whole history of overland immigration, no such instance is related, nor anything approaching to its boldness, so far as the different tribes are concerned. It seems indeed at the very first glance, even did no other circumstances suggest the idea, that white men must have been concerned in the outrage. The emigrants were from Missouri and Arkansas, and against the people of these states the Mormons have long cherished a blind and indiscriminate hatred. They have sworn vengeance against the entire race and have always declared an intention of future revenge. Circumstances have recently occurred inducing the suspicion that the saints have decided upon a change in their line of policy, and this may be one of the first concerted outbreaks. That they employed the Indians as tools cannot be doubted, for they have always claimed, and many recent matters show the claim to be well based, that in case of any outbreak the entire body of savages, dwelling upon the Plains, would be found acting with them. It seems also that two or three of the Mormon Elders traveled this same route by themselves only a day or two after the massacre and were allowed to pass unharmed.

Vengeance for this massacre was twenty years in coming. On March 23, 1877, John D. Lee, former Bishop of the Mormon church, looked into the muzzles of an execution squad's rifles, on the scene of the massacre. The Denver *Rocky Mountain News* printed a dispatch on March twenty-fourth, concerning the execution:


## THE MOUNTAIN MEADOW MASSACRE
## AVENGED

---

### Execution of John D. Lee—"Aim At My Heart"

---

SALT LAKE CITY, March 23—At 11 A. M., precisely, Lee was brought out upon the scene of the massacre at Mountain Meadows, before the execution party, and seated on his coffin about twenty feet from the shooters. After the order of court was read to him, and the company present, by Marshal Nelson, Lee made a speech of about five hundred words, denouncing Brigham Young and calling himself a scapegoat for the sins of others. He hoped God would be merciful. He denied he was guilty of bloodshed to the last and maintained that his visit to the Meadows was one of mercy. After the speech, Parson Stokes, a Methodist, made a prayer, commending the soul of the condemned man to God. Immediately after this, the handkerchief was placed over Lee's eyes. He raised his hands and placed them on top of his head, sitting firm, Nelson giving the word "fire" at exactly 11 o'clock. Five guns were fired, the balls penetrating the body in the region of the heart. Lee fell square back upon the coffin, dead. Death was instantaneous. The body was placed in the coffin and the crowd dispersed. There were about seventy-five persons, all told, on the ground. Not a child or a relative was there. Lee's last words were, "Aim at my heart."

Brigham Young outlived his accuser by only a few months. The New York *World* reported on August 30, 1877:

> Salt Lake City, August 29—President Brigham Young died this afternoon at 4:01 o'clock. He had been violently ill for several days, and his death was looked for.

---

## III

# A DEAD DESPERADO

(St. Louis *Globe-Democrat*)

---

The exploits and notoriety of the Dalton and James gangs were almost exactly those of Dillinger and Karpis and the others of our century. The Daltons' ill-fated attempt to raid Coffeyville differed in technique from a modern bank robbery only in the lack of sub-machine guns and automobiles; Jesse James, like Dillinger, was delivered to his death by the hand of a betrayer.

After his years of terrorizing the West as the most feared gunman of his time, James was shot to death in his St. Joseph hideaway on April 3, 1882. The Chicago *Tribune* for April fourth described James' background in this article:

> Kansas City, Mo., April 3—Here the James boys were reared and here has ever been their harbor of refuge when chased from pillar to post and State to State by detectives. Here many of their old guerrilla comrades live, and here, too, they have friends and relatives residing.
>
> The James boys were raised in Clay County, within twelve miles of Liberty; the Youngers in Jackson County, within four miles of Independence. There is something

suggestive in the names of their homes, for liberty and independence with them have been carried beyond the limits of criminal license.

Frank James joined Quantrell's guerrillas when he was 20 years old. He soon became noted for his daring and murderous ferocity. Jesse, only 14 years old, sought service at the same time, but was rejected as too young. Returning home, he became serviceable as a spy for the guerrillas infesting Clay and adjoining counties. His step-father, Dr. Samuels, was a pronounced Secessionist, and old Mrs. Samuels gave unbridled license to her tongue in advertising her sympathy for the South. The family, thus making themselves conspicuous, were marked for vengeance by the Union militia of the State, who were stationed at Kearney and other towns in that locality.

. . . In Quantrell's command the James boys found congenial spirits in Cole and Jim Younger, Jarrette, Clell Miller, George Shepherd, and others who have been partners in their robberies since the War. Both were in Quantrell's band of 20 when Lawrence, Kansas, was sacked, burned and nearly every male inhabitant ruthlessly murdered. Jesse James boasted at the time to have shot down thirty-six.

Probably no horror of equal enormity or atrocity was ever perpetrated than the massacre at Centralia, Mo., in a way station on the Wabash Railroad in Boone County. Here, on Sept. 27, 1864, Bill Anderson, assisted by Jesse and Frank James, killed thirty-two invalid soldiers in cold blood. They first raided the village and sacked the stores. Then, waiting for the east-bound train, they stopped it and robbed the passengers of their money. Among the passengers were thirty-two sick soldiers en route from St. Joseph to St. Louis for better hospital accommodations. These poor wretches were marched out and aligned by Frank and Jesse James, and Bill Anderson, with his own hands, shot and killed every man of them, a pistol being handed him by either Frank or Jesse as fast as he emptied the one in hand.

Scarce had the diabolical massacre been finished before a company of Iowa volunteers appeared in the distance, and they, too, became victims of the unerring aim of these bandits. Thus within two hours eighty slain were piled up about the village. Such scenes as these hardened the James boys, and made their latter-day crimes merely trivial in comparison.

Also in the *Tribune* that morning there appeared dispatches from St. Joseph to the Western Associated Press, containing the accounts of James' death. Rearranged here for continuity, these dispatches fully describe the drama and its principal actors :

St. Joseph, Mo., April 3—A great sensation was created in this city this morning by the announcement that Jesse James, the notorious bandit and train-robber, had been shot and killed here in St. Joseph. The news spread with great rapidity, but most people received it with doubts until an investigation established the fact beyond question. Then the excitement became more and more intense, and crowds of people rushed to that quarter of the city where the shooting took place, anxious to view the body of the dead outlaw and to learn the particulars.

The body is that of a man of magnificent physique, who in the pride of health and strength must have been a commanding figure, six feet tall, and weighing 175 pounds, with every muscle developed and hardened by active life. It is a body that would fill with delight the surgeon seeking material for demonstrating anatomy. The features, but little disturbed in death are not unpleasing, and bear the imprint of self-reliance, firmness and dauntless courage. To look upon that face is to believe that the wonderful deeds of daring ascribed to Jesse James have not been exaggerated. The hair is dark brown, the eyes half-opened, glazed, a cold steel gray, upon the upper lip a close-cropped mustache, stained by nasal hemorrhage, and the lower part of the face covered by a close brown beard about four inches long. Over the left eye is the blackened wound caused by the bullet

of Robert Ford, the beardless boy whose cunning and treachery, animated by greed of gold, brought to an ignoble end
the desperado who has so long snapped his fingers contemptuously at the law and its myriad of agents.

A superficial examination of the body would alone afford
strong proof that the dead body is that of Jesse James. He
has been literally shot to pieces in his daring exploits, and
his old wounds would have killed any one cast in a less
rugged mold. Two bullets have pierced the abdomen, and
are still in the body. There is a bullet-hole in the right
wrist, and another in the right ankle. Two more disfigure
the left thigh and knee. The hands are soft and white and
unstained by manual labor, and the middle finger of the left
hand has been shot away at the first joint. Hundreds of
people have passed before the body, and while there was a
unanimous expression of relief that the country was rid of so
formidable a desperado, there were not a few who did not
hesitate to condemn the manner of his taking off. Nevertheless, the young Ford brothers are undeniably the heroes
of the hour. As they sat in the County Clerk's office this
afternoon awaiting their call before the Coroner's inquest,
then progressing in an adjoining room, they were the coolest
and most unconcerned persons present, and the very last that
a stranger would pick out as the slayers of Jesse James. . . .

It was Robert E. Ford, the younger brother, who fired
the fatal shot, but his brother Charles was at his side with
cocked revolver in hand to second his attempt. Charles is
said by old Missourians to bear a wonderful resemblance to
the once-famous Basil Duke.* He is 24 years old, with black
hair banged over the forehead, heavy black eyebrows, a faint
and foppish mustache, high cheek bones, sunken cheeks and
square jaws, denoting great firmness. Robert, the killer, is
but 20 years of age, five feet ten and a half inches tall, and
weighs 135 pounds. His hair is brown and close-cropped,
and his round, ruddy face is smooth-shaven. He has hazel

---

*A Kentuckian, an enthusiastic states-rights man, who took active
part in the seccessionist movement in Missouri, engaging in spectacular
and dangerous operations.

eyes as sharp as a hawk's, which constantly move about with restless and penetrating gaze. There was not the faintest trace of excitement in the young man's manner as he detailed the story of his act. "There is nothing to conceal," he said, "and I am proud of what I have done. I was born in Richmond, Ray County, Missouri, and raised on a farm until 17, when I clerked for two years in a country store. Then I went back on the farm.

"So they say the dead man isn't Jesse James, do they? Then they are mistaken. I first met Jesse James three years ago, and I have made no mistake. He used to come over to the house when I was on my oldest brother's farm. Last November he moved here to St. Joe and went under the name of Thomas Howard. He rented a house on 31st up on the hill back of the World's Hotel, a quiet part of town and not thickly settled. My brother Charley and I had known nearly all of the gang, but had never worked with any of them otherwise. I was in collusion with the detectives, and was one of the party that went to Kentucky and arrested Clarence Hite last February. Hite got twenty-five years in the penitentiary. Jesse never suspected that we were false to him, and as his gang was all broken up, he wanted new material and regarded us favorably. Two weeks ago he came to Clay County to see his mother, Mrs. Samuels, who lives forty miles east of Kansas City. Charley and I told him then we wanted to join him and become outlaws and he said all right. Charley came here with him a week ago Sunday and I followed last Sunday night. We both stayed at his house, a one-story building with seven rooms. Gov. Crittenden had offered $10,000 reward for Jesse, dead or alive. We knew that the only way was to kill him. He was always cool and self-possessed, but always on the watch.

"During the day he would stay around the house and in the evening he would go down town to the news depot and get the papers. He said there were men here who ought to know him, but they never did. He took the Chicago *Tribune*, Cincinnati *Commercial* and Kansas City *Times* and always knew what was going on all over the world. About a week ago he read a piece in one of the papers that Jesse James' career was over, and Charley said he was awful mad about it. He said he would show them before long that Jesse James was not done yet. He had not done any job since the 'Blue Cut' train robbery last September and I don't believe he had over $700 or $800 in money. He was thinking of robbing some bank near by and then running in under close cover. It was for this he wanted our help.

"Well," continued the youth, calmly relighting his cigar, "we knew we had to kill him. But there was no chance to get the drop on him until this morning. His wife, and boy of 7 and girl of 3 were in the kitchen. Jesse was in the front sitting-room where he slept.

"I never knew him to be so careless. He commenced brushing the dust off some picture frames, but stopped and took off his weapons and laid them on the bed. There was a Colt's revolver and a Smith & Wesson, each 45 calibre. He also had in the room a Winchester repeating rifle, fourteen shots, and a breech-loading shotgun. As he turned away from the bed we stepped between him and his weapons and pulled on him. I was about eight feet from him when he heard my pistol cock. He turned his head like lightning. I fired, the ball hitting over the left eye and coming out behind the right ear. Charley had his finger on the trigger, but saw he was done for and did not shoot. He fell dead at Charley's feet. We got our hats, went to the telegraph office and telegraphed Gov. Crittenden, Capt. Henry Craig, of Kansas City, and Sheriff Timberlake, of Clay County. The latter replied: 'I will come at once. Stay there until I come.' "

Ford told this story in the most matter-of-fact and unimpassioned way, without a particle of the dramatic in the delivery.

Ten years later, on October 5, 1892, the Daltons swept into Coffeeville, Kansas, intending to rob both banks in the one raid. There were six in the gang. Robert and Emmett Dalton entered one bank, and Grat Dalton and the other three bandits the second. While they were within, the citizens foregathered in the streets, armed with the ready weapons of the period, and what happened when the gang emerged was told, in a style strikingly like the modern style for such stories, in the Kansas City *Journal* for October sixth:

Coffeeville, Kansas, Oct. 5—The Dalton gang has been exterminated, wiped off the face of the earth.

Caught like rats in a trap, they were today shot down, but not until four citizens of this place yielded up their lives in the work of extermination.

Six of the gang rode into town this morning and robbed the two banks of the place. Their raid had become known to the officers of the law and when the bandits attempted to escape they were attacked by the marshal's posse.

In the battle which ensued, four of the desperadoes were killed outright; and one was fatally wounded but still lives. The other escaped but is being hotly pursued.

It is fitting that in the town where the Daltons lived when they made their entree into outlawing, that they should end their career, and in perhaps no other Town in this country would they have met with the reception they did.

Emmett Dalton cried like a child when shown the bodies of his dead brothers, and identified every man. Following is his statement:

"On the first of October, 1892, I met the boys south of Tulsa and they asked me how much money I had. I told them about $20. I asked them how much they had and they said about $300. I asked them what they were going to do with it and they said this town (Coffeeville) had been talking about them and some of the people had been trying to capture them. I told them I knew it was a lie, for they used to have lots of friends here, but Bob said that he could discount the James boys' work and go up and rob both banks at Coffeeville in one day. I told them I did not want any of it at all. He said I had better go along and help and get some of the money and leave the country; that if I stayed around here I was sure to get caught or killed by myself. On the morning of October 3, we saddled up north of Tulsa, in the Osage nation, and rode about twenty miles toward Coffeeville and talked it over that day. And I went for love of my brothers, for I knew that they [the peace officers] would chase me just as hard as if I was along and I had no money to get out of the country on."

The Coffeeville raid filled much of pages one and two in the *Journal* for that morning. But the editor (resourceful, as all editors are) found space somehow for a little item on page two. The item made two and a half lines of type and read:

London, Oct. 6—Lord Tennyson, poet laureate of England, died at 1:35 o'clock this morning at Adworth.

## IV

# IS IT UNITY?

(New York *Herald*)

————

The old Brooklyn Bridge across the East River, now used somewhat contemptuously by produce truckers and newspaper wagons from the few journals which cling to the vicinity of Park Row, was once the major marvel of the age. In the Eighties, when it was opened to the public, to cross upon it was an event. Editorially, there was as much boom-boom about it as we have ever heard. The discord in the symphony of praise was furnished by union labor, which felt that the date of the opening—May 24, 1883—was undemocratic because it coincided with the date of Queen Victoria's birth.

Brooklyn, even in 1883, was an unwanted stepchild. The New York *Herald,* from the eminence of Manhattan Island, contributed this account of the opening on May twenty-fifth:

The big bridge is opened.

The big bugs have had their glorious jollification, and now to any man or woman on the face of the footstool the aerial highway is free—after the payment of one cent fare. For many years the day of opening that big bridge has been anticipated, but the fondest hope never suggested a more beautiful combination of sun and sky, of air and water, than that which made yesterday a thing of radiant joy and beauty. . . .

The city was one vast flag. Everywhere waved the Stars and Stripes. Churches, ware-houses, public buildings, newspaper offices and horse cars flaunted the patriotic bunting. . . .

Had the arrangements in Brooklyn been a quarter as precise as those in New York, there would have been less confusion and some little appearance of orderliness and comfort.

The President's internal pain bothered him somewhat before he reached the City Hall gate, but when he saw the human density which stretched to the Astor House in front and across the park to the very buildings on the further side of the square, he forgot himself in the majesty of the scene. . . .

Brooklyn has been called the City of Churches, the City of Gush, the City of Talkers. It was a City of Hurrahdom yesterday and everybody in it from the Mayor to the constable metaphorically stood on his head with joy and gladness.

Why?

Because it's now "so easy to get to New York"!

One week later, the crowds crossing the river on this new toy were thrown into fatal confusion. Newspapers of the period do not bear out the legend that an addlepate cried, "The bridge is falling!" but credit the panic to pickpockets or undetermined causes. Whatever its beginnings, it was an unhappy thing to have occur on the newest of the "wonders of the world." Of the panic, the *Herald* said on May thirty-first:

> Shortly after four o'clock yesterday afternoon a panic occurred at the most dangerous point on the footpath of the great bridge, and twelve persons—men, women and children —were trampled to death in a mad rush that was either absolutely needless or, as is believed, was started by pickpockets. . . .
>
> As is well known, the footpath on the bridge proper is raised above the footpath on the two approaches. The elevation is reached by two short flights of steps. On the New York side there are fourteen steps, or two flights of seven each. . . .
>
> Somebody fell, or was thrown down the steps. Some say a child was thrown down by a gang of pick-pockets. . . . Over the prostrate body of the first to fall, another fell. Over him fell another. In an instant there was wild confusion. The crowd added to it by a wild, mad push forward from above; and before anyone realized the gravity of the situation, the half of the crowd on the steps was prostrate and the crowd from above was trampling the fallen to death. The people coming down knew nothing of what was happening until they were right upon the steps. There was no one to stop them. If there had been one strong-voiced enough and clear-headed enough to shout out behind that there had been an accident, and that all must stop, and if the crowd would have heeded and not pushed forward, there would not have been so terrible a story to tell.
>
> For a few moments there was no help. On and on came the crowds. Denser and higher the struggling bodies were piled. Presently, however, assistance came, although for a full quarter of an hour it was impossible to drag out the

dead and dying, help away the wounded and subdue the panic. . . .

It was a hard task, but with the aid of the workmen on the bridge, sections of the railing on either side of the foot-path next to the steps were torn away and paths were ex-temporized across the railroads to the carriage-ways. This relieved the pressure somewhat and enabled those working to take out the bodies of the dead on either side and thus clear the way for the crowds coming in both directions that could not, it seemed, be stayed.

*The Sun* was quick to criticize the poor management that permitted the panic to occur. In its edition for May thirty-first, it said:

It is an ill-omen for the new Brooklyn Bridge that within six days of the time when it was opened amid public jubila-tions by President Arthur, and upon the great national holi-day when the graves of the soldiers of the Union were decorated with flowers, and just after the people of the two cities had enjoyed the martial march of the veterans with their tattered flags through the streets, we should have to record such a shocking thing, with such harrowing features, as the bridge disaster of yesterday afternoon.

We had hoped, upon completion of this great public work, that it would be long free from the stains of blood; but here already are the human sacrifices—women, men and children. Today our reporters give accounts of scenes, in which some of them played their parts, that are too melancholy for pre-tentious description. For long years to come, the memories of yesterday will haunt the minds of those who crossed this bridge, and the catastrophe will always form part of its his-tory. . . .

All practicable means of securing the highest degree of safety for passengers over the bridge must be adopted at once. If necessary, let traffic and travel there be suspended until the proper changes are made.

Last Thursday, it was the bridge of festivity; yesterday it was the bridge of death; henceforth it must be the bridge of safeguards for life.

## V

# THE ITALIAN OPERA WAR

(New York *World*)

———

New York opened more than a bridge in 1883. And, in a sense, there was more than one panic after an opening. In the case of the bridge it was a panic of outpouring people; in the case of the Metropolitan Opera house, it was a panic of out-pouring words. On October 22, 1883, the New York *World* published its interview with the director of the Academy of Music, who was contemptuous of the upstart:

### THE ITALIAN OPERA WAR

———

Both Managers to Advance on the Public Purse To-night

———

Colonel Mapleson in a Talkative Mood—His Comments on His Singers and His Rival

———

Tonight lovers of the opera will turn out en masse and flock towards either the new Metropolitan Opera-House, or the Academy of Music. But the former, judged by the pulse of the regular attendants of the opera, will have the largest attendance. As to the operas to be produced but little need be said. Both have been heard before by New York audiences. "Faust" will be the attraction at the Metropolitan with

Mme. Nilsson as Marguerite and Signor Campanini as Faust. . . .

At the Academy of Music, Mme. Etelka Gerster will appear as Amina in "La Sonnambula" and Signor Vicini as Elvino. . . .

Colonel Mapleson was at his office in the Academy of Music yesterday morning. The floor was littered with scraps of paper and torn envelopes, and the Colonel wore his most suave smile. He conversed freely on the coming opera season and said he felt perfectly contented with the prospect.

"No," said he in answer to a question, "I have not been to the house uptown, but I know just what it is. The Academy is good enough for me. I think the Academy is just perfect. Why, we are modelling our new Opera-House in London after the Academy. The acoustic properties here are perfect. I could have had the new house. They came to me and offered every inducement to have me break my lease here, which had five years to run, but I said 'no.' Then they went to Abbey.

"Support two opera-houses? Why, of course New York cannot support two opera-houses. People may go to the new opera-house to see what it is like, but gradually the novelty of the place will die away, and then they will go where they can hear good music. Now, I've been before the New York public for over twenty years and know just what they want. My chorus is trained and experienced. They have been tried and we all know just what they have done and what they can do again. . . . You see, I discovered Gerster, Christine Nilsson and the rest of 'em and brought 'em out, but there's none like Patti. Christine is losing youth and beauty and her voice is not what it used to be. She sings hardly anything but Marguerite, and you know 'Faust' cannot be given over four times in the season; the public won't have it. Now, I understand, they intend giving it six times.

"Abbey tried hard to get Patti. I had my contract with her for $4,400 written and on my desk, intending to sign it next day. Well, that night what does Abbey do but go to her and offer her $600 a night more than I had contracted to give her. Think of that. Why, such prices are ruinous. Just consider what Patti was paid last year. Why, she took $300,000 away from this country with her. Such salaries cannot be paid and have opera proper.

"Yes, we are all ready to go on, and I've no fear but we'll come out all right. At any rate, I'm going to fight it out to the bitter end, even if I have to come off without a shirt. Will the Opera-House pay? Of course not. The place can't pay and Abbey hasn't got a dime and somebody has to stand the losses. Vanderbilt will soon get tired of doing so. He may give a million, but when it comes to a second million, he won't stand it. You see, that place was gotten up by the *neuve richesse* who found that their money couldn't buy them a proscenium box at the Academy, so they built a house of their own. But just look at that list and you can see who are with us. Why, we have all the best people of New York —all the blue-blood of the city."

The performance, as reported by the *World* for October twenty-third, was fully as brilliant as Colonel Mapleson had hoped it would not be:

At 3 o'clock yesterday there were 20,000 square feet of plaster, shavings, whitewash and dirt, mingled with lumber and paintpots covering the superficial surface of the Metropolitan Opera House. There were 700 women scrubbing the stairways and floors of the entrances.

"It will be ready by 8 o'clock," said Mr. Abbey.

And it was true.

At 7:30 there were 10,000 people in the streets around the building. The scaffoldings that gave a network of ugliness to the Broadway portal in the morning were gone.

The gas was lit. An electric blaze streamed over against the Casino and the carriages were rattling down Thirty-Ninth and Fortieth streets.

Inside all was confusion. Box-holders were running here and there. Ushers were trying to learn the topography of the house. Ticket takers in uniform were straining themselves to keep cool. Gasmen were flying up and down.

At 8 o'clock there was a stream of carriages in both streets and a double stream of full-dressed ladies and gentlemen was pouring into the house.

Seen from the second tier of boxes, the new Opera House with its brilliant assemblage presented a dazzling sight. No such audience had probably ever been seen in America. The triple rows of boxes were all filled. Diamonds flashed, all the way round from one pole of the great horseshoe magnet to the other, and costumes of the richest materials shone in every hue.

The enormous size of the audience-room gave a perspective that was new. From the balcony the parquet spread out like an enormous flower garden, with its bagnoir boxes on either side, like an ornamental hedge.

The prevailing color of the house is a dingy yellow, which gives it an unfinished look.

Indeed the boxes are unfinished, inasmuch as the maroon panels which are intended to form a background for the dresses are not in, and the consequence is there was no effect of shadow, recess or contrast.

The absence of a proscenium is another disadvantage in effect. The stage opening is a square frame without a curve or graceful line in it and its decoration is tame and conventional.

At 8:30 the house was entirely filled. Balcony and gallery were congested, inasmuch as they were the only places where men and women could stand up.

A buzz went over the great assembly. It was the drone of conversation and comment. Lorgnettes were levelled in all directions. Men were standing up in the parquet making sweeping surveys of the house. Ladies leaned over from their boxes to note and smile at their neighbors.

The time passed along and nobody seemed impatient for the curtain to rise, save a few ultra-musical people in the gallery.

Finally, Signor Vinsi came up from a crypt. He was dressed matchlessly and his appearance was the signal for a general round of gloved applause.

He bowed slightly in acknowledgment of the greeting, lifted the baton, held it suspended a moment and then with a graceful flourish commenced the introduction. Before it had reached the andante everyone recognized that it had the two necessary elements of strength and discipline. Composed of eighty musicians, the distribution is somewhat different from that in previous opera bands. The strength of the brass was noticeable; but while giving a sonorous swing it was at the same time handled with great discretion.

Signor Vinsi exhibits considerably more enthusiasm in his work than Signor Arditi, and remembering that everybody was very nervous and the gauge of the house can hardly be said to have been settled, he certainly held his forces well in hand and won at the very outset a tribute to his intelligence and sagacity. When the curtain rose on the performance, the immense height and width of the stage made a visible impression. The first chorus "Interrego ivano" was received with silence. It was not until the Kermesse scene that the ensemble was sufficient to exhibit the capacity of the stage and chorus. The purely scenic effects were admirable and the chorus "Su da vere" was sung with a freshness that was admirable. The act was spiritedly and evenly given. In the later scenes the chorus occasionally fell behind the tempo, but were shipped back by the conductor almost instantly. The forces are particularly rich in bass voices and there was a strong suggestion of Germany about the vigor and solidity of the soldiers' chorus.

When Mme. Nilsson first appeared here as Marguerita, in Gounod's "Faust," it was under Mr. Max Strakosch, in 1871. It will be remembered that she came to the country to sing in concert and so great was her success at Steinway Hall that there was a general and open desire to hear her on the Italian stage. When she appeared in "Faust," it was with Capoul, M. Jamet, M. Barre, and Annie Louise Carey. Recalling the enthusiasm over the Swedish singer of twelve years ago, it must be acknowledged that few, if any vocalists ever came to this country who met with a more cordial reception, who excited more musical enthusiasm or who won more admirers in social life. There was something almost ideal about Nilsson's popularity at that time. In any role she was the beautiful Norse woman of fable. In Gretchen she was the typical Marguerite made familiar by German painters and etchers. . . .

When the soprano walked on in her well-remembered attire, she was received with generous but genteel plaudits. It cannot be said that her reception was an enthusiastic one. It is doubtful if a full dress audience ever is enthusiastic.

There was apparent indecision on the part of her friends to determine whether the quality of the voice was the same. Marguerite had grown stouter. It was useless to deny it. The maidenly charm which twelve years ago made Nilsson seem the ideal Gretchen had given place to a robust maturity, not alone of form but of voice. Her audience followed her tentatively up to the "Jewel Song" and the "King of Thule" and then decided. It may be said that the decision was a generous one. The "Bijou Song" won a round of applause and the "King of Thule" was sung with more of the old charm than any other number. But neither of them is an exacting number, vocally speaking. Not only were they lacking in quality but what they gained in breadth of utterance they lost in spontaneity. The timbre of Mme. Nilsson's voice is not what it was twelve years ago, and it was the timbre of her voice that was its great charm. . . . Something, it is true, must be allowed to an artist of extreme sensibility in the place and surrounded by trying circumstances, and it is only fair to say we may look for better results in Mme. Nilsson's repetitions.

At the conclusion of the "Jewel Song" there was a recall and after the applause there was handed up from the orchestra a huge casket containing a solid gold wreath and two massive gold pins of elaborate and costly workmanship. This gift was placed upon the stage, and in repeating the "Jewel Song," Mme. Nilsson addressed herself to the gift.

It was accompanied by an anonymous letter. The wreath is a beautiful imitation of laurel and the casket bore the inscription "To Christine Nilsson, in commemoration of the opening of the Metropolitan Opera House."

All efforts to find out who the giver was proved fruitless.

# ONE STAR

The weather today in New York (including
points within thirty miles of this city)
promises to be fair and colder, preceded
by partial cloudiness near the coast. Tomorrow it promises to be slightly warmer
and generally fair.

—New York *Herald*
March 11, 1888

# I

## THE BURIED CITY

(New York *Herald*)

---

All snows are measured with the yardstick of the Blizzard
of 1888, whose magnitude was such that the New York
press printed stories about little else for days. The New York
*World* reporter, while the gale and the snow hurled themselves
against the windows at his back, wrote this account of the
storm for the edition of March 13, 1888:

Between the warm and gentle raindrops that peppered on
the dry pavements on Sunday afternoon, and the sharp,
needle-like spears of ice that cut into the face as the shrew-
ish gale drove them at a forty miles-per-hour pace on yesterday afternoon, the broad gamut of storm notes was
played. It was a sort of diabolical symphony, with all the
movements thrown in—andante, allegro, scherzo and finale
—and if any one wanted some kind of weather which he
didn't get it must be because he didn't ask for it. It began
with a raw, soft atmosphere that was neither wintry nor
springlike. Then came rain, and then more rain, ad libitum.
Then the mercury began to get discouraged and at midnight,
while the wind was making music among the thousand
strings of the telegraphic Aeolian harp, the rain had turned
to snow. The wind, taking heart of grace, began to bite the
snow flakes into dust as it grew stronger, and the early
milkman found himself plowing through a powdery atmosphere that was uncomfortable but not disheartening, while
the drift grew from ankle-deep towards knee and thigh. At

seven a. m. the wind was sprinting down from the northwest at forty miles an hour and the temperature was 24 degrees above zero. At least the wise men of the Signal Service said it was from the northwest, though to the humble observer in the streets it looked more like galleywest. And still the combat deepened. By 9 o'clock the scherzo movement was under way and the aerial orchestra was playing every kind of joke of which it was capable—and its capacity is large. It coated the telegraph wires with tons of ice, until they snapped beneath the strain and came curling down to plague the legs of horses and pedestrians. It coated the windows with curtains of snow, tore awnings to ribbons, and sent puffs of feathery blizzard into every crack and crevice in door and window. It turned huge windrows of exasperation over the sidewalks and car tracks and banked vehicles in ever-changing but never lessening hummocks. Deeper and deeper every moment, the drifts soon put an estoppal upon traffic that was not to be denied. Loaded wagons stopped first, then the horse cars, and finally steam succumbed; and the spindle-shanked railroads briefly called the "L" but more appropriately termed if that letter can be slightly asperated, proved how utterly useless they can be in a time of trial. "Oh, for an Underground road!" New York sighed yesterday. Oh, for something, indeed, better than a little box on stilts not capable of pulling four or five cars, and not capable of holding them (as so sadly proved in the Third Avenue tragedy*) on a slight down grade! Finally, having exhausted its ingenuity in grand and lofty tumbling, the weather permitted the bottom to drop out of things in a thermometrical way; the mercury, which was 24 degrees at 7, was 16 degrees at 2 p. m., and going lower. Soon there was ice under foot, and then didn't Boreas have a carnival! Hoighty, toighty, what a mad dance he led the human family! . . .

---

*Blinded by the snow, the engineer of one Third Avenue train did not see another, stopped at the 76th street station, until it was too late. The engineer was killed and the collision persuaded the railroad officials to abandon service until the storm subsided.

To adequately describe the spectacle which New York's streets presented will require many of THE WORLD's broad columns, but it will be matter well worth the reading. Never before has such a storm been seen and probably a generation will pass away and not view another such. Saving Broadway and Third, Sixth and Eighth avenues, the streets were almost wholly given up to the wind, the drifts and the scurrying snow. Here and there stood a vehicle which had been stalled and abandoned. Street cars, beer wagons laden high with loaded kegs, great trucks piled with carcasses from the slaughter houses, broken-down hacks, found place in this mournful display of the abandoned. Up and down the middle of Broadway poured a strange procession of coaches, hacks, cabriolets, coupes and cabs, with here and there a sleigh—for it was cabby's golden harvest day—and on each sidewalk was an Indian file of pedestrians, those going south on the west and those going north on the east side of the street. A more fantastic procession you would go far to find. Some wore blankets tied about their heads. Some had their back hair protected by vari-colored kerchiefs. Some stalked in huge rubber boots. Others showed the part of wisdom by having their trousers legs tied tightly around the ankle and not a few, emulating the wise and foxy tramp, bundled their feet in squares of carpet and were very happy. . . .

Among the bold ones who turned out and braved the storm, were a few school children and quite a number of working girls and women. Weary work the latter had, impeded as they were by skirts and cloaks, to make headway; and some turned back and some reached their destinations breathless and trembling with weariness, only to find the stores closed and locked, for many merchants refused to go through the empty folly of keeping store. In most of the public schools there was no attempt to go through the usual exercises, but the little ones were allowed to sing or listen to reading until 2 o'clock, the hour when they could always be dismissed, if the Board of Education were not a board of old fossils who don't know the meaning of the word enough.

And on another page, this reporter—or one of his colleagues—bragged, in somewhat questionable taste:

It is pleasant to state the big storm wasn't big enough to snow in THE WORLD reporter. It was big enough, to be sure, to block up Mayor Hewitt in his home, to close the doors of the Stock Exchange at noon, to paralyze business as though it had a blow from a bludgeon, to stop traffic on the "L" roads, to bury horse cars along the avenues, to zip all the telegraph wires from the poles, to keep all trains in stations, to rule almost the entire city with a rod of ice—but not quite big enough to snow in the reporters of THE WORLD. In the words of the poet, they got there just the same. It may be well when remembering this fact to bear in mind that the youth who carried the banner Excelsior into Alpine heights has not been heard from, but THE WORLD reporters are around and some of their trips were considered quite as perilous as was that of the young man of the poetry.

Further details, from the pen of a reporter apparently fascinated by morbid possibilities, appeared in the New York *Herald* for March fourteenth, when the fury of the storm had been spent:

With men and women dying in her ghostly streets, New York saw day breaking through the wild clouds yesterday morning. Nature had overwhelmed the metropolis and citizens were found dead in the mighty snow drifts. White, frozen hands sticking up out of the billowed and furrowed wastes testified to the unspeakable power that had desolated the city.

Had Jules Verne written such a story a week ago, New Yorkers would have laughed and pronounced it a clever but impossible romance.

Yet here was the stupendous reality. Within forty-eight hours the city was converted into an Arctic wilderness, cut off from all railway and telegraph communication. The white hurricane had strewn her busiest and gayest thoroughfares with wreck and ruin. Courts of justice were closed and the vast machinery of commerce was paralyzed. Groans of mutilated humanity filled the air.

The artillery of Europe could not have reduced New York to such an awful state of helplessness in such a short time. Think of reporters on snow-shoes, and rescuing parties being organized to save men from dying of exposure in the heart of the city! When firemen dragged their engines to fires it looked as if they were soldiers hurrying cannon through the wilderness as they sat on their horses laboring the leaders and following the dim figures of mounted scouts in the mad tempest.

It was all so white, strange, picturesque and grandly terrible as the ugly sky frowned upon the pulseless, haggard miles of half-buried houses. Everybody knew that corpses would be dug out of the streets.

Just after dawn yesterday, the snow ceased to fall, but the great wind that had roared ceaselessly for two days and two nights still shook the earth and whirled the great flakes upward again in weird, fantastic shapes. At six o'clock the thermometer was one degree above zero.

Thousands upon thousands of men, wrapped in the oddest of costumes that imagination can picture, turned out to dig paths through the streets. In many places the diggers had to cut through gigantic drifts in order to release people who were imprisoned in their own homes.

Tremendous hills of snow were thrown up in the streets and between them were paths through which the population crept along. Sometimes these hills were so high that a man would walk for half a block without being able to see anything but the sullen sky above him and the dazzling white walls on either side of him. Horses were employed in dragging away the fallen trees and telegraph poles. Thousands of abandoned wagons were dug out and dragged by double teams to places of shelter.

Rescue parties in sleighs were sent out in all directions to relieve the snow bound unfortunates. The railway companies battled heroically with the snow in their efforts to push the trains through. Here and there engines were chained together and hurled against the drifts at full speed. The New York Central company upset one of its heaviest locomotives while trying to butt a hole through the snow packed in the Fourth Avenue tunnel. How many have died in the drifts while trying to reach help from these blocked trains will not be known for days yet.

All the sleeping cars in the railway depots were given to the public as hotels. Exhausted men and women gladly crept into them to get warm and snatch a few hours sleep. The great depots in New York and Jersey City were crowded with homeless strangers, driven away from the hotels. Women and children lay on the hard floors and thankfully ate cheese and crackers distributed by the railway companies.

The telegraph wires simply were raveled into tangled webs that caught the feet of horses and human beings in the snow. Editors cabled London in hope of getting news from Boston. The operators slept all night beside their instruments, but no sound broke the deadly silence. . . .

As the storm increased in fury on Monday night, and the mercury fell lower and lower, the cheap lodging houses on the Bowery were invaded by people who had been unable to get beds in the regular hotels. It was indescribably funny to see gorgeously attired young men of fashion humbly arranging for cots in the haunts of the tramp and street arab. All night the lodging house dormitories were crowded, with snow bound dandies who scratched and grumbled and tossed about on hard pallets in the ill smelling cubby holes. . . .

In front of all the clubs, in fact everywhere throughout the city, people could be seen feeding the starving sparrows, which flew against the windows in the most pitiful way. This awful violation of the law—for it is at present a criminal offense in New York—was ignored by the police. Nay, a

HERALD reporter saw a policeman in cold blood criminally feeding crumbs to a sparrow in Twenty-third street near Ninth avenue. . . .

There had been a universal carouse in the saloons all day. Men had filled themselves with whiskey in order to resist the effects of the cold. Drunken men reeled out of the rum shops and staggered into the deep snow. While daylight lasted, these men were soon discovered and rescued. But when darkness closed in and the storm raged over a city in utter blackness the police began to realize the frightful responsibility thrown upon them of saving human life.

A heart rending wail began to go up all over the great city. People were missed and no trace could be found of them. Husbands, fathers, wives, mothers, sons and daughters poured into the police stations, haggard, hollow eyed and desperate with fear and anxiety. The Morgue will soon be choked with victims.

Brooklyn was in a frightful plight, being completely cut off from New York. There was an effort made to run cars on the big Bridge, but one train was derailed on the west side and further work in that direction was given up. To walk across on the bare and unsheltered promenade in the storm that shrieked through the ponderous steel rigging meant suffering and possibly death. The police advised women not to try it.

Here nature, which had shut off the ordinary channels of travel and rendered the monumental bridge of the century useless, provided a substitute in the shape of an ice bridge just like the crystal floe across which Henry Ward Beecher and a few thousand of his fellow citizens walked from shore to shore on that famous cold day in 1874.

A great floe of jumbled and hillocky ice drifted out of the North river and swung around the Battery into the East river at half-past seven o'clock yesterday morning. It gathered up floating ice in its glittering skirts till the East river was filled from shore to shore. Several hundred men and boys walked over to New York.

Editorialists find a moral in everything, and the *Herald,* with this splendid opportunity at hand, did not neglect it. The value of the blizzard to humanity was totaled, in an editorial on March fourteenth:

> The storm taught the cheerful, abundant energy of our people. If nature, either as fire, wind or earthquake, gives us a tumble, we rise at once and go to work, meaning to hold our own even with nature.
>
> And although our whole metropolitan system, about which we are so fond of boasting, was upset in a whirl; the east side piled up on the west side; the elevated railway turned into gymnastic arenas; New York as much in isolation as Sebastopol under her seige and as sadly damaged in money losses; millions wasted and discomfort in every respiration, how cheerful we were! There was more real fun in New York on the day of the blizzard than has been known for a generation. Cheeriness, good will, readiness to help, a kind of an impression that the blizzard was, take it all in all, the funniest thing we had ever known. This grave old Manhattan tousled and rolled in the snow like a schoolboy romping at play—could anything be more laughable?

## II

# THE AWFUL PENNSYLVANIA FRESHET

(*The Sun,* New York)

Johnstown, Pennsylvania, is an unbeautiful little city, huddled among surrounding mountains. Today it is given up to steel mills and coal mining, and since the beginning of the depression it has been distinguished by the vast number of its relief clients. The main street of the town, at either end of which towers a mountain, runs for perhaps eight blocks.

When the mills are running, the city is darkened by a pall of smoke—of this a poet might make a symbol of perpetual mourning for the two thousand and more who died in the flood.

Walking through the streets of Johnstown today, the visitor will be impressed by the many shops housed in what seem to be English basements. To reach them, it is necessary to descend a flight of steps. Once these shops were even with or a bit higher than the street; but when the "Awful Pennsylvania Freshet" had subsided, it left silt and bones and debris enough to lift the physical level of much of the town, in some cases by ten feet.

Several years before the flood, a syndicate of Pittsburgh sportsmen purchased an old dam and acreage behind it. This dam stored the waters of the Conemaugh River, an insignificant little stream. It was a structure built of earth and stones and considered by many engineers, even before it burst, as unsafe. In the late days of May, there were heavy rains; the water deepened behind the dam and pushed harder against it; on May 31, 1889, it gave. The first "flash" into newspaper offices sent reporters scurrying toward the town—with what difficulty may be gathered from the New York *World's* report of June third:

## THE STRUGGLE FOR NEWS
### (For Our Personal Information Only)

Chambersburg, Pa., June 2—Have been in a pocket at Martinsburg since Saturday noon. *Herald, Tribune* and *Times* men with me. The Cumberland Valley bridge over the Potomac was carried away twenty minutes after we walked over it. Took horses there for Martinsburg, Va. The Baltimore and Ohio Railroad is cut up in every direction. Not a wire out of Martinsburg. No trains east or west since Friday. In some places the water is eighteen feet deep on the tracks. We got to Shenandoah Junction with the Chief Engineer of the Cumberland Valley. He was also in a fix. High bridge over river there, and he telegraphed for an engine on Shenandoah Valley road and brought us to Hagerstown. There we learned that 6,000 people were lost and also learned that at Chambersburg we could get horses to Johnstown, seventy-eight miles away. We determined to do that unless countermanded at Chambersburg, as I wired at Hagerstown. The whole country is in a terrible condition. At the Cumberland Valley bridge two houses were swept away and seven people drowned. At Shephardstown, W. Va., where we crossed today, the destruction is widespread, though no lives have been lost. Two massive stone mills are scattered like so much straw. The canal is overflowed and every now and then a canal boat can be seen tossing down in the flood. The Potomac is seven feet higher than it ever was before. At Harper's Ferry the Baltimore and Ohio last night had fifteen engines and a long train of coal cars on the structure to keep it down. Even then the water rose to the boilers of the engines and put out the fires. It was feared this morning that the bridge might have gone during the night, as the river continued rising till midnight. Travel is entirely suspended. I am now traveling in a special car with the Chief Engineer to Chambersburg. All through the Cumberland Valley the little "runs," ordinarily like a thread, are now roaring torrents, and the streams have spread far and wide over the fields. The loss in dollars and cents is incalculable. One farmer alone told me that the flood meant a clear loss of $1,000 to him. There are many thousands of such men throughout the Potomac and Cumberland valleys. Why not a good idea to tell the story of THE WORLD's efforts to get to Johnstown? You can trace the route on a map and then tell about driving across the country. Thursday night there was a cyclone at Falling Waters and the largest kind of trees were uprooted. Two men were killed. We brought the body of one to Hagerstown.

R. A. F.

Later—McConnelsburg, June 2—I shall be in Johnstown some time tonight. How many of our men have got through? Have you had any details? Answer to Bedford, Pa., by 9 o'clock.

R. A. F.

[And from a second correspondent]:
Dunkirk Depot, N. Y., June 2—I learned at Buffalo that road between Buffalo and Pittsburgh blocked; so going on to Cleveland and thence to Pittsburgh. Our train now over half hour late. Will reach Pittsburgh at 2:30 P. M. tomorrow.

The Philadelphia *Public Ledger*, on June third, published a graphic description of the inundated city:

Johnstown, Pa., June 2—I have just come from Johnstown proper, over a rope bridge which was completed this afternoon. I reached there at 5 o'clock last night, and tell only what I did see and do know.

The mighty wave that rushed through the Conemaugh Valley on Friday evening cut a swath of death 13 miles long. In its way lay one of the most thickly populated centres of the Keystone State, and within a few minutes from the time the dam at Lake Conemaugh broke, houses were rolling over one another in a mad whirl, as they were carried by the seething waters down the gorge between the endless hills.

At Johnstown the whole centre of the city was cut, as if a mammoth scythe had passed over the land. At that place was a large stone bridge of the Pennsylvania Railroad Company, one of the strongest that the company owns. The Conemaugh River is crossed by it at an angle. Into this angle houses, trees and fences that came down the left side of the river rushed and were piled on high until rafters and timbers project above the stone. Then the houses, nearly all crowded with people, crashed, one after another, until the terrible wreckage extended a half mile up the stream. No pen can tell the horror of the shrieks of the thousands who were in the mass of floating ruins.

Shortly after the blockade had formed the dry timbers of the houses caught fire, and the mass nearest the railroad bridge became a glowing furnace. Hundreds of people, who had not been drowned or crushed to death in the mad rush downstream, were burned alive. Their shrieks as the flames reached them made the most stout-hearted wring their hands in agony at their inability to render assistance. The wind blew from upstream. The air became filled with the gruesome odors until at last the horrors to sight, hearing and smell became so great that persons in the vicinity were forced to leave the place. Meanwhile, the greater bulk of the houses had gone down along the right bank. One mad rush carried away a portion of the stone bridge, and then the flood bore down upon the thousands of homes and floated them further westward in the Conemaugh. It was only a little after 5 Friday afternoon when the first warning came, and as it had been raining heavily all day the citizens of Johnstown and the neighboring hamlets thought that the slowly rising waters only meant a light flood.

Thus the inhabitants were either grouped in windows or in the open doors watching what was expected would be an imposing spectacle, but nothing more. No one seemed to think it necessary that they should take to the hills, and so all were caught in the fearful rush.

The committee at Johnstown, in their bulletin, place the number of lives lost at 8000. In doing so they are figuring the inhabitants of their own city and the towns immediately adjoining. But it must be remembered that the flood swept ten miles through a populous district before it even reached the locality over which this committee has supervision. It devastated a tract the size and shape of Manhattan Island. Here are a few facts that will show the geographical outlines of the terrible disaster. The Hotel Hurlburt, of Johnstown, a massive three-story building of 100 rooms, has vanished. There were in it 75 guests at the time of the

flood. Two only are known to be alive. The Merchants'
Hotel is levelled. How many were inside it is not known
but as yet no one has been seen who came from there or
heard of an inmate escaping. At the Conemaugh Round
House forty-one locomotives were swept down the stream
and before they reached the stone bridge all the iron and
steel work had been torn from their boilers.

It is almost impossible in this great catastrophe to go
more into details. I stood on the stone bridge at 6 o'clock,
and looked into the seething mass of ruin below me. At
one place the blackened body of a babe was seen; in another
14 skulls could be counted. Further along the bones became
thicker and thicker, until at last at one place it seemed as if
a concourse of people, who had been at a ball or entertain-
ment, had been carried in a bunch and incinerated. At this
time the smoke was still rising to the height of 50 feet, and
it is expected that when it dies down the charred bodies will
be seen dotting the entire mass of burned debris. A cable
had been run last night from the end of the stone bridge
to the nearest point across—a distance of 300 feet. Over
this cable was run a trolley and a swing was fastened under
it.

A man went over, and he was the first one who visited
Johnstown since the awful disaster. I followed him today.
I walked along the hillside and saw hundreds of persons
lying on the wet grass, wrapped in blankets or quilts. It
was growing cold, and a misty rain had set in. Shelter was
not to be had, and houses on the hillside that had not been
swept away were literally packed from top to bottom. The
bare necessities of life were soon at a premium, and loaves
of bread sold at fifty cents.

Fortunately, however, the relief train from Pittsburgh
arrived at 7 o'clock. Otherwise the horrors of starvation
would have been added. All provisions, however, had to be
carried over a rough, rocky road a distance of four miles
(as I know, who had been compelled to walk it) and in
many cases they were seized by the toughs, and the people
who were in need of food did not get it.

The disaster was covered as fully and as well as any other great catastrophe in our history. Stories poured out of the town—grim stories, all, but wrought of humor and heroism and horror. The New York *World,* for June fourth, contained an interview with Engineer Henry of Express Train No. 8, running between Pittsburgh and Altoona:

Some time after 3 o'clock Friday afternoon I went into the train dispatcher's office to learn the latest news. I had not been there long when I heard a fierce whistle from an engine away up the mountain. Rushing out I found dozens of men standing around. Fear had blanched every cheek. The loud and continued whistling had made every one feel that something serious was going to happen. In a few moments I could hear a train rattling down the mountain. About five hundred yards above Conemaugh the tracks made a slight curve and we could not see beyond this. The suspense was something awful. We did not know what was coming, but no one could get rid of the thought that something was wrong at the dam.

Our suspense was not very long, however. Nearer and nearer the train came, the thundering sound still accompanying it. There seemed to be something behind the train, as there was a dull, rumbling sound which I knew did not come from the train. Nearer and nearer it came; a moment more and it would reach the curve. The next instant there burst upon our eyes a sight that made every heart stand still. Rushing around the curve, snorting and tearing, came an engine and several gravel cars. The train appeared to be putting forth every effort to go faster. Nearer it came, belching forth smoke and whistling long and loud. But the most terrible sight was to follow. Twenty feet behind came surging along a mad rush of water fully fifty feet high. Like the train, it seemed to be putting forth every effort to push along faster. Such an awful race we never before witnessed. For an instant the people seemed paralyzed with horror. They knew not what to do, but in a moment they realized that a second's delay meant death to them. With one accord they rushed to the highlands a few hundred feet away. Most of them succeeded in reaching that place and were safe.

The *North American,* in Philadelphia, offered a tribute to what it called "JOHNSTOWN'S PAUL REVERE," on June fourth:

JOHNSTOWN, PA., June 3—A nameless Paul Revere lies somewhere among the nameless dead. Who he is may never be known, but his ride will be famous in local history. Mounted on a grand big bay horse he came riding down the pike which passes through Conemaugh to Johnstown like some angel of wrath of old, shouting his portentous warning: "Run for your lives to the hills! Run to the hills!" The people crowded out of their houses along the thickly settled street, awe-struck and wondering. Nobody knew the man, and some thought he was a maniac and laughed. On at a quick pace he rode, and shrilly rang out his awful cry. In a few moments, however, there came a cloud of ruin down the broad streets, down the narrow alleys, grinding, twisting, hurling, overturning, crashing, annihilating the weak and the strong. It was the charge of flood, wearing its coronet of ruin and devastation, which grew at every instant of its progress. Forty feet high, some say, thirty according to others, was this sea, and it travelled with a swiftness like that which lay hidden in the heels of Mercury. On and on raced the rider, and on and on rushed the wave. Dozens of people took heed of the warning and ran up to the hills. Poor faithful rider; it was an unequal contest. Just as he turned across the railroad bridge the mighty wave fell upon him and horse, rider and bridge all went out into chaos together. A few feet further on several cars of the Pennsylvania Railroad train from Pittsburgh were caught up and hurried into the cauldron.

The deaths of two women, who wanted only to keep their feet dry, were reported in the Philadelphia *North American* for the fifth:

Mr. Edward M. McCullough, of the Westmoreland Coal Company, was among the passengers on the day express east on Friday morning. He states positively that there were two sections of the day express, and the Johnstown accommodation was caught in the flood. Said he: "It is my opinion that at least twenty people were drowned from the trains—in fact I can count that many myself. And the death rate may go as high as forty.

"There were one parlor car and three sleepers on the express and several other cars. We did not know of the flood until about thirty seconds before it was upon us. We heard the whistling of the engine and all who could ran to the hills. Among the passengers were two ladies, one of whom I think lived in Pittsburgh. . . .

"They heard the warning and ran out of the car, but it was muddy and they went back for their overshoes, and before they could get away, they were caught by the water and drowned. The next morning we found both of them cold in death. The lady from New Jersey had a bouquet which she had brought from Pittsburgh, and it was lying beside her."

Perhaps the most pitiful of all stories printed about the flood was this, appearing in the *World* for June fourth:

A pretty, pale little woman told part of her sad story today, as she nervously clasped and unclasped her hands and cried in a quiet, heartbreaking way. Years ago in the Virginia Valley, somewhere near Winchester, this sad little soul met and loved a hard-working, intelligent engineer named Fenn. They were married some years ago and came to Johnstown, where they had a neat, comfortable home. Fenn made good wages, their seven children were always well-clad, and their mother lived with her life concentrated upon them. On the afternoon of the flood, Fenn went to the butcher's and passed out of this short history into the waters.

When the flood came into the Fenn house the mother gathered her chicks in the parlor and told them not to be afraid, as God was there and would guard them. Up came the torrent and they went to the second floor, and again the little mother talked of hope and bade them be of good cheer, for papa would soon come in a boat and take them away. Up, up and up rose the water, and now the family were forced to the top story. The rooms were very low and soon the heads of the mother and children were beating against the ceiling.

"Mama," said the eldest child, a girl, "wouldn't it be better to go outside and die in the open air?"

"Yes, dear," said the mother. "We'll make a raft and all get on together."

She fought her own and her children's way to the window and opened it. She caught a piece of plank and on it put the eldest child with a hasty kiss and a "God bless you." Then she let it float away into the darkness. Six times were these frail barks freighted with precious cargoes and argosies of pious trust. The children were frightened, but obedience was part of their creed and they made but little protest. Now came the turn of the last child, Bessie, the four-year-old. One can fancy what it meant—the last and dearest. The mother put her on a plank.

"I loved them all," said the mother, "but I had two kisses for Bessie, for she was Tom's favorite, and was such a good child. She put her arms about my neck and said, 'You know you said God would take care of me always, Mama; will he take care of me now?'

"I told her He would, and she need not fear, and then she was carried away. 'I'm not afraid, Mama,' she called out and I heard her, although I could not see her, and that's all, except that the roof was torn off and I floated off on it, and some Italians saved me at Kernville, sixteen miles from here."

"And the children, Mrs. Fenn—I hope they all escaped?"

"We have found two of them dead, Bessie and George, and there is not a mark on Bessie's face. They're all gone, every one, eight of them [presumably meaning her husband as well] and I am going home to Virginia after all these years to rest and try to think."

The reporter for the New York *Herald*, walking through the streets, found material for this dispatch, sent for the issue of June fifth:

On the west side of the lower town one or two streets are left from the flood. They are crowded all the time with survivors. As I have gone among them I have heard nothing but such conversations as this, which is literally reproduced:

"Hello, Will! Where's Jim?"

"He's lost."

"Is that so? Goodbye."

Another was:

"Good morning, Mr. Holden; did you save Mrs. Holden?"

"No, she went with the house. You lost your two boys, didn't you?"

"Yes. Good morning."

Two women met on the narrow rope bridge which spans the creek. As they passed one said:

"How about Aunt Mary?"

"Oh, she's lost; so is Cousin Hattie."

It gives an outside listener a strange sensation to hear people talking thus with about as little emotion as they would talk about the weather. But the people of Johnstown have had so much to do with death that they think about nothing else.

## III

# NOW FOR OKLAHOMA

(St. Louis *Republic*)

---

Thousands wanted land in Oklahoma. The announcement of the proclamation by President Harrison opening the territory to homesteaders was forecast in a brief dispatch to the St. Louis *Republic* for March 23, 1889, reading:

At last the news comes from Washington that President Harrison will today issue the proclamation opening about 1,800,000 acres of land in Oklahoma. The boomers are reported flocking into the promised land as rapidly as ever, notwithstanding their recent eviction by the soldiers. They are said to have formed a secret league to kill those who shall inform on their violations of the bill under which the land is to be opened for settlement.

The proclamation fixed April twenty-second as the date for the land rush. The St. Louis *Globe Democrat,* on that day, included in its columns this dispatch, from its correspondent with the homesteaders:

*(Special Dispatch to the Globe-Democrat)*
Arkansas City, Kans. April 22—Few of the thousands of seekers of something for nothing, who have used this city as their last halting place prior to making the rush into Oklahoma, went to bed last night. They spent the night on the street, at the depot and in and out of hotel lobbies. Yesterday's influx of visitors was enormous. . . . The regular trains have had to run in sections. And this extra accommodation has not sufficed. The aisles have been crowded to excess, and the suffering of the cooped up speculators and

boomers must have been great.   Fortunately, there were very few women in the crowds. . . .

The depot was crowded all night and the sale of tickets kept steadily on, nine-tenths of those issued being to Guthrie and most of the balance to Arthur.   This latter is just five miles over the line, and as all trains will stop before leaving the Cherokee strip, the holders of tickets to Arthur propose to jump off at the line. . . . Everyone seemed to be talking, and there was a perfect babel, but the grand rush commenced about 6, when the people who had slept up town joined their less fortunate brethren.   Some carried absolutely nothing in their hands, evidently thinking they could do the rushing better for not being handicapped. . . . But a marked characteristic of the crowd was the great number of spades and axes carried. . . . The [railroad] company's arrangements to prevent a general rush to one train was to so arrange matters that no one could know which train could pass first, and the secret has been admirably kept.

The trip south commenced, amid shouting and cheering. There could not have been less than 5,000 men who failed to secure seats, although a score of flat cars had been fitted up with plank seats, which were crowded with eager boomers.

Two men got on the cowcatcher of a locomotive, but had to be removed.   On a later train, however, a man rode the whole journey of 89 miles on the cowcatcher. . . . There were only two ladies on the train. . . . Each had a light boomer's outfit and expressed confidence in the gallantry of the men to enable them to locate claims.   The conductor collected 1024 tickets on this train.

At 12:15 precisely there was a loud whistle from the engine, answered by a shout from the train, and we were in Oklahoma, at last.   Before the train had crossed the line 50 yards a man sprang off, regardless of the danger.   He fell pretty heavily, but was on his feet in a few seconds; collected his baggage, which he had thrown out ahead and was turning sods before the train was out of sight. . . . A little farther south a man had evidently just alighted from the mule which was standing by him, and whose pack he was unloading. So far it was just possible that every boomer seen had waited till 12 o'clock before he crossed the line, but squatters pure and simple now came in view. They sprang out of the woods on every side and it was evident from the appearance of some of them that they had been in hiding for weeks. . . .

When the word was given to advance at the north line, the boomers started forward at various rates of speed. All who desired to locate anywhere near the track in the north end of the Territory found themselves forestalled. Some turned back in disgust and others pushed farther on into the interior. But for absolute contempt of the President's reminder of the dangers of premature occupation, Guthrie takes the lead. It could not legally be reached by road in advance of the train, yet when the town site came in view, it was literally covered with lot claimants. . . . The location is well suited for a town. The railroad runs along a valley on the west of which is a creek, which forms a picturesque background to the depot. The town, or town site, is on the other side of the track, and the ground slopes gradually up to the summit of a little ridge. At the summit is the land office.

What happened when the train began to slacken beggars all description. Boys, middle-aged men and old fellows threw themselves off the platform and commenced a wild rush. They fell upon each other, scrambled to their feet and made off, some carrying their grips and others dropping everything in the eagerness of the chase. As the train went on toward the depot the passengers kept jumping off. . . . The town lot craze seemed to lend speed even to cripples. A man with a wooden leg was among the first to make the dangerous jump, and he held his own in the race. Not a passenger by this first train went past Guthrie, so that the population of the new city was increased by this rush to the extent of nearly 1,000. [The 1024 tickets mentioned previously evidently included those of newspaper correspondents.]

All roads seemed to lead to the land office at which a line over 100 yards long was already formed. For a second the runners paused.

Then they commenced a wild tear out east, and each man, as he found an unclaimed lot, proceeded to stake it out and hold it down. The process of securing the lots, as in general adoption, is simple in the extreme. First of all a stake is driven in the ground, with or without a placer attached, setting forth the name of the claimant. Then the new owner paces off the ground he proposes to occupy for a residence or business house. There is at least a charm of variety about the laying out of Guthrie. Some people contented themselves with 25 feet frontage, others took 40 feet, and others 50, but most of the claimants had a fair idea of where the streets ought to be and left the necessary space for them. . . . By the time the men on train No. 1 had each selected his lot the town site had extended away beyond the half section reserved and long before the majority had quit running, train No. 2 pulled in, quite as heavily loaded as its predecessor. The same process was carried out to the letter. . . .

Among those hurrying up the hill were two ladies, who succeeded in securing a claim each and will hold it. These ladies are from California. They are going into business at once. . . .

There was a considerable interval before another train arrived, but the third and fourth came in close together, each discharging its cargo of passengers to add to the astounding crush. The limits of the city kept on increasing, and by the time the fifth and sixth trains had unloaded the city extended far away to the distance. Altogether ten trains got in before 3 o'clock and making allowance for those who went on to Oklahoma City, there must have been at least 6,000 people in Guthrie three hours after the territory was legally opened for settlement. It was wonderful the manner in which disputes among the newcomers were settled in this early part of the proceedings. Sometimes half a dozen men would pounce on a lot simultaneously, or nearly so.

Each would commence to stake out, but after a little while a general agreement would be come to, and every applicant but one would rush off and secure an undisputed lot. There has been so far no unpleasantness of any kind.

Speculation in town lots commenced at once. Hacks met the trains and drivers shouted:

"This way for lots at a dollar apiece." .

For a dollar, lot-hunters were driven to vacant lots and left to get their dollar's worth themselves.

The St. Louis *Republic,* on the same date, reported that the first homestead entry at the Guthrie office was in the name of a Kansan—an old soldier, one Johnson. A general picture of Oklahoma was given in another story:

## AND SO IT CAME TO PASS

### The Beautiful Land of the Chickasaws
### Tilled by the White Man

Down in Oklahoma City, rival town site companies are preparing to enforce their respective claims with Winchesters and six-shooters, and in consequence an additional force of deputy marshals has been dispatched there to help preserve order. From the banks of the Canadian came vague, indefinite accounts of bloody encounters between old and new boomers, but owing to lack of telegraph service the reports cannot be confirmed. Everything is in confusion and turmoil. Forty thousand men are sleeping in the open air. Some of them are without even so much as a blanket to protect them from the night air. Thousands who are gathered at the station are bewildered and hardly dare to move out of sight of the troops and marshals. They are like men at sea on a raft without rudder or compass. The vast expanse of green plain offers them no relief or consolation. It is little more than a dreary desert in their eyes. Scores of them are penniless and are moving from tent to tent pitifully begging for something to eat. Many spent all they had to get to the beautiful land, and now, through an adverse fate, they are anchored to it as firmly as the tallest cottonwood.

The scrambling crowds poured over all the four borders. All were eager; all were determined. From the Cherokee Strip came the great fleet of schooners across the Canadian; from the Chickasaw Nation came troop after troop of sturdy ponies, each one carrying a boomer; from the Arapahoe and Cheyenne reservations on the west came a yelling mob of horsemen, who fired volley after volley to celebrate their final victory. The Kiowa of the southwest and the Cherokee and Creek nations on the east also furnished their contingent of boomers. Upon the northern line the boomers' wagons seemed to be less than 100 feet apart, and the whole line extended east and west from the railroad track as far as the eye could see. At the starting signal they moved all together as if propelled by a common force. The big draft horses lashed by their merciless drivers sprang ahead and the lumbering wagons rolled over the green turf with a speed that would have done credit to roadsters. Across the line they went all together, great waves of cheering breaking open the air. Guns were discharged—at first at regular intervals—and then volleys that sent the horses prancing ahead faster than before. There was no halting, no hesitation.

The wagons continued on over the level green plain until they were about halfway across the northern tier of claims, and then upward of 100 of them were brought to a standstill. The others rolled on to the lower tiers. Men, women and children poured from the stationary schooners, and, in an incredibly short time, the foundations of the pioneer homes of Oklahoma had been laid by willing hands. Every farm had more than one claimant, some had two or three, and others as many as 10. They are all ready to swear that they crossed the borders first and that theirs were the first

improvements. So it is, all over the Territory, and especially in the sections adjoining Guthrie and Oklahoma City.
The land offices will have many difficulties to decide before
the end of the week.

## IV

## FATHER TIME OUTDONE!

(New York *World*)

---

Nellie Bly, the great sob sister of the Nineties, became
famous through the efforts of the *World* and in spite of the
eloquent silence of the opposition press. When she completed
her trip around the world in seventy-two days, the other newspapers in New York paid no attention to her—she was a
*World* stunt, and as such to be ignored. But the *World* told
about it. On January 26, 1890, the morning after Nellie's
arrival, this story appeared:

A Monsieur Jules Verne, Amiens, France:
Mademoiselle Nellie Bly est arrivée à New York
aujourd'hui. Elle a fini son tour du monde en
soixante-douze jours, six heures et quelques minutes.
Le New York WORLD présente ses compliments et
désire votre opinion sur le voyage accompli. Réponse
est payée à votre discrétion.
DIRECTEUR DU WORLD

Amiens, Jan. 25—Jaimais doute du succes de Nellie
Bly. Son intrépidité le laissait prevoir. Hurrah pour
elle et pour directeur du "World"! Hurrah! Hurrah!
JULES VERNE

It is finished.
Sullen echoes of cannon across the gray waters of the bay
and over the roofs and spires of three cities.

People look at their watches. It is only 4 o'clock. Those cannot be the sunset guns.

Is some one dead?

Only an old era. And the booming yonder at the Battery and Fort Greene tolls its passing away. The stage-coach days are ended and the new age of lightning travel begun.

A little woman is stepping from the platform of a railroad train in Jersey City. Ten thousand eyes are on her. A mad crowd surges to and fro about her as if it would sweep her against the great grim wheels of the locomotive which whirled her thither. Men push and strain against each other in a struggle fierce as if it were for life and death. Hats are knocked off, eyeglasses vanish. Big policemen wave their locusts wildly, and are brushed about in that clutch of the eager, irresistible throng.

And amid all the tumult walks the little lady, with just a foot of space between her and the madly joyous mob. She is carrying a little walking stick in one hand and with the other waves her checkered little fore-and-aft traveling cap, and laughs merrily as her name is hoarsely shouted from innumerable throats. Tense faces stare from the long galleries that bend ominously beneath their awful load of humanity. The tops of passenger coaches lying on side tracks are black with men and boys.

Grimy railroad men, their smutty and bewhiskered faces wreathed in smiles, swing their dirty caps and cry hurrah to the little traveler. Policemen are almost at fisticuffs with the crowd there. From the balconies bunches of flowers are thrown into the struggling crowd.

But the little girl trips gayly along. The circuit of the globe is behind her. Time is put to blush. She has brushed away distance as if it were down. Oceans and continents she has traversed. She has tripped through war-trodden Europe, where the armies of centuries have tramped up and down in ceaseless and unavailing bloodshed. London has squinted sleepily at her from the fog. Paris has cried "Voilà!" Old Rome has breathed her its benediction. Naples has smiled out at her own Capri, and the blue Mediterranean which tossed the pious Æneas has kissed the prow of her bark and lulled her to sleep o' nights. The Pyramids with their hoary centuries have lifted up sleepy heads to wink at her. Suez has opened its gates to welcome her on to Aden. The Indian Ocean, China and Japan have ushered her ever eastward, and the great fatherly Pacific took her in strong, peaceful arms to hand her back to her native land.

Faster, ever faster. Her latest journey was her swiftest. She has turned the wildest dream of a French fiction-master into sober truth, and Nellie Bly's fact of today has made the fancy of a quarter of a century ago seem like a twice-told tale. And now she is home, a happy little heroine, with a sunburnt nose and a proud, glad heart. There are smiles and plaudits and love and fame for a welcome. . . .

One day last November the people knew that Nellie Bly, with all her former honors thick upon her, was going to undertake a new and gigantic task.

M. Jules Verne was credited with the most limitless of imaginations. It reach out to infinity, and took in the moon and all the planets. It plunged into depths of the sea which no McGinty could hope to fathom. Nellie Bly, THE WORLD said, was going to show M. Verne that he had not imagined half wildly enough; that this Puck of his, this globe-girdler, this Phineas Fogg, was a slow old poke.

So with an outfit made up to avoid the cumbersome delays of baggage travel, the young woman made a neat apology to Jules Verne, invoked the auspices of her stars and started.

On a bright November morning—it was the 14th—in 1889 she set sail on the steamship Augusta Victoria. Fond hands waved her goodbye, she steamed down the Narrows with all the world before her, and the great race against time and fable was begun.

Here is the itinerary Nellie Bly carried in her one solitary little grip-sack. It shows what she thought she might do. What has been done has outstripped her wildest anticipations!

Nov. 14—Leave New York by steamship Augusta Victoria, 9:30 A. M.

Nov. 21—Due Southampton; London by rail in three hours.

Nov. 22—Leave Victoria station, London, 8 P. M. on India Mail

Nov. 23—Calais, Paris, Turin.

Nov. 24—Brindisi, 10:14 P. M.

Nov. 25—Leave Brindisi, steamship Cathay, 2 A. M.

Nov. 27—Ismailia

Dec.  3—Aden

Dec. 10—Colombo, Ceylon

Dec. 16—Penang

Dec. 18—Singapore

Dec. 25—Hong Kong

Dec. 28—Leave Hong Kong for Yokohama

Jan.  7—Leave Yokohama for San Francisco by steamship Oceanic

Jan. 22—Due at San Francisco

Jan. 27—Due at THE WORLD office in New York.

Nov. 14 to Jan. 27—New York to New York—75 days.

And now she is home. The ghost of Phineas Fogg may sit and sip ghostly hot-Scotches somewhere in the realm of fancy, and sigh over his old age and his glory now outdone.

When Nellie Bly's honest little feet plumped down on the grimy planking of the Jersey City Station yesterday, she had made the tour of the globe in 72 days, 6 hours, 10 minutes and some seconds.

V

# THE FIRST ELECTROCIDE

(New York *World*)

The first man to pass through the little green door at Sing Sing did so on August 6, 1890. The manner in which the execution was carried out showed the backwardness of the last century: the State did not kill the man at all neatly, and the press was as a result outraged.

Executed was William Kemmler. Kemmler eloped with one Tillie Ziegler, another man's wife. In 1889, at Buffalo, he tired of this woman and sought to solve his amorous problem with an axe. The *World,* one of the leaders in the fight against electrical execution, spared no feelings when it described how this man had died, on August seventh:

The first execution by electricity has been a horror. Physicians who might make a jest out of the dissecting room, officials who have seen many a man's neck wrenched by the rope, surgeons who have lived in hospitals and knelt beside the dead and dying on bloody fields, held their breaths with a gasp, and those unaccustomed to such sights turned away in dread.

The doctors say the victim did not suffer. Only his Maker knows if that be true. To the eye, it looked as though he were in a convulsive agony.

The current had been passing through his body for fifteen seconds when the electrode at the head was removed. Suddenly the breast heaved. There was a straining at the straps which bound him, a purplish foam covered the lips and was spattered over the leather head-band.

The man was alive. Warden, physicians, everybody, lost their wits. There was a startled cry for the current to be turned on again. Signals, only half understood, were given to those in the next room at the switchboard. When they knew what had happened, they were prompt to act, and the switch-handle could be heard as it was pulled back and forth, breaking the deadly current into jets.

The rigor of death came on the instant. An odor of burning flesh and singed hair filled the room. For a moment a blue flame played about the base of the victim's spine. One of the witnesses nearly fell to the floor. Another lost control of his stomach. Cold perspiration beaded every face. This time the electricity flowed four minutes.

Kemmler was dead. Part of his brain had been baked hard. Some of the blood in his head had been turned into charcoal. The flesh at the small of his back was black with fire.

The editorial opinions of the various newspapers differed; the three following are typical:

### (New York *Press*, August 7, 1890)

It will not mend matters at all to say that there was ignorant bungling on the part of the executioners; that the first current was not kept on long enough or the third current too long. It was argued in behalf of this mode of execution that death was to be instantaneous, lightning-like, painless, and that the maudlin hero-worship attending the dramatic march of the nervy murderer to the scaffold was to be done away with, and a secret and mysterious taking off, devoid of sensational features, to be substituted. The act went so foolishly far as to prohibit the newspapers from publishing the details of such an execution—a prohibition which, by the way, they most properly and completely ignored yesterday. . . . The age of burning at the stake is past; the age of burning at the wire will pass also.

### (New York *Times*, August 7, 1890)

No doubt the advocates of this method of executing the death penalty are for the moment put upon the defensive, but they have not a failure of method to face. Nothing that they have claimed has been refuted. The first trial was of necessity an experiment and was not conducted with that care and coolness that was requisite to insure success. But it was made clear that with the current that had been recommended for the purpose, with appliance free from defect in construction and operation, and with a firm and confident application of the process, there could hardly be any question of instant and painless death. It would be absurd to talk of abandoning the law and going back to the barbarism

of hanging, and it would be as puerile to propose to abolish
capital punishment, because the new mode of execution was
botched in its first application.

(New York *World,* August 7, 1890)

The first experiment in electric execution should be the
last. Its result strongly condemns this method of putting
criminals to death as very cruel and very shocking.

The theory of unconsciousness from the first moment of
shock is at best a mere assumption. It was not sustained in
Kemmler's case by outward indications. Apparently the man
died in agony, by slow torture.

The effect upon the witnesses was sickening. The effect
upon the public is even more shocking, chiefly because of an
attempt to do this judicial killing by torture in secret and to
conceal the facts, whatever they may be, from the public in
whose name and by whose authority the killing was done.
The folly and wickedness of that attempt are sufficiently
emphasized by the result.

The electric execution law ought now to be repealed on all
accounts. So long as it stands, convictions for capital of-
fenses will be difficult to the point of impossibility. Juries
will not willingly condemn men to death by torture. So long
as capital punishment is maintained, old-fashioned hanging
is good enough, provided it is administered by trained and
skillful hangmen.

## VI

# THE ATTENUATION OF COXEY

(Washington *Post*)

---

Jacob S. Coxey was a figure of depression. He could be
likened to the other messiahs we have known in our own
time. Coxey's prescription for the curing of mankind's ills

was a Good Roads program, an unlimited currency and non-interest bearing bonds for public improvements. It occurred to Coxey in 1894 that the best way to present this plan to Congress would be to march there at the head of an enormous army —leaving Massillon, Ohio, on March 25, 1894, he predicted that one hundred thousand men would be at his back when he reached the steps of the Capitol. His army moved across the country and gave the newspapers much to print. Among its members was a youngster named Jack London, who had missed the Western Division under General Charles T. Kelly at Sacramento, and joined up at Council Bluffs after a chase on blind baggages and freight trains.

Coxey arrived in Washington, leading a ragtag army of a pathetically small number. The Washington *Post,* on April 30, 1894, the day before Coxey was arrested for walking on the Capitol grass, published a scornful summation of his achievements:

It may not be an heroic, but it is at least a comfortable consummation that the Coxey movement should have dwindled from a great moral crusade to a cheap catch-penny show. When Coxey set out from Massillon, Ohio, the country was given to understand that he proposed to impress the American people with a new theory of government, and to awake the Congress into adopting the theory by means of a popular demonstration at once tremendous and irresistible. Now, after some weeks of suspense and more or less apprehensive expectation, we are told that Coxey and his crowd are at last corralled in some enclosure just outside of town and used to stimulate business for a suburban railway. Advertised as prophets and apostles of a new and splendid dispensation, they turn out to be a collection of freaks and curiosities. Heralded as the evangelists and liberators of the generation, they show up as properties for a third-rate dime museum.

And while Coxey and his immediate retinue are being fenced in at Brightwood Park so as to prevent the populace from seeing the show without buying a ticket, the various contingents on their way to re-enforce the holy propaganda are receiving treatment anything but respectful at the hands of their fellow-citizens. Some of them, who seem to think they are entitled to help themselves to other people's property without reference to any of the vulgar formalities observed by ordinary human beings, have been gathered in by the police. Others, who have so far escaped the myrmidons of despotism, are the objects of an earnest and painstaking pursuit. And still others, who have so far done nothing to merit serious consideration, are meeting with a playful if somewhat contemptuous reception, which must make them question the reverence of those who extend it. Altogether, the much-talked-of Commonweal movement appears to have degenerated into a particularly forlorn burlesque. With one lot under arrest for grand larceny, and another in full flight from the constables; with a section here receiving a charivari at the hands of the college boys, and another there being held up for purpose of disinfection by the sanitary authorities; and, finally, with Coxey's own immediate Commonwealers safely caged for exhibition in a suburban resort like so many five-legged calves or wild men of Borneo, it really does begin to seem that the great moral demonstration of 1894 is likely to figure in history as the most ridiculous of humbugs.

It may possibly develop some more serious and dignified features later on. It may even attain the comparatively majestic proportions of a public nuisance and earn hard knocks instead of careless merriment. But just at present the Coxey apotheosis looks more like a fiasco than anything else we can think of.

# TWO STAR

CARRIE NATION

There came to our town an old pelican
Whose manner was scarcely angelican;
    To a man who sold beer
    She said: "Say, look here!
If you want me to save you from helican."
         *—Ironquill* in the Topeka *Capital*

# I

# THE MAINE BLOWN UP!

(Washington *Evening Star*)

---

Between February, 1895, and February, 1898, the United States watched with growing wrath (cunningly encouraged by Messrs. Hearst and Pulitzer) the struggle of the Cubans for independence. The feeling on the mainland was crystallized into the action that was the Spanish-American War, after a messenger had delivered to a sleepy Secretary of the Navy, at two A. M. on February 16, 1898, a telegram announcing the destruction of the battleship *Maine*.

Before this message was delivered—a full week before—the New York *Journal* published an ominous editorial:

> The relations between Spain and the United States are becoming so strained that the rumor that the Administration is worried over the approaching visit of the Spanish cruiser Vizcaya to New York is quite credible. If the Vizcaya got inside our line of defences and anchored in the North River just before Spain found it convenient to begin hostilities, she could give us several unpleasant hours before we could effectively call her to order.

> One way of providing against this danger would be to strew a few submarine mines at judiciously selected points in the North and East Rivers and assign the Vizcaya an anchorage over a nest of them. But a better way would be to bring the Cuban affair to a head before the arrival of the "friendly visitor" from Spain. Let the President recognize

the independence of Cuba and call upon Spain to withdraw her army at once. Then we shall know before the Vizcaya gets here whether we ought to salute her with blank cartridges or shell.

The news of the explosion reached morning newspapers in the East too late for full treatment in their columns. But the evening papers covered the event completely, as this story from the Washington *Evening Star* for February sixteenth testifies:

## THE MAINE BLOWN UP

### Awful Disaster to United States Battle Ship in Harbor of Havana

### Number of Killed or Missing, 253

### Lieutenant Jenkins and Engineer Merritt Among the Number

### Cause of the Disaster Unknown

### Question Whether It Was Accident Aboard or Blow Without

### Comment of Various Officials

The Secretary of the Navy received the following telegram from Capt. Sigsbee early this morning:

"Maine blown up in Havana harbor, 9:40, and destroyed. Many wounded and doubtless more killed and drowned. Wounded and others on board Spanish man-of-war and Ward line steamer. Send light house tenders from Key West for crew and few pieces of equipment still above water. No one had other clothes than those upon him. Public opinion should be suspended until further report. All officers believed to be saved. Jenkins and Merritt not yet

accounted for. Many Spanish officers, including representatives of Gen. Blanco, now with me and express sympathy.
(Signed)   SIGSBEE."

Later advices today place the number of killed and missing at 253, including Lieutenant Friend W. Jenkins, and Assistant Engineer Darwin R. Merritt. . . .

The Secretary immediately sent the following telegram in reply:

"Capt. Sigsbee, Havana: Deepest sympathy and anxiety. We await particulars and cause. Advise fully. Spare no efforts to relieve sufferers and learn facts.
LONG."

Secretary Long received the news with apparent calm, and his first act was to comply with Capt. Sigsbee's request that assistance be sent from Key West. He immediately wired Capt. Forsythe at Key West to proceed with the naval tender Fern to Havana harbor.

Secretary Long then sent for Capt. Dickens, acting chief of the bureau of navigation, and the two discussed Capt. Sigsbee's brief telegram giving news of the greatest disaster which has befallen the American Navy since the disaster at Apia,* many years ago. The Secretary is inclined to believe that most of the officers of the Maine were on shore at the time of the accident, as it was still early in the night. While neither the Secretary nor Captain Dickens are inclined to discuss the probable cause of the accident, several suggestions were ventured upon. They believe that it may have been caused by a fire in the bunkers, heating the bulkhead near a magazine, or that an accident may have occurred while inspecting high explosives for torpedoes. Of course, this is mere speculation, and the Secretary is anxiously awaiting a more detailed report from Captain Sigsbee.

Later the Secretary sent another telegram to Key West, directing that the tender Mangrove also be sent to Havana.

---

*At Apia, Samoa, on March 15, 1889, three United States and three German warships were driven ashore in a storm, killing fifty Americans and ninety-six Germans.

The orders for the lighthouse tenders were at once sent to Key West in plain language, thus avoiding the delay that would have arisen from the use of cipher.

Captain Dickens, after carrying out the instructions of Secretary Long, with regard to relief measures for the survivors of the Maine, went at once to the White House, where the President was aroused and informed of the disaster. President McKinley received the news calmly, and expressed his deep sorrow, but said nothing further except that he was thoroughly satisfied with the measures adopted by the Navy Department.

In an editorial called "Our Relations with Spain," the New York *Journal* on February eighteenth placed the blame where its editors thought the blame belonged:

The evidence accumulates that Spain, or at least some Spanish hand, has struck us a blow, cruel, cowardly and treacherous, as is fitting. A foreign paper, printed in New York, protests on this point:

"It is simply inconceivable that the Spanish authorities in Cuba, high or low, could have countenanced any plot to destroy the Maine. Make them out as wicked as you please, they are not lunatics; and official connivance in torpedoing the Maine, or in firing a mine under her would have been an act of madness, far more fatal to Spain than it could possibly be to this country."

Why would torpedoing the Maine be an act of madness? Because if brought home to the perpetrators it would cause a war in which Spain would be crushed? But what if the men who committed the deed cherished the belief, rampant in Havana, and prevalent in the highest official circles in Spain, that war was already inevitable? Would it not be desirable then to reduce the naval superiority of the United States as far as possible before hostilities began? Would it not be better to fight four battle ships than five? The chances of destroying the Maine in battle would be extremely slim.

To take an opportunity that would never come again of disposing of one enemy in advance would be deviltry, but anything but lunacy.

If the destruction of the Maine can be brought home to the Spaniards, war on that point will be inevitable. But the fate of the Maine, heartrending as it is, profoundly as it has moved the American people, is only an episode in a drama that would have moved more swiftly to its destined end without it. Intervention in behalf of Cuban independence was our duty before the Maine was destroyed; it was our duty before DeLome wrote his letter,* and it is our duty now. It has merely been hastened by events that have reached to the very bottom of the popular heart.

The patience of this nation has seemed illimitable. It has apparently been proof against the spectacle of a whole people dying in the tortures of a slow starvation. It has endured insults and injuries of every sort. It has allowed an impassive Executive to throttle all its generous impulses. But at last it had been tried too far. The American people are issuing their commands to their servants in Washington, heretofore seemingly their masters, in terms that cannot be misunderstood. From every State Capital comes the call to arms. This Union wants no war. That is why it is roused at last. It is resolved that peace shall be restored in Cuba and that the possibility of the repetition of such disasters as that to the Maine shall be dispelled. If Spain desires peace as ardently as we do, she will begin the evacuation of Cuba tomorrow.

In the same column, the paper defended itself against the critics, who were jeering at its heavily-typed page-one offers of fifty thousand dollars for the exposure of the bomber:

The Journal's offer of $50,000 for the detection of the persons, if any, criminally responsible for the destruction of the Maine has met with the usual reception. It has been

---

*Reflecting upon President McKinley, for which Ambassador DeLome was recalled by Madrid.

criticized by jealous New York newspapers and praised by the press of the rest of the world, as well as by the public everywhere. The papers of London, Paris and Berlin unite in generous recognition of the offer and its motives. The Paris Temps praises the Journal as "conspicuous in the American press for its enterprise." The Berlin papers call the proposition "the greatest piece of journalistic magnificence of the age." The Anzeiger says: "This generous offer of reward is the exponent of the noblest sentiments of loyalty and patriotism, and this departure in journalism cannot fail to create a sensation in both hemispheres" and adds the hope "that the Journal will succeed in finding the perpetrators of this dastardly outrage."

Meanwhile the Mail and Express hastens to brand the Journal's attempt to aid the government of its country in discovering facts of momentous importance as "a vulgar bit of self-seeking enterprise", and alleges that "no one connected with the conspiracy would betray it, because it would sound his death knell", and hints that the reward may be intended as a bait "to corrupt investigating officers."

Not with the chimerical idea of setting right malicious contemporaries that prefer to be wrong, but for the purpose of enabling the public and those to whom the offer is addressed to understand clearly what it is hoped to accomplish, the Journal deems it well to show why its reward may be expected to show good results.

There would be no object in attempting to corrupt the investigating officers. The Government's investigation can show nothing except that the explosion took place in a certain way. It can show that certain plates are bent outward or inward, but it can throw no light upon the question *who caused the explosion that bent them?* The Journal proposes to begin where the Government leaves off. It will find out, if possible, who carried out the plot and who planned it.

Even if the name of the informant were to be made public at once, there is no reason to suppose that fear of "going to his death" would deter him from claiming the fortune within his reach. Conspirators in all ages and countries have betrayed their comrades at the risk of their lives for much less than $50,000. Russian Nihilists, French Anarchists and Italian Mafists have turned informers knowing that death awaited them at every turn.

But in the present case no such sacrifice is asked. Unless it proves absolutely necessary to make known the name of the informant, to verify his information, his identity will be kept strictly secret. He will be able to' take his $50,000 and live in secure and luxurious seclusion in any part of the world he may select.

If the Maine was blown up intentionally, several men were engaged in the crime. The Journal offers any one of them $50,000 if he will furnish to it exclusive information that will lead to the detection and conviction of his accomplices. In a country where soldiers sell their cartridges to the enemy, it believes that such an offer will have great attractions. The Journal believes that if a crime has been committed this reward will uncover it, and in making the offer, it feels that it is rendering a patriotic service—the best one at present within its power.

And finally, to make its editorial day complete, the *Journal* published this statement concerning the *Vizcaya:*

The "accident" to the Maine has solved the problem of how to receive our "friendly visitor" the Vizcaya, if, as now seems unlikely, she shall insist on carrying out her original program. One accident of that sort is a sufficient strain on credulity. Another following immediately after would find no believers anywhere. For the sake of our national reputation no accident must happen to the Vizcaya while she is here. Consequently she must not be allowed to enter the upper bay, where miscreants with skiffs may beset her with infernal machines. Let her be safely anchored under the guns of the forts at the Narrows, and requested not to move out of range. We must keep her where we can give her efficient protection, if it takes every battery we have to prevent her from running into danger.

II

# RAIDED A JOINT

(Topeka *Daily Capital*)

---

The hatchet of Mrs. Carry Nation furnished much amusement for the newspapers and their readers in the early days of the century. From Kansas where she first practiced her "hatchetation" (her own abominable word!) she traveled widely, including in her tours visits to the model for all modern Sodoms—Manhattan. In the Topeka *Daily Capital* for December 28, 1900, there appeared a Wichita dispatch concerning her big-city raid:

Special to the Capital, Dec. 27—Mrs. Carrie Nation, president of Barber County Women's Christian Temperance Union, began today a raid on the saloons in Wichita. As a result of her work she is now under arrest and placed behind the bars at the county jail.

At 9:45 this morning she entered the saloon in the basement of the Carey hotel and without a word of warning pulled from a bundle of papers which she carried in her hands two large stones. Before the clerks and bartenders could realize what was going on, Mrs. Nation sent one of the stones whizzing through a large oil painting of Cleopatra nude at the Roman bath. The painting was valued at $100. As a result of the stone hitting the painting the picture is completely spoiled.

After damaging this picture, the woman suddenly turned herself about and with much force sent another large stone through a valuable $1,500 mirror which is situated directly back of the bar. She then left the saloon.

While in the saloon she also broke about $25 worth of bottled goods and also a window. As soon as she left the saloon she was arrested. . . .

Last night Mrs. Nation visited all the saloons in Wichita and demanded that they close their doors. She called at the Carey barroom last night where she saw this costly picture hanging on the wall. She told the bartender to remove it. The bartender refused to do so. Today, while the stones were being hurled, the bartender, Edward Parker, hid himself behind the bar.

Mrs. Nation, when seen by a reporter for the Capital, said:

"I am a law abiding citizen and I have not gone out of the bounds of the law. I have a husband who is a lawyer and he says they cannot prosecute me. . . ."

She dared the officers to place her in a cell. She said if they did, she would sue the city for false imprisonment. . . .

Members of the Women's Christian Temperance Union of Wichita who heard of the actions of Mrs. Nation say they do not approve of them, and believe there are other ways to shut up the saloons in Wichita.

Mrs. Nation was removed to the county jail tonight. . . .

"I came to the Governor's town," she said, "to destroy the finest saloon in it, hoping thus to attract public attention to the flagrant violation of a Kansas law, under the very eye of the chief executive of the state."

The damage done to the saloon is hard to estimate. It was finished with stucco secured from the World's Fair buildings and many blocks of it are shattered. The painting of Cleopatra cost Mr. Noble, its author, nine months' time painting it and was still his property, being rented by the saloon. It has been seen at nearly all the street fairs from Canada to the Gulf.

The *Capital* quoted Mrs. Nation at the jail:

"I came to Wichita expecting to get into trouble and here I am. I have brought my clothes and some eating along so as to be as comfortable as possible. . . . I studied the law and asked competent lawyers if I can be prosecuted for destroying the property of the jointists and they say I cannot for the reason that the saloon men here have no rights under the state laws. I telegraphed my husband this morning not to come here and interfere with my work, but to leave me alone."

The course of Mrs. Nation's fight for temperance started from the cause of the death of her first husband twenty-five years ago, who died from the result of delirium tremens. His name was Dr. Charles Glayd and she was married to him at Holden, Mo., against the wishes of her parents. . . . Word is received in Wichita that Mrs. Nation is well respected in Medicine Lodge. [Her home was in that community.] She is considered eccentric at some times.

Her next major offensive was against the blind tigers of Topeka. Mrs. Nation's war on the saloonkeepers was not all one-sided; she was rendered impotent and ridiculous by such retaliations as this, described in the *Capital* for February 5, 1901:

## MRS. NATION'S FIRST ATTACK
## REPULSED BY THE JOINTISTS

### They Stole Her Hatchet

### And It Now Adorns the Bar of the Big 803 Joint

It was a strenuous afternoon. . . .

At the Topeka Cash Store Mrs. Nation stopped and purchased half a dozen bright and shiny hatchets, paying therefor $2.50. She armed each of her followers with one, and the procession moved on, each woman carrying her hatchet in plain sight on her arm. By this time the crowd numbered 500. . . .

At Sixth street, the "Home Defenders" went directly to Murphy's place. . . . Mrs. Nation glanced at the window and raised her hatchet to throw it. A man behind her, who runs the roulette table in the gambling room at 803 Kansas avenue, reached over her shoulder and wrested it from her, and slipped away through the crowd with the hatchet under his coat. . . .

Mrs. Nation's hatchet, adorned with a blue ribbon, hangs over the bar in the joint at 803 Kansas avenue. Mrs. Nation wanted to swear out a warrant for the man who had taken it from her, but evidently forgot it in the rush of events.

The fame of the "Smasher" spread and she traveled. She did no smashing in New York, but under the wily guidance of the reporters she graced that city with two visits of equal lunacy. On August 29, 1901, her first tour was covered thoroughly in the *World's* best gibing manner:

Here is what Carrie Nation did during a six-hour stay on Manhattan Island yesterday:

Gave Police Commissioner Murphy the most uncomfortable quarter of an hour in his life.

Scared Chief Devery into dodging her.

Gave John L. Sullivan a bad attack of the frights.

Kept Acting Mayor Guggenheimer in a state of nervous agitation.

Had a row with her manager and left town, happy as a lark.

With a two-foot hatchet strapped to the girdle under her linen jacket, her beaded black poke bonnet pushed down firmly on her head, her broad jaw set at its most pugnacious angle, the Smasher strode into Col. Murphy's room at Headquarters at 11 A. M., plumped into a chair close to him and in ringing tones demanded:

"Don't you think New York is an awful bad place?"

"I don't think anything of the kind," testily answered the Colonel.

"Yes, it is," insisted the Smasher. "It's full of hell holes and murder factories."

"Stop right there. I don't want to listen to you or to hear that kind of talk in this place," almost shouted the Commissioner.

"You won't listen to me?" queried the Smasher in surprise. "Why I came here a-purpose to discuss these matters with you. Do you mean to say you won't discuss these murder shops, these hell holes, these sinks of depravity in New York?"

"That's just what I mean." . . .

"I only came here to do New York good. I want to do something for you."

"You don't know what you are talking about," said the Colonel in a rage. "Go back to Kansas. . . . You are not in your right mind."

"Do you think I am crazy?" shouted the now furious Smasher.

"Yes, I do." . . .

All this time Deputy Commissioner Devery was hiding in a corner where he could listen without being seen. As the Smasher went out she passed a man smoking a cigarette. Turning on him, she shouted:

"You horrid, nasty man! Don't you know that your fate will be an eternal smoking?"

"Now take me to see John L. Sullivan," said the Smasher to her manager. "He once said some mean things about me."

Up to the Forty-Second street saloon formerly owned by the ex-champion, the Smasher went. The saloon was recently closed, but John L. still has a room on an upper floor. A messenger took up word to the pugilist, who said:

"Not on your life. Tell her I'm sick in bed." . . .

Proprietor Caddigan, of the Hoffman House, was in a nervous frenzy last night. He did not know that Mrs. Nation had left the city, and jokers had told him she intended to invade the cafe at 9 P. M., smash the famous $10,000 painting "Nymphs and Satyr" and rip to pieces the $100,000 worth of art treasures. Mr. Caddigan posted a man at all the entrances until some one told him Mrs. Nation was on her way to Ohio.

On her second visit *The Sun* followed her about as faithfully as had the *World* on her first. This article was dated September 2, 1901:

> Carrie Nation came to town yesterday to lecture, and be stared at and the day furnished more excitement for her than any previous day she had had since she abandoned the saloon-smashing that made her famous. While it is true that the only thing she smashed was a house rule at the Democratic Club, she compensated by lecturing the bar-tenders of half a dozen saloons, visiting several dance halls, and being placed under arrest and being released again before she reached the police station.
>
> It was 10:30 yesterday morning when the Southwestern Limited puffed into the Grand Central Station, and Mrs. Nation, wearing a small-size reproduction of her famous hatchet across the front of her yellow traveling duster stepped out and strode the platform. . . .
>
> It wasn't a minute before the news of the arrival had spread through the station. Cabbies from all around the neighborhood ran to join those standing at the entrance and soon the familiar cries of "Keb, kerriage; keb, kerriage" were drowned by a swelling chorus of "Carrie! Carrie! Carrie!" The bane of the vineyard smiled her acknowledgements. . . .
>
> "Why, that Lake Shore line's nothing but a regular barroom on wheels," was the first remark Mrs. Nation made after reaching the hotel. "The smell of whiskey and cigarette smoke was something awful. They drank all day and they drank all night. Why, they mixed their toddies right under my nose. Yes, I spoke to the porter about it, but that didn't do any good. I tell you I was strongly tempted to perform a little hatchetation on them. And cigarette smoke? Phew! There was a young man named Straus who had a

private compartment right next to me and he did nothing but smoke cigarettes—with the door open—all the time. I told him to stop, but he wouldn't. Then I got up and shut the door. He opened it, and I shut it again. Finally I had to put my foot against it to keep it shut. Then he rang for a porter and told him to put me off the car. Of course the porter didn't do it." . . .

An open saloon on the southeast corner of Seventh avenue and Fiftieth street struck Mrs. Nation's fancy and she boldly entered the family door. Half a dozen workmen were in the back room eating sandwiches and drinking beer. Mrs. Nation remained calm.

"Well, well, well," she began, "so this is the way you hard-working boys spend your hard-earned money for poison!"

"It's the only pleasure we have, ma'am," said one of them.

Mrs. Nation stepped to the barroom door. The bar was lined with men drinking. A crowd had followed her and many members of it pushed their way inside.

"Isn't this against the law?" Mrs. Nation opened up on the bartender. "Where are the police, I'd like to know, that they allow such a criminal factory to keep open today? Aren't you satisfied to run six days in the week without selling your poison on the seventh?"

"Oh, mind yer business," said the bartender.

"This is my business. How would you like me to start smashing in here?"

The Kansas terror stepped around behind the bar and seized a whiskey bottle, but the hooting and jeering brought the proprietor.

"Damn it," he yelled, "git t'ell outer here!"


The *World* added to this the account of her arrest by three New York policemen:


A deafening medley of voices that merged into a terrific "Hurrah for Carrie Nation!" A mob of thousands, beating this way and that, tearing, trampling each other for a sight of that determined squat little figure, marching on with the exaltation of a conquering hero, and the Kansas smasher was steered straight into the arms of three burly New York policemen and promptly "pinched".

It happened at Devery's corner, Twenty-eighth street and Eighth avenue, at 5:30 yesterday afternoon. The dauntless Carrie unmolested had:

Precipitated a riot in three saloons.

Invaded two Sunday concert halls.

Paraded the highways and byways with a tumultuous rabble at her heels.

It was only when she invaded the district of the Big Chief that the arm of the law became effective.

"I am not disturbing the peace," asserted Mrs. Nation indignantly, whisking about in her Quakerish linen gown with its quaint cape, and fixing on the bluecoats an invincible eye.

"You are raising a crowd and creating a riot, and I arrest you," was the response of one of her captors. . . .

At Twenty-fourth street, satisfied by Mrs. Nation's friends that she was about to return to her hotel, the policeman released her and put her on a car amid a volley of "Hurrahs".

The Smasher's progress down Broadway was a veritable triumphal procession. . . .

"Take me to some more hell holes," she demanded of her escort. Darting into a saloon at Twenty-ninth street and Sixth avenue, she cried:

"Ain't this against the law? Where are the police? I am Carrie Nation, and I protest against the selling of that hell-broth."

"We are selling lemonade," insisted the barkeeper.

"Lemonade!" echoed the reformer scornfully. "It's beer!" and walking over to a table where some sailors were drinking, she seized one of the steins and took a sup. "I know the taste of beer as well as you do, and you men are disgracing Uncle Sam's uniform every drop you drink." . . .

At the Apollo Music Garden—the French quarter of Eighth avenue, with a legend that reads *"Entrée libre au Café Chantant"*—she went in search of women sinners, but quiet reigned and an irritable proprietor turned her out of his "private house".

# FIVE STAR FINAL

"LINDBERGH FLIES ALONE"

Alone?

Is he alone at whose right side flies Courage, with Skill within the cockpit and Faith upon the left? Does solitude surround the brave when Adventure leads the way and Ambition reads the dials? Is there no company with him for whom the air is cleft by Daring and the darkness is made light by Emprise?

True, the fragile bodies of his fellows do not weigh down his plane; true, the fretful minds of weaker men are lacking from his crowded cabin; but as his airship holds her course, he holds communion with those rarer spirits that inspire to intrepidity and by their sustaining potency give strength to arm, resource to mind, content to soul.

Alone? With what other companions would that man fly to whom the choice were given?

—*The Sun,* New York,
May 21, 1927

# I

# FLYING MACHINE SOARS THREE MILES

(Norfolk *Virginian-Pilot*)

---

It is only yesterday that such devices as the China Clipper, flying from San Francisco to Manila in five days, were considered undangerous dreams only if written by the engaging Jules Verne. And it is only an hour or two ago that the brothers Wright, in their lonely test field on the Carolina sand dunes, hurled their suicidal box kite into the air and kept it there.

The Norfolk *Virginian-Pilot* was the one newspaper in America to cover this flight seriously and thoroughly. Its reporter, who tried to sell his story to other papers, found many of them too skeptical to buy it. The story was published on December 18, 1903, the morning after Wilbur Wright immortalized himself as the first man to fly; it was complete; nothing that could help it can be added three decades later:

The problem of aerial navigation without the use of a balloon has been solved at last.

Over the sand hills of the North Carolina coast yesterday, near Kitty Hawk, two Ohio men proved that they could soar through the air in a flying machine of their own construction, with the power to steer and speed it at will.

This, too, in the face of a wind blowing at the registered velocity of twenty-one miles an hour.

Like a monster bird, the invention hovered above the breakers and circled over the rolling sand hills at the command of its navigator and, after soaring for three miles, it gracefully descended to earth again, and rested lightly upon the spot selected by the man in the car as a suitable landing place.

While the United States government has been spending thousands of dollars in an effort to make practicable the ideas of Professor Langley, of the Smithsonian Institute, Wilbur and Orville Wright, two brothers, natives of Dayton, O., have, quietly, even secretly, perfected their invention and put it to a successful test.

They are not yet ready that the world should know the methods they have adopted in conquering the air, but the Virginian-Pilot is able to state authentically the nature of their invention, its principles and its chief dimensions.

The idea of the box kite has been adhered to strictly in the basic formation of the flying machine.

A huge framework of light timbers, 33 feet wide, five feet deep and five feet across the top, forms the machine proper.

This is covered with a tough, but light canvas.

In the center, and suspended just below the bottom plane, is the small gasoline engine which furnished the motive power for the propelling and elevating wheels.

These are two six-bladed propellers, one arranged, just below the center of the frame, so gauged as to exert an upward force when in motion, and the other extends horizontally to the rear from the center of the car, furnishing the forward impetus.

Protruding from the center of the car is a huge, fan-shaped rudder of canvas, stretched upon a frame of wood. This rudder is controlled by the navigator and may be moved to each side, raised or lowered.

Wilbur Wright, the chief inventor of the machine, sat in the operator's car, and when all was ready his brother unfastened the catch which held the invention at the top of the slope.

The big box began to move slowly at first, acquiring velocity as it went, and when half way down the hundred feet the engine was started.

The propeller in the rear immediately began to revolve at a high rate of speed, and when the end of the incline was reached the machine shot out into space without a perceptible fall.

By this time the elevating propeller was also in motion, and keeping its altitude, the machine slowly began to go higher and higher until it finally soared sixty feet above the ground.

Maintaining this height by the action of the under wheel, the navigator increased the revolutions of the rear propeller, and the forward speed of the huge affair increased until a velocity of eight miles was attained.

All this time the machine headed into a twenty-one mile wind.

The little crowd of fisher folk and coast guards, who have been watching the construction of the machine with unconcealed curiosity since September, were amazed.

They endeavored to race over the sand and keep up with the thing in the air, but it soon distanced them and continued its flight alone, save the man in the car.

Steadily it pursued its way, first tacking to port, then to starboard, and then driving straight ahead.

"It is a success," declared Orville Wright to the crowd on the beach after the first mile had been covered.

But the inventor waited. Not until he had accomplished three miles, putting the machine through all sorts of manoeuvres en route, was he satisfied.

Then he selected a suitable place to land and, gracefully circling, drew his invention slowly to the earth, where it settled, like some big bird, in the chosen spot.

"Eureka!" he cried, as did the alchemist of old.

The success of the Wright brothers in their invention is the result of three years of hard work. Experiment after experiment has been made and failure resulted, but each experiment had its lesson, and finally, when the two reappeared at Kitty Hawk last fall, they felt more confident than ever.

The spot selected for the building and perfecting of the machine is one of the most desolate upon the Atlantic seaboard. Just on the southern extremity of that coast stretch known as the graveyard of American shipping, cut off from civilization by a wide expanse of sound water and seldom in touch with the outer world save when a steamer once or twice a week touches at the little wharf to take and leave government mail, no better place could scarcely have been selected to maintain secrecy.

And this is where the failures have grown into success.

The machine which made yesterday's flight easily carried the weight of a man of 150 pounds, and is nothing like so large as the ill-fated "Buzzard" of Potomac River fame.

It is said the Wright brothers intend constructing a much larger machine but before this they will go back to their homes for the holidays.

Wilbur Wright, the inventor, is a well-groomed man of prepossessing appearance. He is about five feet, six inches tall, weighs about 150 pounds and is of swarthy complexion. His hair is raven hued and straight but a piercing pair of deep blue eyes peer at you over a nose of extreme length and sharpness.

His brother, Orville, on the other hand, is a blonde, with sandy hair and fair complexion, even features and sparkling black eyes. He is not quite so large as Wilbur, but is of magnificent physique.

The pair have spent almost the entire fall and winter and early spring months of the past three years at Kitty Hawk working upon their invention, leaving when the weather began to grow warm and returning in the early fall to work.

Their last appearance was on September 1st, and since then they have been actively engaged upon the construction of the machine which made yesterday's successful flight.

There was no apparatus used in yesterday's test to give the machine a starting velocity. From the top of an inclined plane, constructed upon a hill of sand, the start was made.

For several years, flying provided the world with an entertaining spectacle, not to be taken too seriously. Barnstormers appeared, and lifted their ungainly crates into the air from state fairgrounds. The true practicality of the heavier-than-air flying machine remained to be proved; and it was, in the spectacular demonstration of a Frenchman, in 1909. The New York *Times* offered, on July twenty-sixth of that year, M. Bleriot's account of his passage across the English Channel:

## BY LOUIS BLERIOT

DOVER, England, July 25.

At 4:35 "all's ready". My friend Le Blanc gives the signal and in an instant I am in the air, my engine making 1,200 revolutions, almost the highest speed, in order that I may get quickly over the telegraph wires along the edge of the cliff.

As soon as I am over the cliff, I reduce speed. There is now no need to force the engine. I begin my flight, steady and sure, toward the coast of England. I have no apprehensions, no sensation—pas du tout—not at all.

The Escopette [French navy escort] has seen me. She is driving ahead at full speed. She makes perhaps 42 kilometers (26 miles) an hour. What matters it? I am making at least 68 kilometers. Rapidly I overhaul her, traveling at a height of 80 meters (260 feet). Below me is the surface of the sea, disturbed by the wind, which is now freshening. The motion of the waves beneath me is not pleasant. I drive on.

Ten minutes are gone. I have passed the destroyer and turn my head to see whether I am proceeding in the right direction. I am amazed. There is nothing to be seen—neither the torpedo boat destroyer nor France nor England. I am alone; I can see nothing at all.

For ten minutes I am lost; it is a strange position to be in—alone, guided without a compass in the air over the middle of the channel.

I touch nothing, my hands and feet rest lightly on the levers. I let the aeroplane take its own course. I care not whither it goes.

For ten minutes I continue, neither rising nor falling nor turning—and—then, twenty minutes after I have left the French coast, I see green cliffs and Dover Castle, and away to the west the spot where I had intended to land.

What can I do? It is evident the wind has taken me out of my course. I am almost at St. Margaret's Bay, going in the direction of Goodwin Sands.

Now it is time to attend to the steering. I press a lever with my foot and turn easily toward the west, reversing the direction in which I am traveling. Now I am in difficulties, for the wind here by the cliffs is much stronger and my speed is reduced as I fight against it, yet my beautiful aeroplane responds still steadily.

I fly westward, chopping across the harbor, and reach Shakespeare Cliff. I see an opening in the cliff. Although I am confident I can continue for an hour and a half, that I might, indeed, return to Calais, I cannot resist the opportunity to make a landing upon this green spot.

Once more I turn my aeroplane, and describing a half circle, I enter the opening and find myself again over dry land. Avoiding the red buildings on my right, I attempt a landing, but the wind catches me and whirls me around two or three times. At once I stop my motor and instantly my machine falls straight upon the ground from a height of 20 meters (75 feet). In two or three seconds I am safe upon your shore.

Soldiers in khaki run up and policemen. Two of my compatriots are on the spot. They kiss my cheeks. The conclusion of my flight overwhelms me.

This ended my flight across the Channel—a flight which could easily be done again. Shall I do it? I think not. I have promised my wife that after a race, for which I have already entered, I will fly no more.

The transatlantic fliers, with their incredible and not very beneficial achievements of the Lindbergh-Byrd-Chamberlin era, were not yet born, some of them, when an explorer named Walter Wellman embarked upon a fantastic and heroic exploit. With a crew of five men (and a cat for luck) Wellman started from Atlantic City in a dirigible, on October 15, 1910, heading for Europe. With rare foresight, he equipped his ship with Marconi's new wireless device, with which he kept in communication with ships and the mainland for the first two days of his voyage. On the sixteenth, he spoke the Nantucket station; on the seventeenth he was silent; and on the eighteenth he was discovered by the *S.S. Trent* to have been silent for the sufficient reason that he was derelict in the Atlantic. *The Sun* (New York), had a word for Wellman on its editorial page for October nineteenth:

Count Zeppelin, who has devoted nearly forty years to the study of aeronautics and has designed many powerful dirigible balloons and sailed many miles in them, would never dream, we are sure, of attempting to cross the Atlantic in any airship he has as yet constructed.

What the future of aeronautics will be is only conjecturable, nothing certain can be known about it. The problem of retaining for several days the gas distending the envelope is still unsolved, as Sir Hiram Maxim has pointed out. A thoroughly reliable motor has not been invented. The propeller and its shaft are more or less fragile, since weight has to be considered, and in spite of its great size the whole fabric is insecure. Most of Count Zeppelin's flights have been disappointments to him. The motor has failed to work satisfactorily, or some part of its complicated mechanism has got out of order and it was necessary to descend to make repairs. He has also had experiences that were almost tragic in high winds. With the experiments of this great inventor and navigator in mind, we never regarded very seriously Mr. Walter Wellman's undertaking to cross the Atlantic in a dirigible balloon. When the *America* was released from its hangar and launched into the fogs of the Atlantic without a preliminary trial, it was not easy to believe that Mr. Wellman had started for Europe in sober earnest. But the mad enterprise had begun, inevitable defeat was being faced, and the risk of drowning was taken.

Mr. Wellman and his loyal crew should have credit for great daring; perhaps it was the courage of desperation; but, whatever it was, it excites a certain admiration, although we do not think compliments are in order, except for a safe issue from a foolish adventure. We congratulate Mr. Wellman upon his escape—not even the *America's* cat was sacrificed.

## II

# HEART IS TORN FROM MIGHTY CITY

(Los Angeles *Times*)

At his breakfast plate that morning, the San Franciscan had his favorite newspaper—the *Call,* the *Chronicle* or the *Examiner*. In the one of these to which he subscribed, there was to be found the usual grist of a morning journal: crime in the way of a jewel robbery, minor accidents of one sort or another; building permits; editorial wisdom; deaths and progress. If he read the *Examiner* by choice, he could learn from its informed columns that the committee chairmanned by the enterprising journalist, William Randolph Hearst, had obtained $23,344 for the relief of the sufferers in Naples, who had seen their city devastated ten short days before by Vesuvius' deadly lava. (Being a San Franciscan, the reader of the

*Examiner* would feel justifiable pride that his city was fourth in all the land, with contributions of $2,223.)

From his window, he could see the Golden Gate and the majesty of the city's hills. He could glance again at his paper, and recall last night's *Carmen,* and agree with Ashton Stevens, critic of the *Examiner,* who felt that Caruso's "Don José" had made the performance.

Thus, an average San Franciscan on April 17, 1906.

Within twenty-four hours, a hotel manager in New York was to walk into a convention gathered in secret session, and without a word of apology for his intrusion say, "Gentlemen, San Francisco has just been destroyed by a fire."

By some miracle of journalism, the combined staffs produced, on the morning of the nineteenth and while the city was still dissolving into fire-blackened junk, a *Call-Chronicle-Examiner* extra. It was an excellent job of emergency publication, but one must travel nearly five hundred miles for an objective view of what had happened: to Los Angeles and the *Times* of April nineteenth:

SAN FRANCISCO, April 18—(Special)—During six hours of mortal dread and nameless terror, San Francisco was today tossed upon the seismic waves of the most disastrous earthquake known to the history or traditions of America's west coast. In the mad confusion and helpless horror of this night uncounted bodies of dead men and women are lying in morgues and under uplifted walls. It is believed that nearly 1000 lives have been lost. The number cannot fall far short of that, and it may prove to be much greater. Fire and flame have added to the destruction, the ruination and despair. The material losses are beyond computation. Wounded and hurt inexpressibly, the chief city of the West lies at this hour humbled to the dust, blackened, battered and charred, her glory of yesterday but a hideous dream, and the moans from her stricken heart filling the pitying world.

The first shock came while still the mighty city lay deep in slumber, weary with the revelries and pleasures of the night before. In the quiet homes, in the crowded hotels, men had not yet awakened to the strifes and endeavors of the new-dawned city. The stars had but waned, and the morn was just breaking through the mists and fogs that hung in gray curtains across the waters of the placid bay and over the waiting hills. In through the Golden Gate were blowing the first piping winds; with the greeting of the sea to the green-clad heights and flower-strewn fields that skirted the shores and stretched away into the dim distances beyond. The sailors still slept in their hammocks in the harbored ships. A few wan-eyed wanderers of the night were stealing through the streets, a few early toilers were astir. But that was all.

Then came the rumble of deep thunder from the mighty bowels of the startled earth. The city shook like an aspen leaf, and her gray highways suddenly cracked and split as though the batteries of Satan and his upper hell had been opened against them from underneath. Along shore the wharves warped and creaked and the rakish shacks of the water front fell like stacks of cards. The hills of Sausalito and Piedmont, the Oakland heights and the dim bluffs of San Jose rocked like forests in the wind. The waters of the bay were whipped into lashes of white foam against the Barbary Coast. The clock in the tall tower of the Ferry Building stopped as though the spirit of a demi-god were passing. The majestic structures of steel and stone that reared their domes against the sky along Market street and up and down Montgomery and the other splendid thoroughfares that line and intersect the mart-crowded town, swayed and swung like pendulums. Then the batteries from below broke forth again, and still again. Shock followed shock, as though the enemy that lay masked beneath the buttresses of the earth were determined to annihilate the city by storm.

Rude was the awakening from the slumber-bound night—rude and cruel with messages of death and doom. Into the rent and reeling streets men, women and children rushed, half-clothed, with blanched faces and white and speechless lips. The mighty terror that they had sometimes dreaded and had often laughed at was face to face with them at last. Their black day of trouble had come, indeed. In the paralysis of fear and in the dumb grip of an unspeakable horror they will lie down tonight with the now dead friends of yesterday.

There is no witness of this day's story whose tongue or pen can describe the wreck and ruin, the death, the doom, the despair and suffering that lies on every hand. All through the horror-stricken hours the living hunted for the dead. Deeds of human bravery, countless and beyond praise, have been performed. The police, firemen and private citizens have vied with one another in rendering that service which nothing can repay. Heroes without number have leaped into the jaws of death to save their fellow human beings, and in more than one instance sacrificed their lives in the vain effort to save others. Death and sorrow have leveled all differences, social or otherwise. Saint and sinner are huddled alike in the gloom of this sad night, the same grief tugging at the heart of each. The holy men of the tabernacles and the ungodly denizens of the shadows walk side by side, the same livid fear blanching their lips. Lady of quality and woman of the slums, the vestal virgin and the painted harridan are weeping their tears together.

Fair and beautiful, from thrice her seven hills, the city of St. Francis yesterday looked down upon the sunset sea. Tomorrow she will lie a blackened, ruined thing, the pity of the world. Her shining streets, buttressed with towering structures of granite and marble and brick, hooped with steel and bolted with iron, are riven as though by the hand of devastating demons. Generation after generation, she builded with infinite care and tireless patience until the sons of the four winds came to look upon her loveliness and the wonder of her beauty. But in the space of a few short hours she has been undone. Tonight there stands no keeper at the Golden Gate. From tower and dome and window there gleam no lamps of welcome. No song creeps out upon the mirroring waters. Where life was, there is now death. The dead are at peace, but the living stand with sleepless eyes, waiting for the dreaded dawn of another day.

By the next day, the *Examiner* had found type and presses and paper, and went into the ghosts of streets with a magnificent edition, containing page after page of fresh, staccato news. It was not a well-written paper, except in spots, and it was garishly over-displayed, with its enormous headlines, but from two of its stories a complete picture of what had happened to the city could be obtained. The first of these stories, on page one, announced that:

The destruction of San Francisco is complete.

At the time of going to press the flames had leaped over Van Ness avenue and were whirling out Broadway, devouring everything in their path. When the people heard that the efforts to stop the fire at Van Ness avenue had failed they lost heart. It now looks as though practically every building in the city save a few on the water front and some south of the park will not be standing within twenty-four hours.

Already two-thirds of its great buildings have been converted into heaps of charred timbers and streamers of bent and twisted steel. Miles of its dwellings throughout the districts south of Market street, the Western Addition and Nob, Russian and Telegraph Hills have been swept away. The waste of ruin stretched over the Mission district and reaches from Townsend street to the Presidio. Practically everything east of Van Ness avenue has been wiped out.

But far worse than the destruction of the buildings is the condition of the 300,000 homeless gathered in the city's public squares and parks.

The problem of feeding these unfortunates must be solved immediately. They must have bread and meat and drink. Already Congress has appropriated $1,000,000 toward a relief fund. All of the towns of consequence throughout the country are contributing within their means to alleviate the sufferings of the helpless victims of the fire. Sacramento is sending a steamer load of bread and meat. The Los Angeles Examiner has sent a relief committee to care for the injured, and also a boat filled with provisions. Oakland was among the first to offer substantial aid. Unfortunately, San Jose, Santa Rosa and other neighboring towns have been rendered powerless to furnish outside relief. In a smaller way they are as badly off as San Francisco.

All day yesterday and through the night the flames made terrifying progress. They carried everything before them in their sweep from Jefferson Square to the Presidio. The historic mansions of Nob Hill and the glorious Fairmount Hotel offered little or no resistance. The Hopkins Institute of Art passed out of existence like a tinder box. The old Stanford Home gave little more resistance. The mad rush of the flames over Russian Hill and throughout North Beach was appalling.

The only hope the fire fighters held out was that if the flames could be stopped at Van Ness avenue, a portion of the residence district might be saved. But it was only a half-hearted hope and few regarded it seriously.

The estimated property loss is without limit. It easily exceeds $200,000,000.

At an early hour yesterday morning the throng of homeless gathered in Union Square were forced to abandon their improvised tents and couches when the flames got hold of the surrounding buildings. The campers in Jefferson Square met a like fate.

From dawn to nightfall famine prices prevailed. Bread brought 75 cents and a dollar a loaf. Soda crackers sold for five and ten cents each. Canned goods that under ordinary conditions bring ten cents were disposed of at $1 apiece.

The soldiers did excellent guard duty and forced a number of recalcitrants who refused to assist the fire-fighters to join the heroes at the point of their revolvers.

A number of thieves were shot and killed by the Federal troops.

On a back page, C. E. Van Loan wrote what he had seen:

San Francisco, city of the Argonauts, is nothing but a memory. Through the red haze of a hundred fires, the tottering ghost of its once fine buildings look down on a burning city. Between sun and sun every great block in the business section was destroyed. A roaring, seething hell of flame swept its way from the ferry station westward, and the magnificent fire department of San Francisco, pitifully handicapped by lack of water and scarcity of dynamite, was forced back to the residence district, fighting every inch of the way. It was a bitter warfare, but the odds were with the fire fiend. All night long the losing battle continued, until firemen dropped exhausted in the street, still clinging to the nozzles which they refused to desert. So the flames crept over the hill from Kearny street.

South of Market there is nothing but desolation. Not a building stands in that dreary waste of smoking ruins, and miles to the southwest dozens of marching smoke columns mark the destruction of the Potrero and the Mission.

At nine o'clock the fire was threatening Nob Hill and its dozens of historic residences. Here the firemen made one last desperate stand. Down the hill as far as the eye could reach the city was afire. The rumbling crash of dynamite told that the department was fighting the advance all along the line, but it was on Nob Hill that the real battle took place.

From six o'clock in the morning an engine and crew of men watched the Mark Hopkins Institute of Art. The fire was all around it at eight o'clock, but still the firemen refused to give up. For three hours longer the fire fighters held the fort.

At eleven o'clock the big building was a seething mass of flames and the firemen sullenly retreated into California street, dragging their engine after them. The fire had won.

At ten o'clock the official heart of the city had been moved out to the North End Police Station. Here the Mayor met the committees and conferred with the citizens, and from this point went the kegs of powder with which the fire department hoped to make an end of the burned district at Polk street.

The people of San Francisco slept out of doors that awful first night. For the almost unbelievable thing about it all is that they did sleep. Women, worn out with hysteria; men overworked to the breaking point, dropped down to the streets of that burning city and slept. Some of them lay on the porches, wrapped in blankets, but for the most part they slept in the open air, and not even the sight of a greater than the Chicago fire could rouse them. They had seen the Palace Hotel writhe and drop back into its bed of ashes; they had watched the skyscraper section crash into chaos, carrying millions of dollars with it. They had seen the worst, so they went to sleep. When the fire came too near, the soldiers roused the sleepers and they arose, rubbed red eyes, took a careless look at the terrible panorama, yawned once or twice and went away to find another untenanted doorstep.

At two o'clock in the morning, the streets were filled with men and women making their way to the ferry. The only route was down Broadway and thousands tramped it that night, dragging their trunks behind them. A very few favored ones had horses and wagons, but some of the horses dropped dead in the streets, because since Wednesday morning there had been no water for them. But the ninety and nine trudged down old Broadway, carrying all their earthly possessions on their backs, for there was no other way. They left their houses to burn—and left them without a backward glance. Women hushed their babies in the shadow of the Ferry Building and the mere rumor that a boat was about to go out brought cries of thanksgiving.

They wanted to get away—anywhere. . . . Toward noon the patrols began to break into grocery stores in the doomed district.

"They'll be burned anyway," said the officers. "Let the people have a chance to get something to eat."

And let me tell you what I saw on Ellis street. I saw women with diamonds on their fingers and pearls about their throats begging a big sergeant of the guard to allow them to go into those stores for just one can of green corn. I saw a woman wrapped in sealskins eating baked beans from a tin can, and with her fingers, too. These were women of refinement. Money they were plentifully supplied with, but money will buy nothing in this stricken city these two weeks to come. I saw men—well dressed men—scrambling like children for handfuls of walnuts tossed out of a wrecked fruit store. All that was left was a sack of walnuts. Those men came near fighting for them. I saw one man creep away by himself to eat his walnuts out of his hat. Plenty of money—money, everywhere, but no food.

This is the truth: the people of San Francisco are hunrgy; inside of two days there will be another gaunt spectre to deal with—starvation.

San Francisco—great, generous-hearted San Francisco— is hungry. The city which has never failed to answer the cry of the needy, the city which sent the first trainload of supplies thundering to Galveston, the city which last week was raising a mighty fund for the Naples sufferers—this city is hungry.

Now let the response be swift, for hunger is swift, and these people have already been thirty-six hours without any sort of a food supply.

—EPITAPH—

. . . Hope and industry cannot be burned nor drowned. They are immortal because the world lives on them. The rebuilding of Chicago began in the winter when the temperature was below zero and the bricks were laid in hot mortar. Here nature smiles on us. Let us smile back and put our hands to the task of building, not rebuilding. We have finished Revelation and now go back to Genesis. . . .

San Francisco *Call*
April 23, 1906.

## III

# "YOU RUINED MY WIFE," THAW CRIES

### (*The Sun,* New York)

---

We have been made familiar with the setting (those of us who cannot remember it for ourselves) by the thoughtfulness of Hollywood. There were, on the Madison Square Garden roof that June night, champagne bottles in shiny buckets and gentlemen in tailcoats. The ladies were dressed in the Gibson Girl manner. There was the robust gaiety of the Floradora period—too much eating, too much wine, and entirely too much of what passed for stage humor. Into this setting stepped Harry Kendall Thaw, the Pittsburgh playboy, in neat evening dress complete with pistol. *The Sun,* on June 26, 1906, told in detail the story of Stanford White's murder:

Stanford White, the architect, was shot and killed instantly last night by Harry Thaw, of Pittsburgh, on the roof of the Madison Square Garden at the performance of "Mamzelle Champagne", a new musical summer show that opened last night.

Mr. White had been spending the evening at the Manhattan Club and went over to the roof garden to see how a theatrical performance would go on top of this big building which he himself designed.

It was 11:05 o'clock when Mr. White arrived at the roof and was escorted to a table and chair about two feet from the stage on the left hand side. A sextet billed as the "Big Six" were dancing and singing in the chorus of a song that Harry Short was leading in.

A tall young man walked down the aisle between the tables at this time, and, approaching White, drew a revolver.

Raising it with great deliberation to the level of his shoulder, he fired one shot and then, after a short interval, two more close together. A host of persons in the house saw White roll from his chair to the floor, toppling over the table in front of him as he did.

While a few in the audience had recognized Thaw as he came down the aisle, and others had observed White when he came in, the majority of those in the audience thought at first that the shooting was some sort of horseplay in connection with the show.

After he had fired the shots Thaw looked down at the prostrate form of the architect and said,

"You deserve this; you have ruined my wife!"

Thaw, after the shooting, walked leisurely to the back of a clump of potted shrubbery and around behind toward the elevator.

Lionel Laurence, the stage manager of the show, knew that the shooting wasn't part of the show, and he told this fact to Fireman Druddy and Policeman Debs, who were on duty on the roof. Just as Thaw approached them, Druddy knocked the revolver from his hand and grabbed him.

Thaw was very pale; but otherwise cool. He made no attempt to resist the fireman and the policeman and willingly stepped into the elevator and was hustled downstairs.

Meanwhile the people in the audience on the roof had come to the realization that a tragedy had taken place, and then came wild panic. Policeman Debs, as soon as he reached the ground floor, telephoned for ambulances and extra policemen. Two ambulances were sent to the Garden and the reserves from the Tenderloin station were hurried over.

A doctor in the audience had made his way to the side of Mr. White and saw at a glance that he was dead. He and the ambulance surgeon, who arrived soon afterwards, said that the architect had been killed instantly.

Harry Stevens, who has the bar privileges at the Garden, happened to be sitting at the same table with White. He says that the first shot missed the architect. There were two bullet wounds found in the left breast.

The attendants at the Garden, assisted by cool headed men in the audience, worked heroically to prevent a panic. A stampede to the elevator and stairways had started, but the excited ones were fully convinced that there was no danger and took their time in getting out. After the three shots had been fired the show ended then and there.

Thaw, led by Policeman Debs, was walked to the Tenderloin station. News of the shooting had spread to the street and a crowd quickly formed at Thaw's heels. He walked with his head bowed and said nothing during the time consumed in reaching the station house. He was very pale, his face matching the broad shirt front of his evening clothes.

At the station house, when arraigned before the sergeant, Thaw gave his name as John Smith, of 18 Lafayette Square, Washington, D. C. and said that he was 18 years old and married. He refused absolutely to make any statement or answer questions as to his identity. In his pocket were found numerous articles engraved with his initials and a card case full of cards bearing the name "Harry Kendall Thaw".

Thaw was placed in the back room of the station house, and stretched himself out on a bench. The police did not put him in a cell and said they would let him remain in the back room until the arrival of the Coroner and a representative of the District Attorney. Thaw asked the police to send for lawyers F. W. Longfellow and Lewis L. Delafield. He said he would make no statement until he had conferred with them.

The body of Mr. White was removed from the roof garden and taken to his residence in Gramercy Park.

Stanford White was the son of Richard Grant White, the
distinguished author and critic.   He was born on November 9, 1853, in New York city and was educated in public
schools, supplemented by private tutors. . . .

Among the buildings designed by Mr. White is the house
in Madison avenue built for the late Henry Villard, but
recently occupied by Whitlaw Reid, now Ambassador to
Great Britain.   Mr. White also designed the Madison Square
Garden, in which he was killed, the Century and Metropolitan Clubhouses, some of the principal buildings of the
University of New York and the University of Virginia.

He also designed the architectural work to be used in
connection with the statues of Augustus St. Gaudens, notable
among which are the Farragut statue in Madison Square and
the Lincoln statue in Chicago.   The Memorial Arch in
Washington Square was also his work.   He designed it in
1889.   He has also made numerous designs for book covers,
as well as those for the covers of the Century and Scribner's
magazines. . . .

Harry K. Thaw has got considerable notoriety in the past
few years, chiefly because of the events leading up to his
marriage with Florence Evelyn Nesbit, the artist's model.

He first began to get before the public about three years
ago when he gave a dinner in Paris which was said to have
cost $25,000.   At it was got together more fair women than
even the Bohemia of Paris ever saw in one place before.

For his extravagances he has been mainly dependent on
his mother, Mrs. William Thaw, of Pittsburgh, who is a
strict Presbyterian.   Under his father's will he was to get
only $2,500 a year until he should be 35 years old.   His
mother made his income $80,000.

Miss Nesbit, whose mother is Mrs. Charles J. Holman, of
Pittsburgh, was well known here as a model.   She drifted
to the stage and was a flower girl in "Floradora".   Thaw
met her about that time.

Two years ago she went abroad to study music and Thaw followed her.

Last summer he was arrested in Switzerland for speeding his auto and it was reported at the time that he was accompanied by "Mrs. Thaw," a woman of unusual beauty.

Word came last fall that Harry Thaw and Evelyn Nesbit had registered at the Carlton Hotel in London as man and wife. Shortly afterward they came to New York on the same steamer but in different apartments.

They got here on November 3, but refused to say whether they were married or not. They went to the Hotel Cumberland, where Thaw refused to register her as his wife. He was allowed to stay there that night, but had to occupy a room on another floor. In the morning he still refused to write "and wife" on the register, and they were told to leave the hotel before noon. They left.

A friend took care of Miss Nesbit and Thaw went to Pittsburgh. The family had something to say to him. It was generally understood that the family ultimatum was to leave Miss Nesbit or get along on $2,500 a year. There were reports of an offer of $25,000 to Miss Nesbit to give him up.

Anyhow, a settlement of some kind was effected, for on April 4, Thaw and Miss Nesbit were married in Pittsburgh in the study of the Rev. William L. McEwan, pastor of the Third Presbyterian Church. Mrs. William Thaw witnessed the ceremony and after it kissed her daughter-in-law. The other witnesses were Joseph C. Thaw, a brother, and Mr. and Mrs. Charles J. Holman, stepfather and mother of the bride. Since the wedding, the Thaws have furnished very little space for the newspapers.

It then came out that this was really the couple's second marriage, which had to be performed before Mrs. Thaw would agree to continue his income of $80,000. It is presumed that the first marriage was in London. Mrs. Holman had this notice published in a Pittsburgh newspaper:

Re-Married in Pittsburgh

Mr. Harry K. Thaw and Florence Evelyn Nesbit, on Tuesday, April 4, at 5 P. M. at the parsonage of the officiating minister, the Rev. W. L. McEwan. There were present Mr. and Mrs. C. S. Holman (Mrs. Holman is the mother of the bride) and Mrs. William Thaw and Josiah C. Thaw (mother and brother of the groom).

Harry Thaw was prominent in the marriage of his sister, Alice Cornelia Thaw, to the Earl of Yarmouth, a few years ago. The Earl was a friend of his, and he stuck out for the match against the opposition of the rest of the family. He was booked to give the bride away at the ceremony, but didn't show up, and a younger brother took his place. It was said that he was angry because of the marriage settlement upon which the Earl insisted.

The Thaws are one of the wealthiest families in Pittsburgh and one of the most religious. Harry was brought up strictly. From the time the boy passed 14, he was guarded by companions whose only instructions were to keep him from evil influences and the girls.

Two days later, with a flavor now known to us only in parody, the Pittsburgh *Post* told of "THEIR FIRST MEETING":

New York, June 27—The girlhood of Florence Evelyn Nesbit ended so early; the joyousness of her childhood was so soon taken out of her life, that few think of her ever as "yet a child and still unknown to fame" but, paradoxical as it may seem, it was that same sweet child of a struggling lawyer and his modest, unassuming wife who was brought to the attention of the artistic and pleasure-seeking world.

It was when her mother, proud of her wonderfully beautiful daughter, took her to a photographer for her first real pictures that Evelyn Nesbit flashed into public view. The pictures were so perfect in feature that the artist exhibited them in his studio.  Little wonder that Charles Dana Gibson, then in the zenith of his fame, looked upon Evelyn's photograph in rapture and wished immediately to meet the original and arrange, if possible, to have her pose for him.

The meeting was arranged and as a result Miss Nesbit became one of Gibson's most successful models.  His "Eternal Question" which adorns the walls of half the dens and studios of the country is perhaps the most exquisite thing that the artist ever drew, and it was Evelyn Nesbit from whom he gained his inspiration.

One day the little model was about to leave the studio when she was met by a man on his way in.

"By jove, Gibson, who is this little vision of the Empyrean blue?  Tell me!  I must know the little sprite!" the man cried.

The usual unconventional studio introduction followed.  The man who gazed in admiration at the flowerlike beauty of the young girl was Stanford White, the architect.

Soon she was esconced in a high-class apartment hotel—alone, away from her mother—and Stanford White paid the bills and was a constant visitor to the magnificently appointed apartment.

There she lived in ease and the artist-architect brought his men friends to see this girl, and he boasted that she was his "by right of discovery".

Finally, a stage career was mapped out for her; White managed it and Evelyn Nesbit's fame spread as she flaunted her lithe form and graceful beauty in the "Floradora" sextet.

It was at this time that Harry Thaw made her acquaintance.  The late hours and the endless, restless round of pleasure had told upon the fragile girl, and she fell ill.

A European trip was planned for her, and Stanford White was one of the party.  In a few weeks they returned to New York and Evelyn was sent to a boarding school, where White hoped that she would regain her health sufficiently to reappear upon the stage.

At this time Evelyn was a mere slip of a girl, just 16, with a wealth of golden hair and great brown eyes. It was in Mrs. Henry C. de Mille's select school that White chose to have his "ward" educated.

It soon began to be whispered that Evelyn Nesbit was a soubret, and exceptions were taken to the visits of Stanford White and Harry Thaw and other men of their type.

One day White went to the school in a big touring car and invited some of the pupils for a ride. During that ride, his conversation was of such a nature that three of the girls insisted on being permitted to alight and to return to the school on foot.

This caused such an uproar in the school that Evelyn was asked to leave. Just then she was prevented from going by an attack of appendicitis.

During her illness, Thaw was indefatigable in his attentions. When the girl was forced to leave, Thaw was there to defray whatever expenses had been incurred.

White, meanwhile, had deserted the girl and refused to pay her tuition which then amounted to $3,000. He declared he was Evelyn's guardian by courtesy only.

His failure to keep his word to defray the girl's expenses was a severe blow to Mrs. de Mille whose school was forced to suspend.

In the meantime, Thaw, who had been since he had first met the girl, desperately in love with her, took her back to her mother and told her of his love, and begged her to take Evelyn to Europe as his guest. It was in Paris sometime later that he married the girl who had been left friendless by the man who had claimed her "by right of discovery".

# DR. COOK'S CONFESSION

(New York *Times*)

Nineteen Nine was enlivened by the polar controversy of Dr. Frederick A. Cook and Robert E. Peary. Cook announced on September 1, 1908, that he had reached the North Pole on the preceding April twenty-first. As he was retelling his enthralling story to Danish scientists in Copenhagen, on April 6, 1909, Peary wirelessed from his camp that he had been successful and intimated strongly that Cook had lied. The New York *Herald,* a leader in the original journalistic acclaim for Cook, hastened to press on the seventh with:

Tidings flashed from the bleak coast of Labrador by Robert E. Peary that on April 6, 1909, he had reached the North Pole, electrified the civilized world yesterday as kings of Europe were lionizing Dr. Frederick A. Cook, another American, who a year before the date had won in the same battle with the inhospitable Arctic realm.

Names of two intrepid explorers who reached the goal of a thousand years and planted at the axis of the world the Stars and Stripes are proclaimed by the trumpet of fate within a few days and all the earth is ringing with their praises and with congratulations to the land of their birth.

News from Mr. Peary was so sudden that when it first began to come through the channels of communication those who received it were scarce able to realize its meaning. From Indian Harbor, in the exuberance of his joy in again coming in touch with his fellow countrymen, Mr. Peary telegraphed the news of his success to the Associated Press, to his wife at South Harpswell, Maine; to Herbert L. Bridgman, secretary of the Peary Arctic Club, and to the

New York Yacht Club, whose burgee his vessel, the Roosevelt, was even then flying at her masthead. A member of his expedition, H. B. McMillan, of Worcester, Mass., also sent some messages.

The intelligence girdled the earth and Dr. Frederick A. Cook, fêted in far Copenhagen, was one of the first to send a congratulatory message, for he asked that the Herald convey his congratulations to Mr. Peary upon his success.

Laconic as were those of Dr. Cook, were the messages which Robert E. Peary sent to apprise his countrymen that he had reached the end of many an arduous journey over the frozen floes. There was in them the succession of dramatic suspense, indicating that he was not unaware of the announcement that on April 21, 1908, Dr. Cook unfurled the Stars and Stripes where one man, by a single step, changes hemispheres.

For a year and a half, Dr. Cook stuck to his guns. Then, with too much doubt present in his world, he impelled the editors of the New York *Times* to write this editorial, on December 1, 1910:

## DR. COOK'S CONFESSION

After mature thought, I confess that I do not know absolutely whether I reached the pole or not. This may come as an amazing statement, but I am willing to startle the world, if, by so doing, I can get an opportunity to state my case. By my case I mean not my case as a geographical discoverer, but my case as a man. Much as the attainment of the north pole once meant to me, the sympathy and confidence of my fellow men mean more.

Fully, freely, and frankly, I shall tell you everything— and leave the decision with you. If, after reading my story, you say, "Cook is sincere and honest; half crazed by months of isolation and hunger, he believed he had reached the pole; he is not a fakir," then I shall be satisfied.—DR. FREDERICK A. COOK in Hampton's Magazine for January.

DR. COOK's arctic state of mind, due to cold, hunger and suffering, spreads before us a most engaging panorama of aberration. Far away to the left we see a low ridge of unauthenticated land, rising abruptly from the Arctic Ocean. We see dog trains, sleds, packs and pemmican, pressure ridges, and pen leads. Over the remote north hangs a cloud; it veils the pole. The square object, half concealed amid icy blocks off to the right is, of course, the box of missing records at ANORATOK. Through the fog of Crown Prince Gustav Sea we dimly descry the figure of Capt. LOOSE. It is night. The lamp but half reveals his face as he bends over his heroic tasks of revising the data. Then a council chamber appears. Men of grave mein gathered about a table are examining the celebrated records. They have long white hair, which they occasionally tear, plucking out a handful or two now and then to denote their interest in astronomic records such as never before came within their learned ken. They are the Faculty of the University of Copenhagen. Behind and above them towers Mount McKinley. Upon its peak stands the great explorer, proudly wearing his wreath of roses and brandishing what appears to be a brass tube. There are other figures, other details in the composition, but these are enough.

DR. COOK's forthcoming contribution to psychiatrical literature is a confession and an appeal for consideration and sympathy. It should be followed by an apology. The Doctor certainly owes an apology to the New York Herald and to that part of the American press and the public which was through it deluded into an acceptance of his polar story.

V

# UNIONIST BOMBS WRECK THE TIMES!

### (Los Angeles *Times*)

---

It was at one o'clock in the morning, when good burghers were in their beds and the streets were given up to policemen, reporters, prostitutes, and other more or less respectable specimens of the night, that the first of six detonations shook the city of Los Angeles. The roar was still echoing against the surrounding hills when houses began to empty of their alarmed inhabitants. The sufficiently curious, who went to the scene of the explosions, saw the gray stone building of the Los Angeles *Times* partly blown apart and with what remained standing etched in flames. Thus ended twenty lives, given up on the battleground in the war between capital and labor.

In 1890, the Typographical Union of Los Angeles struck for higher wages. Publishers made settlements of one sort or another, and in a few days the strike was ended. Ended, that is, except in the shop of the doughty General Harrison Gray Otis, publisher of the *Times,* who replied to labor's threats by forever banishing union men. For twenty years thereafter, the *Times* dedicated itself to unending war against the unions. The bombing of the plant, to which the brothers McNamara, J. J. and J. B., pleaded guilty and went to San Quentin, occurred on October 1, 1910, as the final edition of the paper was being put to bed.

Students of labor's struggles may write of the causes, defeats, victories and treasons of the campaign in Los Angeles. But to the compiler of a scrapbook, no story that appeared about the explosion could exceed in interest this document against violence, published in the *Times* itself on October third:

New York, Oct. 2—But a few minutes previous to the explosion in Los Angeles, a message had been received from the news editor of the Times there to the news editor of the New York Times, stating that the Los Angeles Times was planning to issue a special extra giving the details of the Vanderbilt Cup Race at Mineola.

"Send us a good account of the race. At the crack of the pistol begin sending the actual scenes on the track, describing in detail any accidents as they occur," the message read. . . .

Operator R. L. Sawyer was selected as the man to copy the dispatch, for he was considered one of the best telegraphers on the Coast.

At 4:00 A. M. came the last message from the paper, giving final instructions. It was also the last message from Operator Sawyer, the last he will ever send.

At 4:03, but an instant after this message had been finished, a harmless little click snapped over the wire and it went open.

"Wire open," cried the operator in the New York Times office to the editor, who was busy but a few feet away, compiling the first dispatch for the then annihilated and famous Pacific Coast paper.

"Get after them quickly," was the editor's reply. "No time can be lost now; here's the first installment about ready."

But before he could hardly get these words out of his mouth, the main office of the Western Union at Los Angeles, which connects the wires to the newspaper loops, came in and cut the paper loop off. That, of course, closed the circuit again, and simultaneous with its closing the New York Times operator started calling "TS", the sign letters for the Los Angeles Times office. He had made but a few calls when the wire chief at the main office came in on the circuit and informed him that he would never raise that office again, and "poor old Sawyer," as he mournfully put it, "will answer no more calls."

He stated that the paper had been blown up by a bomb and that the building was then lying a mass of ruins. . . .

# ALL STAR FINAL

" . . . The loss of the said ship was due to
collision with an iceberg, brought about
by the excessive speed at which the ship
was being navigated."
—The London *Times*

# I

## TITANIC HITS ICEBERG?

(New York *Times*)

---

For this, the concluding major event in the period of which this book treats, the author deems it fitting that he should step aside entirely, and let the story of the *Titanic* be told precisely as the reporters told it. It is an exciting story, and it begins in—

(London *Times,* April 11, 1912)

The propelling machinery consists of the same combination of reciprocating engines and turbines as is fitted in the Olympic, and in view of the modifications introduced in the propellers of the latter vessel after she had been in service, with the result of increasing her speed, it will be interesting to see whether the Titanic, in which no doubt these improvements have already been embodied, will show still better results.

(London *Times,* April 12, 1912)

The White Star Liner Titanic on her maiden voyage to New York, left Queenstown yesterday. She had a good passage from Cherbourg and arrived at the Irish port shortly before noon. On her departure at 1:30 she had on board 350 saloon, 200 second and 740 third-class passengers, 903 crew and 3,814 sacks of mails.

(New York *Times,* April 15, 1912)

## TITANIC HITS ICEBERG?

Montreal Hears of an Accident to the
New White Star Liner

Montreal, April 14—The new White Star Liner Titanic is reported in advices received here tonight to have struck an iceberg.

(New York *Herald,* April 16, 1912)

In the darkness of night and in water two miles deep, the Titanic, newest of the White Star fleet and greatest of all ocean steamships, sank to the bottom of the sea at 20 minutes past two o'clock yesterday morning.

Despatches received late last night from the Cape Race wireless station in Newfoundland and admissions reluctantly made at the same time by the New York officials of the White Star Company warrant the fear that of the 2,200 persons who were aboard the great vessel when she received her mortal wound in collision with an iceberg, more than 1,500 have gone to their death in her shattered hulk, while 675, most of whom are women and children, have been saved.

Should these grim figures be verified, the loss of the Titanic—costliest, most powerful, greatest of all the ocean fleet—while speeding westward on her maiden voyage, will take rank in maritime history as the most terrible of all recorded disasters of the sea. . . .

The first reports of the disaster, received early yesterday morning, indicated that the Titanic had been in collision with an iceberg not long after 10 o'clock Sunday night. It appears, therefore, that this most splendid of modern steam power creations, equipped with every device for the safe-guarding of life at sea, remained afloat only a little more than four hours after she sustained the mortal thrust. . . .

Of the conditions which made the disaster possible, as little definite information is available as is accurate knowledge of its terrible results. It is a natural assumption that such a collision could not happen except in a dense fog. The HERALD'S weather service station, at Cape Race, N.F., reported that at noon yesterday the weather was fair and that a fresh wind was blowing from the west. The temperature was slightly above the freezing point, recording thirty-three degrees fahrenheit.

The barometer at that time registered 30.20 inches, indicating an absence of fog.

### (San Francisco *Chronicle,* April 16, 1912)

New York, April 15—Wealth aggregating something like half a billion dollars is represented by seven of the passengers on the Titanic. If calamity befell only a few of these, even, it would materially affect the vast business enterprises in the United States and England. The seven are:

Colonel John Jacob Astor—$150,000,000.
J. Bruce Ismay—$40,000,000.
Colonel Washington Roebling—$25,000,000.
Isador Straus—$50,000,000.
George D. Widener—$50,000,000.
Benjamin Guggenheim—$95,000,000.
J. B. Thayer—$10,000,000.
Total—$420,000,000.

If the fortunes of the first-class passengers alone were placed together they would easily make $1,000,000,000.

### (*The Sun,* New York, April 16, 1912)

On her maiden trip, the Titanic, built and equipped at a cost of $8,000,000, a floating palace, found her graveyard. Swinging from the westerly steamship lane at the south of the Great Banks of Newfoundland to take the direct run to this port, she hurled her giant hulk against an iceberg that rose from an immense field drifting unseasonably from the Arctic. Running at high speed into that grim and silent enemy of seafarers, the shock crushed her bow. Through rent plates and timbers water rushed so swiftly that her captain, E. J. Smith, the admiral of the White Star fleet, knew there was no hope of saving her. That much the faltering wireless has told us, but its confused and fragmentary whimperings left blank the story of the few hours that the doomed vessel staggered among the icebergs.

When she went down she carried with her, it is feared, two-thirds of her people. The women and children had been lowered in the small boats, these and a few men, less than 700 in all, which appear to have been picked up by the Virginian and transferred to the Carpathia. But whether the Virginian saved others besides these was not known last night. No word had come from that ship to the White Star line or to the wireless stations along the coast.

The officials of the White Star line were struggling all night to get into communication with the Carpathia and learn the names of some of those who were or who were not on board. All they could get by wireless was the fact that the Carpathia, which left New York on April 13, for the Mediterranean, was retracing her course to this port, bringing here the mournful cargo of women and children. The Marconi stations were striving also to get in touch with either the Carpathia or the Allan liner Virginian to find out if all those rescued were on board the Carpathia or whether the Virginian carries others that were saved. But they were unsuccessful and it is not positively known whether the Virginian transferred all those she picked up to the Carpathia. The Carpathia should reach here some time on Wednesday afternoon.

Staggering in the ice field into which she had driven, the Titanic sped call after call to the hurrying liners of the upper roads—the Cunarder Carpathia, the Virginian and the Parisian, of the Allan line, the great Baltic, the Good Samaritan of the Atlantic, and the big Germans that were ploughing their way between the continents. And the wireless once more proved its worth, for the Carpathia and the Virginian, wheeling in their courses, sped through the night, venturing unknown dangers, and raced up in time to save the lives of all those who were known to be safe.

It has been many years since the world was left in such suspense and dread as followed the first faltering calls for help from the crushed Titanic. At 10:40 P. M. on Sunday night, the Virginian, speeding on her way to Glasgow, picked up the White Star steamship's insistent, frantic C Q D, the Marconi signal of distress and peril that clears the air of all lesser messages and that turns ships at sea out of their courses. Dash by dash and dot by dot, the wireless operator of the Virginian caught the cry for help:

"Have struck an iceberg. Badly damaged. Rush aid."

Seaward and landward, J. G. Phillips, the Titanic's wireless man, was hurling the appeal for help. By fits and starts—for the wireless was working unevenly and blurringly—Phillips reached out to the world crying the Titanic's peril. A word or two, scattered phrases, now and then a connected sentence, made up the messages that sent a thrill of apprehension for a thousand miles east, west and south of the doomed liner. Other rushing liners beside the Virginian heard the call and became on the instant something more than cargo carriers and ocean greyhounds. The big Baltic, 200 miles to the eastward and westbound, turned again to save life, as she did when her sister of the White Star fleet, the Republic, was cut down in a fog in January, 1909.* The Titanic's mate, the Olympic, the mightiest of seagoers save the Titanic herself, turned in her tracks. All along the northern lane, the miracle of the wireless worked for the distressed and sinking White Star ship. The Hamburg-American Cincinnati, the Parisian, from Glasgow, the North German Lloyd Prinz Frederick Wilhelm, the Hamburg-American liners Prinz Adelbert and Amerika all heard the C Q D and the rapid condensed explanation of what had happened.

---

*The first great sea rescue resulting from a wireless distress call. The *Republic*, rammed by the *Florida* off Nantucket, and sinking fast, flashed a C Q D; the *Baltic* responded, saving fifteen hundred persons. Wireless, when it carried the death cries of the *Titanic* to the world, was still a mysterious novelty to the average person.

But the Virginian was nearest, barely 170 miles away, and was the first to know of the Titanic's danger. She went about and headed under forced draft for the spot indicated in one of the last of Phillips' messages—latitude 40:32 N. and longitude 61:18 W. She is a fast ship, the Allan liner, and her wireless has told the story of how she stretched through the night to get up to the Titanic in time. There was need for all the power of her engines and all the experience and skill of her captain. The final fluttering marconigrams that were released from the Titanic made it certain that the great ship with 2,180 souls aboard was filling and in desperate peril.

Farther out at sea was the Cunarder Carpathia, which left New York for the Mediterranean on April 11, and which had felt the chill in the air which all sailors know means the proximity of ice. Round she went and plunged back westward to take a hand in saving life. And the third steamship within short sailing of the Titanic was the Allan liner Parisian, away to the eastward, on her way from Glasgow to Halifax.

While they sped in the night with all the drive that steam could give them, the Titanic's call reached to Cape Race and the startled operator heard at midnight a message which quickly reached New York:

"Have struck an iceberg. We are badly damaged. Titanic, Latitude 41:46 N., Longitude 50:14 W."

Cape Race threw this appeal broadcast wherever his apparatus would carry.

Then for hours, while the world waited for a crumb of news as to the safety of the great ship's people, not one thing more was known save that she was drifting, broken and helpless and alone in a waste of ice. And it was not until seventeen hours after the Titanic had sunk that the words came out of the air as to her fate. There was a confusion and tangle of messages—a jumble of rumors. Good tidings were trodden upon by evil. And no man knew clearly what was taking place in that stretch of waters, where the giant icebergs were making a mock of all that the world knew best in shipbuilding.

## (*The Sun,* New York, April 19, 1912)

The Titanic had been making good time and everyone on board was happy in the hope of making New York in record time. The ship had worked beautifully. Sunday was calm and clear. There was no moon as the night fell, but it was perfectly clear. The sea was smooth. No icebergs had been sighted during the day or evening, at least none that were in a dangerous distance of the ship.

The Titanic was making twenty-two knots an hour as the night fell upon the seas. The passengers promenaded the decks in the evening, gathered in the lounging rooms or smoking rooms. There was music in the music rooms and some singing. They had not begun to retire for the night at 10 o'clock, except for a few women and children. The beautiful night kept many on deck. . . .

There was a watch set forward and in the crow's nest. These men had powerful night glasses. They kept a careful watch on the sea ahead. So far as they could see, there was no ice near the ship. But at 11:57 there loomed up directly in the path of the Titanic an enormous iceberg. It was of a color almost of the water itself. It could not be perceived one moment, but the next it was seen to be a mountain towering at least 100 feet above the sea and almost the area of a city block.

There was only time for the men in the crow's nest and the watch forward to shout "Ice ahead!" and for the quartermaster to bring his wheel down hard, when the Titanic smashed into this big berg. First came a smash on the port side forward, which split the berg and ran the Titanic into the berg itself, after which there was a heavy crash to the starboard. The Titanic had split off a part of the berg that was above the water. Hundreds of tons of ice were in this way precipitated on the forward upper deck. The Titanic, it was afterward discovered, had literally climbed up on all that part of the berg that was under water and below her keel, tearing loose the entire forward part of the immense ship below the water line.

The collision had ripped out plates forward, had buckled the keel and in fact had caused water to flow into every forward bulkhead of the ship.

Men came out of the smoking room asking: "What the devil was that? Did we hit something?" Women in the various lounging rooms, grill room and music room said, "Mercy! What could that have been?" There was no excitement. The electric lights did not even flicker at this time and it was more in the perfunctory manner of people who were bored and wanted something to divert themselves that they arose in a leisurely way and walked out on the upper decks to see what it was. They could see stewards walking rapidly about and they stopped them and asked them what was the matter, only to get a reply: "I don't know. We may have run into a little bit of ice, perhaps."

It was at 12:25 that Captain Smith, who had returned to the bridge, transmitted orders through Chief Officer Murdock that all persons should be assembled on the upper deck. Four hundred stewards and kitchen men immediately rushed through the ship, from lower to higher deck, summoning all persons on deck. There was yet no excitement. Women arose leisurely under orders to dress themselves in their warmest clothing. One woman who was rather indignant at being awakened was half way to the deck when she remembered that she had not locked her trunk. She returned and performed this service and climbed leisurely to the upper deck.

Second Stewart Dodd reported to Mr. Murdock, the first officer, fifteen minutes later that every person was on deck. Still there was no panic, no excitement, or fear. The electric lights still burned and passengers all massed starboard and port on the upper deck. There was a little feeling of fear through the crowd ten minutes later, however, when Chief Officer Murdock called sharply:

"Crews to the boats! Women and children first!"

At this time, little murmurs of dissent came, particularly from the women. Wives announced that they would not be separated from their husbands, mothers said they would not leave their sons; sisters their brothers. A few threw their arms around their men folks and that sentiment showed itself among all classes on the ship.

There was no distinction when the time came for the boats to be filled. The crew of the first boat simply grabbed the first woman they saw, hurled her up in the air and dropped her in the boat. They turned again and grabbed another. Thereafter that was the general scene on both sides of the upper deck, members of the crew grabbing any woman who might have her arms around the neck of a man and passing her into the boat. In this the men were assisted by husbands, brothers and sons.

Mrs. John Jacob Astor positively declined to leave her husband and he, with a steward, simply picked her up, carried her over and put her in boat No. 1. Every man, every crew seen last night, remembered that during all this ordeal John Jacob Astor was not only cool, but did a valiant work in assisting the crew in getting the women to the boats.

A band of men from the steerage made for one of the boats. The majority spoke the language of Continental Europe. Murdock faced them. He looked into the faces of the English speaking men and said:

"Don't forget you are Britons." That was enough for the men. They fell back, but others came on.

Murdock brought his revolver up to a level, with the curt declaration: "I'll kill the first man that rushes."

Three men rushed. There were two shots. Two men dropped, one shot through the head, the other with his jaw torn off. There was no use to shoot the third man. Quicker than the bullet could reach him a fist of a husky quartermaster landed on the point of the third man's jaw and he went down like a poleaxed ox. Then the work of filling the boats went on. . . .

The order to lower the boats came from Captain Smith at 2 o'clock and they all took the water. Members of the crew aboard each of the sixteen boats and the collapsibles got them away from the sides and rested on their oars fifty feet distant. "Go on!" was the command and the crew, obeying the orders, began to pull on their oars.

The eyes of all those in the little boats remained fixed on the Titanic. They could see then that she had sunk about twenty-five feet at the head, raising her enormous stern high up out of the water. But not a soul on those small boats thought even then that the great ship could sink. There was no moon, but still the night was clear. The light of the stars and the long rows of lights from the decks and portholes of the Titanic enabled them to see the men they had left moving along her deck further aft, but still showing no signs of excitement. Nobody in the small boats thought it possible that they were soon to see the greatest tragedy of the sea.

And then without warning, as the last boat got a mile away from the Titanic the men and women in those small boats saw the bow of the Titanic dip down as if it had been pulled by a giant hand, while the last flicker of electric lights disclosed a great gap two-thirds aft. The great ship had split in two. The forward part simply slipped into the water like a flash and as it swung under the water there came a series of explosions. The forward boilers had blown up. That part of the boat carried with it the hundreds of men in the engine room and stokehole.

The after part of the ship, upon which all the passengers and crew who were on the deck had taken refuge, bobbed back from the spot, bent forward, and then a weak cheer came from the horror stricken people in the boats as the hulk appeared to right itself, stood up on an even keel and floated. But prayers of thankfulness and cheer were changed almost in an instant. There came from the front of the remaining hulk a great puff of steam, as the roar of another great explosion came to them. The huge mass of steel was rent asunder. The fragment of ship suddenly choked up and the whole thing slid down under the water, carrying with it the thousand or more men who had remained on it. As she went down her band was heard to play.

(*The Sun,* New York, April 21, 1912)

A man in woman's clothes was among the survivors in lifeboat 10, according to Mrs. Mark Fortune, of Winnipeg, who was rescued with her three daughters on that boat. Mrs. Fortune's husband, a Winnipeg real estate broker, and her son, Charles, were lost. They were not allowed to mount to the upper deck until the women and children were safely bestowed, according to her statement. Her daughters, Alice, Mabel and Ethel, unite with her in saying that a man saved his life by his woman's dress, one of the daughters having the seat next to him in the lifeboat.

The lifeboat, said Mrs. Fortune, was greatly overcrowded. Four of the crew were in her and the rest were supposed to be women, with the exception of one stoker and a Chinaman. There was a figure forward dressed in a brown mackintosh with a shawl like that of a steerage passenger over its head. The face was completely hidden. Miss Alice Fortune sat directly beside the supposed woman.

Soon after the boat had left the ship the four sailers were transferred to another boat and it was at this time it was discovered that the figure was that of a man. When somebody asked who he was, he refused to reply. The stoker and the Chinaman, who were the only men at the oars, demanded that the impostor bear a hand. He said he did not know how to use an oar and the stoker struck him in the face.

(London *Times,* April 19, 1912)

The English Board of Trade passengers' certificate on board the Titanic allowed for a total of approximately 3,500. The same certificate called for lifeboat accommodation for approximately 950 in the following boats:—fourteen large lifeboats, two smaller boats, four collapsible boats. Life preservers were accessible in apparently sufficient number for all on board. . . .

The number saved was about 80 per cent of the *maximum* capacity of the lifeboats. We feel it is our duty to call the attention of the public to what we consider the inadequate supply of life saving appliances provided for modern passenger steamships, and recommend that immediate steps be taken to compel passenger steamers to carry sufficient boats to accommodate the *maximum* number of people carried on board. . . .

[Statement signed by Mr. Samuel Goldenberg, Chairman of the Passengers' Committee, and twenty-five others.]

### (New York *Herald*, April 19, 1912)

Freighted with her argosy of woe, disaster and death, bringing glad reunion to some but misery unutterable to many, the Carpathia with the survivors of the lost Titanic aboard came back to a grief stricken city and nation at nine o'clock last night.

The story she brought home was one to crush the heart with its pathos, but at the same time to thrill it with pride in the manly and womanly fortitude displayed in the face of the most awful peril and inevitable death.

As the Titanic went down, according to the story of those who were the last to leave her wounded hulk, the ship's band was playing. Captain Smith stood to his post calm, resolute, efficient to the last, and when all that mortal man could do for the two thousand lives intrusted to his care had been done, he raised his revolver and shot himself while standing on the bridge.

### (New York *Times*, April 20, 1912)

Report of Captain A. H. Rostron, of the Carpathia:

"I beg to report that at 12:35 a. m. Monday, 15th inst., I was informed of urgent message from Titanic, with her position. I immediately ordered ship turned around and put her in course for that position, we being then fifty-eight miles E. 52-1. "T" (true course) from her; had heads of all departments called and issued what I considered the necessary orders to be in preparation for any emergency.

"At 2:40 a. m. saw flare half a point on port bow. Taking this for granted to be ship, shortly after we sighted our first iceberg. I previously had lookouts doubled, knowing that Titanic had struck ice, and so took every care and precaution. We soon found ourselves in a field of bergs, large and small, and had to alter course several times to clear bergs. Weather fine and clear, light airs on sea, beautifully clear night, though dark.

"We stopped at 4 a. m., thus doing the distance in three hours and a half, picking up the first boat at 4:10 a. m., boat in charge of officer, and he reported that the Titanic had foundered. At 8:39 a. m. last boat picked up. All survivors aboard and all boats accounted for, viz.: fifteen lifeboats, one boat abandoned, two Berthon boats alongside (saw one floating among wreckage) and, according to second officer (Senior officer saved) one Berthon boat had not been launched, it having got jammed, making sixteen lifeboats and four Berthon boats accounted for.

"By the time we had cleared the first boat it was breaking day and I could see all within area of four miles. We also saw that we were surrounded by icebergs, large and small, and three miles to the northwest was a huge field of drift ice with large and small bergs in it, the ice field extending from northwest around west and south to southeast as far as we could see either way.

"At 8 a. m. the Leland steamship California came up. I gave him the principal news and asked him to search and I would proceed to New York. At 8:50 proceeded full speed. While searching over the vicinity of disaster, and while we were getting people aboard I gave orders to get spare hands along and swing in all our boats, disconnect the falls, and hoist up as many Titanic boats as possible in our davits; also, get some on fo'castle heads by derricks. We got thirteen lifeboats, six on forward deck and seven in davits. After getting all the survivors aboard, and while searching, I got a clergyman to offer a short prayer of thankfulness for those saved, and also a short burial service for their lost, in the saloon.

"Before deciding definitely where to make for, I conferred with Mr. Ismay and though he told me to do what I thought best, I informed him, taking everything into consideration, I considered New York best. I knew we should require clean blankets, provisions, and clean linen, even if we went to the Azores, as most of the passengers saved were women and children and they hysterical; not knowing what medical attention they might require, thought it best to go to New York. I also thought it would be better for Mr. Ismay to get to New York or England as soon as possible, and knowing I should be out of wireless communication very soon if I proceeded to the Azores, it left Halifax, Boston and New York, so I chose the latter.

"Again, passengers were all hysterical about ice, and I pointed out to Mr. Ismay the possibilities of seeing ice if I went to Halifax. Then I knew from the gravity of the disaster that it would be best to keep in touch with land stations as best I could. We have experienced very great difficulty in transmitting news, also names of survivors. Our wireless is very poor, and again, we had so many interruptions from other ships and also messages from ashore, principally press, which we ignored.

"I gave instructions to send first all official messages, then names of passengers, then survivors' private messages and the press messages, as I considered the three first items most important and necessary. We had haze early Tuesday morning for several hours; again more or less all Wednesday, from 5:30 a. m. to 5 p. m., strong south-southwesterly winds, and clear weather Thursday, with moderate rough sea."

(April 19, 1912)
BY CARLOS F. HURD
(Staff Correspondent of the New York *World* on Board
the Carpathia)
(Copyright, 1912, by the New York *World*)

... Facts which I have established by inquiries on the Carpathia, as positively as they could be established in view of the silence of the few surviving officers are:

That the Titanic's officers knew, several hours before the crash, of the possible nearness of icebergs.

That the Titanic's speed, nearly twenty-three knots an hour, was not slackened.

That the number of lifeboats on the Titanic was insufficient to accommodate much more than one-third of the passengers, to say nothing of the crew. MOST MEMBERS OF THE CREW SAY THERE WERE SIXTEEN LIFEBOATS AND TWO COLLAPSIBLES; NONE SAY THERE WERE MORE THAN TWENTY BOATS IN ALL. THE 700 WHO ESCAPED FILLED MOST OF THE SIXTEEN LIFEBOATS AND THE ONE COLLAPSIBLE WHICH GOT AWAY TO THE LIMIT OF THEIR CAPACITY.

That the "women first" rule, in some cases, was applied to the extent of turning back men who were with their families, even though not enough women to fill the boats were at hand on that particular part of the deck. Some few boats were thus lowered without being completely filled, but most of these were soon filled with sailors and stewards, picked up out of the water, who helped man them.

That the bulkhead system, though probably working in the manner intended, availed only to delay the ship's sinking. The position and length of the ship's wound (on the starboard quarter) admitted icy water which caused the boilers to explode, and these explosions practically broke the ship in two.

Had the ship struck the iceberg head-on, at whatever speed and with whatever resultant shock, the bulkhead system of water-tight compartments would probably have saved the vessel. As one man expressed it, it was the "impossible" that happened when, with a shock unbelievably mild, the ship's side was torn for a length, which made the bulkhead system ineffective.

The Titanic was 1,799 miles from Queenstown and 1,191 miles from New York, speeding for a maiden voyage record. The night was starlight, the sea glassy. Lights were out in most of the staterooms, and only two or three congenial groups remained in the public rooms.

In the crow's nest, or lookout, and on the bridge, officers and members of the crew were at their places, awaiting relief at midnight from their two hours' watch.

At 11:45 came the sudden sound of two gongs, a warning of immediate danger.

The crash against the iceberg, which had been sighted at only a quarter of a mile, came almost simultaneously with the click of the levers operated by those on the bridge, which stopped the engines and closed the water-tight doors.

Capt. Smith was on the bridge a moment later, giving orders for the summoning of all on board, and for the putting on of life preservers and the lowering of lifeboats.

The first boats lowered contained more men passengers than the later ones, as the men were on deck first, and not enough women were there to fill them.

When, a moment later, the rush of frightened women and crying children to the deck began, enforcement of the women-first rule became rigid. Officers loading some of the boats drew revolvers, but in most cases the men, both passengers and crew, behaved in a way that called for no such restraint.

REVOLVER SHOTS, HEARD BY MANY PERSONS SHORTLY BEFORE THE END OF THE TITANIC, CAUSED MANY RUMORS. ONE WAS THAT CAPT. SMITH SHOT HIMSELF, another was that First Officer Murdock ended his life. Smith, Murdock and Sixth Officer Moody are known to have been lost. The surviving officers, Lightoller, Pitman, Boxhall and Lowe, have made no statement.

Members of the crew discredit all reports of suicide and say that Capt. Smith remained on the bridge until just before the ship sank, leaping only after those on the decks had been washed away. It is also related that, when a cook later sought to pull him aboard a lifeboat, he exclaimed, "Let me go!" and, jerking away, went down.

What became of the men with life-preservers? is a question asked since the disaster by many persons. The preservers did their work of supporting their wearers in the water until the ship went down. Many of those drawn into the vortex, despite the preservers, did not come up again. Dead bodies floated on the surface as the last boats moved away.

To relate that the ship's string band gathered in the saloon, near the end, and played "Nearer, My God, to Thee", sounds like an attempt to give an added solemn color to a scene which was in itself the climax of solemnity. But various passengers and survivors of the crew agree in the declaration that they heard this music. To some of the hearers, with husbands among the dying men in the water and at the ship's rail, the strain brought in thought the words

"So, by my woes I'll be
Nearer, My God, to Thee
Nearer to Thee."

(April 19, 1912)

### BY HAROLD BRIDE

(The surviving wireless operator of the Titanic)

*(Dictated to a reporter for the New York Times, and copyrighted 1912 by the New York Times)*

To begin at the beginning, I joined the Titanic at Belfast. I was born at Nunhead, England, twenty-two years ago, and joined the Marconi forces last July. I first worked on the Hoverford, and then on the Lusitania. I joined the Titanic at Belfast.

I didn't have much to do aboard the Titanic, except to relieve Phillips from midnight until some time in the morning, when he should be through sleeping. On the night of the accident, I was not sending, but was asleep. I was due to be up and relieve Phillips earlier than usual. And that reminds me—if it hadn't been for a lucky thing, we never could have sent any call for help.

The lucky thing was that the wireless broke down early enough for us to fix it before the accident. We noticed something wrong on Sunday and Phillips and I worked seven hours to find it. We found a "secretary" burned out, at last, and repaired it just a few hours before the iceberg was struck.

Phillips said to me as he took the night shift: "You turn in, boy, and get some sleep, and go up as soon as you can and give me a chance. I'm all done for with this work of making repairs."

There were three rooms in the wireless cabin. One was a sleeping room, one a dynamo room and one an operating room. I took off my clothes and went to sleep in bed. Then I was conscious of waking up and hearing Phillips sending to Cape Race. I read what he was sending. It was a traffic matter.

I remembered how tired he was and I got out of bed without my clothes on to relieve him. I didn't even feel the shock. I hardly knew it had happened until after the Captain had come to us. There was no jolt whatever.

I was standing by Phillips, telling him to go to bed, when the Captain put his head in the cabin.

"We've struck an iceberg," the Captain said, "and I'm having an inspection made to tell what it has done for us. You'd better get ready to send out a call for assistance. But don't send it until I tell you."

The Captain went away, and in ten minutes, I should estimate the time, he came back. We could hear a terrible confusion outside; there was not the least thing to indicate that there was any trouble. The wireless was working perfectly.

"Send the call for assistance," ordered the Captain, barely putting his head in the door.

"What call shall I send?" Phillips asked.

"The regulation international call for help. Just that."

Then the Captain was gone. Phillips began to send "C Q D". He flashed away at it and we joked while he did so. All of us made light of the disaster.

We joked that way while he flashed signals for about five minutes. Then the Captain came back.

"What are you sending?" he asked.

"C Q D," Phillips replied.

The humor of the situation appealed to me. I cut in with a little remark that made us all laugh, including the Captain. "Send S O S," I said. "It's the new call, and it may be your last chance to send it."

Phillips, with a laugh, changed the signal to "S O S". The Captain told us we had been struck amidships, or just back of amidships. It was ten minutes, Phillips told me, after he had noticed the iceberg, that the slight jolt that was the collision's only signal to us occurred. We thought we were a good distance away.

We said lots of funny things to each other in the next few minutes. We picked up, first, the steamship Frankford. We gave her our position and said we had struck an iceberg and needed assistance. The Frankford operator went away to tell his captain.

He came back and we told him we were sinking by the head. By that time we could observe a distinct list forward.

The Carpathia answered our signals. We told her our position and said we were sinking by the head. The operator went to tell the Captain and in five minutes returned and told us that the Captain of the Carpathia was putting about and heading for us.

Our Captain had left us at this time, and Phillips told me to run and tell him what the Carpathia had answered. I did so, and I went through an awful mass of people to his cabin. The decks were full of scrambling men and women. I saw no fighting, but I heard tell of it.

I came back and heard Phillips giving the Carpathia fuller directions. Phillips told me to put on my clothes. Until that moment I forgot that I was not dressed.

I went to my cabin and dressed. I brought an overcoat to Phillips. It was very cold. I slipped the overcoat upon him while he worked.

Every few minutes Phillips would send me to the Captain with little messages. They were merely telling how the Carpathia was coming our way and gave her speed.

I noticed as I came back from one trip that they were putting off women and children in lifeboats. I noticed that the list forward was increasing.

Phillips told me the wireless was growing weaker. The Captain came and told us our engine rooms were taking water and that the dynamos might not last much longer. We sent that word to the Carpathia.

I went out on deck and looked around. The water was pretty close up to the boat deck. There was a great scramble aft, and how poor Phillips worked through it I don't know.

He was a brave man. I learned to love him that night, and I suddenly felt for him a great reverence to see him standing there sticking to his work while everybody else was raging about. I will never live to forget the work of Phillips for the last awful fifteen minutes.

I thought it was about time to look about and see if there was anything to catch that would float. I remembered that every member of the crew had a special lifebelt and ought to know where it was. I remembered mine was under my bunk. I went and got it. Then I thought how cold the water was.

I remembered that I had some boots and I put those on, and an extra jacket, and I put that on. I saw Phillips standing out there still sending away, giving the Carpathia details of just how we were doing.

We picked up the Olympic and told her we were sinking by the head, and were about all down. As Phillips was sending the message, I strapped his lifebelt to his back. I had already put on his overcoat.

I wondered if I could get him into his boots. He suggested with a sort of laugh that I look out and see if all the people were off in boats, or if any boats were left, or how things were.

I saw a collapsible boat near a funnel and went over to it. Twelve men were trying to boost it down to the boat deck. They were having an awful time. It was the last boat left. I looked at it longingly a few minutes. Then I gave them a hand, and over she went. They all started to scramble in on the boat deck, and I walked back to Phillips. I said the last raft had gone.

Then, came the Captain's voice, "Men, you have done your full duty. You can do no more. Abandon your cabin. Now it's every man for himself. You look out for yourselves. I release you. That's the way of it at this kind of a time. Every man for himself."

I looked out. The boat deck was awash. Phillips clung on, sending and sending. He clung on for about ten minutes, or maybe fifteen minutes after the Captain had released him. The water was then coming into our cabin.

While he worked something happened I hate to tell about. I was back in my room, getting Phillips' money for him, and as I looked out the door I saw a stoker, or somebody from below decks, leaning over Phillips from behind. He was too busy to notice what the man was doing. The man was slipping the lifebelt off Phillips' back.

He was a big man, too. As you can see, I am very small. I don't know what it was I got hold of. I remembered in a flash the way Phillips had clung on—how I had to fix that lifebelt in place, because he was too busy to do it.

I knew that man from below decks had his own lifebelt and should have known where to get it.

I suddenly felt a passion not to let that man die a decent sailor's death. I wish he might have stretched rope or walked a plank. I did my duty. I hope I finished him. I don't know. We left him on the cabin floor of the wireless room and he was not moving.

From aft came a tune from the band. It was a rag-time. I don't know what. Then there was "Autumn". Phillips ran aft, and that was the last I ever saw of him.*

---

*Bride was injured in both legs getting away from the *Titanic*, but after a few hours' rest aboard the *Carpathia*, he volunteered to help the overworked marconimen, remaining on duty continuously until the rescue ship docked. The account of which this is an excerpt was dictated to a *Times* reporter after Bride, unable to walk, had been carried ashore in New York.

(London *Times,* July 31, 1912)

## THE TITANIC REPORT

### Loss Due to Excessive Speed

### The Master's "Grievous Mistake"

### Lord Mersey and the Board of Trade

The Report on the loss of the Titanic was presented at a final meeting of the Court of Inquiry held at the Scottish Hall yesterday morning. The Report, a long printed document occupying 74 pages was read by the Wreck Commissioner, Lord Mersey. The finding of the Court is as follows:—

The Court, having carefully inquired into the circumstances of the above-mentioned shipping casualty, finds, for the reasons appearing in the annex hereto, that the loss of the said ship was due to collision with an iceberg, brought about by the excessive speed at which the ship was being navigated.

# EXTRA!

It is difficult to discuss the tragedy at
Sarajevo yesterday without laying one-
self open to the reproach of heartless-
ness. For while it is only natural that
one should be stricken with horror at
the brutal and shocking assassination of
Archduke Ferdinand, it is impossible to
deny the fact that his disappearance
from the scene is calculated to diminish
the tenseness of the situation and to
make for peace both within and without
the dual empire.

—*The Sun*, New York,
June 29, 1914

## I

# STUDENT SHOOTS AS AUTO PASSES

(Natchez *Democrat*)

---

Sarajevo, Bosnia, June 28—Archduke Francis Ferdinand, Heir to the Austro-Hungarian throne, and the Duchess of Hohenberg, his morganatic wife, were shot dead today by a student in the main street of the Bosnian capital, a short time after they had escaped death from a bomb hurled at the royal automobile.

It was on the return of the procession that the tragedy was added to the long list of those that have darkened the pages of the recent history of the Hapsburgs.

As the royal automobile reached a prominent point in the route to the palace, an eighth grade student, Gario Prinzip, sprang out of the crowd and poured a deadly fusillade of bullets from an automatic pistol at the archduke and princess. . . .

—Natchez *Democrat*
June 29, 1914

THE END